Rhetoric & Composition
PhD Program

PROGRAM
Pioneering program honoring the rhetorical tradition through scholarly innovation, excellent job placement record, well-endowed library, state-of-the-art New Media Writing Studio, and graduate certificates in new media and women's studies.

TEACHING
1-1 teaching loads, small classes, extensive pedagogy and technology training, and administrative fellowships in writing program administration and new media.

FACULTY
Nationally recognized teacher-scholars in history of rhetoric, modern rhetoric, women's rhetoric, digital rhetoric, composition studies, and writing program administration.

FUNDING
Generous four-year graduate instructorships, competitive stipends, travel support, and several prestigious fellowship opportunities.

EXPERIENCE
Mid-sized liberal arts university setting nestled in the vibrant, culturally-rich Dallas-Fort Worth metroplex.

English
DEPARTMENT
Contact Dr. Mona Narain
m.narain@tcu.edu
eng.tcu.edu

composition STUDIES

Volume 46, Number 2
Fall 2018

Editor
Laura R. Micciche

Editorial Consultant
Bob Mayberry

Book Review Editor
Bryna Siegel Finer

Editorial Assistants
Christiane Boehr
Ian Golding
Rich Shivener

Former Editors
Gary Tate
Robert Mayberry
Christina Murphy
Peter Vandenberg
Ann George
Carrie Leverenz
Brad E. Lucas
Jennifer Clary-Lemon

Advisory Board
Sheila Carter-Tod
Virginia Tech University

Elías Dominguez Barajas
University of Arkansas

Qwo-Li Driskill
Oregon State University

Susan Martens
Missouri Western State University

Aja Y. Martinez
Syracuse University

Michael McCamley
University of Delaware

Jessica Nastal-Dema
Prairie State College

Annette Harris Powell
Bellarmine University

Melissa Berry Pearson
Northeastern University

Margaret Price
The Ohio State University

Jessica Restaino
Montclair State University

Donnie Sackey
Wayne State University

Christopher Schroeder
Northeastern Illinois University

Darci Thoune
University of Wisconsin-La Crosse

SUBSCRIPTIONS

Composition Studies is published twice each year (May and November). Annual subscription rates: Individuals $25 (Domestic), $30 (International), and $15 (Students). To subscribe online, please visit http://www.uc.edu/journals/composition-studies/subscriptions.html.

BACK ISSUES

Back issues, five years prior to the present, are freely accessible on our website at http://www.uc.edu/journals/composition-studies/issues/archives.html. If you don't see what you're looking for, contact us. Also, recent back issues are now available through Amazon.com. To find issues, use the advanced search feature and search on "Composition Studies" (title) and "Parlor Press" (publisher).

BOOK REVIEWS

Assignments are made from a file of potential book reviewers. If you are interested in writing a review, please contact our book review editor at brynasf@iup.edu.

JOURNAL SCOPE

The oldest independent periodical in the field, *Composition Studies* publishes original articles relevant to rhetoric and composition, including those that address teaching college writing; theorizing rhetoric and composing; administering writing programs; and, among other topics, preparing the field's future teacher-scholars. All perspectives and topics of general interest to the profession are welcome. We also publish Course Designs, which contextualize, theorize, and reflect on the content and pedagogy of a course. Contributions to Composing With are invited by the editor, though queries are welcome (send to compstudies@uc.edu). Cfps, announcements, and letters to the editor are most welcome. *Composition Studies* does not consider previously published manuscripts, unrevised conference papers, or unrevised dissertation chapters.

SUBMISSIONS

For submission information and guidelines, see http://www.uc.edu/journals/composition-studies/submissions/overview.html.

Direct all correspondence to:

> Laura Micciche, Editor
> Department of English
> University of Cincinnati
> PO Box 210069
> Cincinnati, OH 45221–0069
> compstudies@uc.edu

Composition Studies is grateful for the support of the University of Cincinnati.

© 2018 by Laura Micciche, Editor
Production and printing is managed by Parlor Press, www.parlorpress.com.
ISSN 1534–9322.
Cover art by Giovanni Weissman and design by Gary Weissman.

http://www.uc.edu/journals/composition-studies.html

composition STUDIES

Volume 46, Number 2
Fall 2018

Contents

From the Editor   10

Composing with   12
   Composing With   12
     Ethan Philbrick

Articles   15
   Naming What We Feel: Hierarchical Microaggressions and the Relationship between Composition and English Studies   15
     Meaghan Brewer and Kristen di Gennaro

   "Higher" School: Nineteenth-Century High Schools and the Secondary-College Divide   35
     Amy J. Lueck

   Translational Learning: Surfacing Multilingual Repertoires   52
     Ryan McCarty

   Inhabiting Ordinary Sentences   79
     Peter Wayne Moe

   Learning about Learning: Composition's Renewed Engagement with Cognition   96
     Ann M. Penrose and Gwendolynne C. Reid

   Intellectual Risk in the Writing Classroom: Navigating Tensions in Educational Values and Classroom Practice   116
     Alexis Teagarden, Carolyn Commer, Ana Cooke, and Justin Mando

Course Designs   137
   Advanced Exposition: Writing through Podcasts   137
     Jacob Greene

   Sociolinguistics for Language and Literacy Educators   163
     Missy Watson

Where We Are: #MeToo and Academia   186

Beyond a Hashtag: Considering Campus Policies
in the Age of #MeToo   186
Laura Rosche

Literacy Narrative: Ways to Write #MeToo   189
Tessa Brown

Misogyny in the Classroom: Two Women Lecturer's Experiences   192
Patricia Fancher and Ellen O'Connell Whittet

A Vindication of the Rights of Faculty   195
Michelle Graber

Academic Spaces and Grad Student Harassment   198
Katelyn Lusher

Centering the Conversation: Patriarchy,
Academic Culture, and #MeToo   200
Anna Sicari

Book Reviews   203

Here We Go Again: More Ways of "Making It," Circa 2018   203

Women's Professional Lives in Rhetoric and Composition: Choice, Chance, and Serendipity, edited by Elizabeth A. Flynn and Tiffany Bourelle

Surviving Sexism in Academia: Strategies for Feminist Leadership, edited by Kirsti Cole and Holly Hassel

Reviewed by Michelle Ballif, Diane Davis, and Roxanne Mountford

Centering Research, Practice, and Perspectives: Writing Center Studies
and the Continued Commitment to Inclusivity and Accessibility   212

The Oxford Guide for Writing Tutors: Practice and Research, by Lauren Fitzgerald and Melissa Ianetta

Writing Centers and Disability, by Rebecca Day Babcock and Sharifa Daniels

Reviewed by Mike Haen

Legible Sovereignties: Rhetoric, Representations, and Native American Museums, by Lisa King   219
Reviewed by Katie Bramlett

Florida, edited by Jeff Rice **223**
   Reviewed by Jacob W. Craig, College of Charleston

Inside the Subject: A Theory of Identity for the Study of Writing,
by Raúl Sánchez **227**
   Reviewed by Thomas Girshin

Facing the Sky: Composing through Trauma in Word and Image,
by Roy F. Fox **230**
   Reviewed by Christy Goldsmith

Announcement 234

Contributors 235

From the Editor

This issue begins with writer and performance artist Ethan Philbrick's treatment of composing as source of both rotting and transforming. His "Composing With" is about how change happens and how art helps. Following this provocative piece are six articles that deal, in one way or another, with liminality as a condition of being. Starting us off is Meaghan Brewer and Kristen di Gennaro's study of microaggressions leveled at composition teachers and scholars by colleagues in literature and creative writing. The authors address how to improve communication and work toward changed relations.

Amy J. Lueck explores the ever-relevant relationship between high school and college writing instruction through a historical study of their blurred lines. Also positioned at the intersection of high school and college, Ryan McCarty's piece follows six bilingual Spanish-English students as they navigate this schooling transition. Peter Wayne Moe continues the focus on students by examining what he calls "ordinary sentences," linking the rhetoric of sentences to ethos. Shifting to graduate students, Ann M. Penrose and Gwendolynne C. Reid describe a ten-year study they conducted with GTAs focused on cognitive variability in writing classrooms; their article adds to the field's ongoing engagement with cognitive theory and pedagogical decision-making. Still sticking with students, Alexis Teagarden, Carolyn Commer, Ana Cooke, and Justin Mando investigate intellectual risk-taking through the experiences of undergraduate students as well as those invested in their success, early-career writing instructors.

This issue also includes two course designs: Jacob Greene's undergraduate course on podcast writing, and Missy Watson's graduate course on sociolinguistics for language and literacy educators. Both offer terrific expansions of writing studies that I hope you will find generative for your own teaching. Speaking of generative, we feature two review essays and four book reviews—your fall reading list! Of special note is Michelle Ballif, Diane Davis, and Roxanne Mountford's "Here We Go Again: More Ways of 'Making It,' Circa 2018." Their review of books about women's professional lives and sexism in the academy is simultaneous with #MeToo, Brett Kavanaugh's confirmation hearings amidst accusations of sexual misconduct by two women, Bill Cosby's prison sentence for sexual assault, and pervasive images of women protesting, being ejected from court rooms and halls of government for disrupting business-as-usual, reprimanded on tennis courts, degraded by President Trump, and calling out abuses of power on every media platform. Everywhere we turn, women's bodies are front and center, women's anger is coalescing into movements, and movements are disrupting the normal presence of sexual violence and harassment in women's everyday lives.

This extraordinary moment was the inspiration for our Where We Are section devoted to #MeToo and Academia. Contributors delve into sexual violence and campus policies (or their absence), the aftermath of rape and the importance of talking about sexual violence in our work on campus and in the field, lack of support for teachers who are objects of misogynistic behavior and speech in the classroom, harassment of graduate students at professional conferences, and writing centers as potential sites where students and teachers can talk safely about sexual harassment and violence. These pieces are infuriating and depressing; we need them. We need more of them. Those of us who have been in the field of rhetoric and composition for a while now know stories of serial harassers whose careers flourish unfettered. We've heard stories passed discreetly among friends at conferences and in hallways. Yet the number of submissions we received for this section didn't break double digits, and the majority of submissions came from those with the least power in our field: graduate students and non-tenure-track faculty. Few addressed peer-to-peer violence and harassment, an open secret in the field (and in academia more widely). The culture of silence and fear is entrenched and difficult to overcome. Will accusers be believed? Be marked as trouble-makers and suffer professionally? My hope is that the stories included in this issue spark a wider sustained conversation including more voices, led by those who occupy (relative) positions of power, and motivate accountability measures that ensure the safety of students and teachers alike.

L.M.
Cincinnati, Ohio
September 2018

Composing with

Composing With

Ethan Philbrick

Composing Is Decomposing

There's a kind of making that happens in rotting, a reconstitution of matter, a generativity in decomposition. When I feel lost I make erasure poems[1]—cutting words out of texts and decomposing a text in order to make a different one, a text that feels like mine when I don't know how to make mine. Maybe one way to think about erasure poems is as a kind of willful rotting, a scrubbing out of words on a page to create a new assembly of words, a becoming-parasite that eats a text and spits part of the unchewed chunks out to make one that works.

When I was 22 and had just gotten married to an emotionally abusive partner and didn't know how to tell anyone about it, I grasped for things to keep me afloat. I found myself at a community garden center's composting workshop. It was me and a bunch of sweet retirees. We ripped up newspaper and combined it with squirming worms in the bottom of plastic containers to make "worm bins" for our basements. When I got home I loaded my bin up with a bunch of vegetables and eggshells and promptly forgot about it for over a year. When I finally happened upon the bin and opened it expecting to find books I thought I had stored in the basement, I found it full of deep brown soil, rich and teeming with dirty life.

Composing Is Improvising

When I'm playing the cello and making up music and not using any notation, am I composing or improvising? Why don't we call improvisation a kind of composition, a composing in time, a composing without marks? Performance studies scholar Danielle Goldman writes wonderfully about the indeterminacy between composing and improvising in *I Want to Be Ready: Improvised Dance as a Practice of Freedom*:

> Improvisation is generally described as a spontaneous mode of creation that takes place without the aid of a manuscript or score. According to this view, performance and composition occur simultaneously—on the spot—through a practice that values surprise, innovation, and the vicissitudes of process rather than the fixed glory of a finished product. This view may initially seem straightforward, but [...] it becomes increasingly complicated the more instances of improvisation one considers. As the ethnomusicologist Paul Berliner states in *Thinking in Jazz*, composition and improvisation "overlap hopelessly at the margins." Many improvisers work with loose scores, call upon idiomatic tradition, or cultivate individual styles. And many compositions begin with improvisation. (5-6)

These complicated and overlapping distinctions between composition and improvisation are always already gendered, racialized, and classed. Musicians of color who work within genres such as jazz are thought of as improvisors rather than composers, with "composition" connoting more of the authority of the author-function while "improvisation" connotes more of the labor-function of a performer.

Composing Is Recomposing

I love to translate a poem into another poem in the same language. Or translate a manifesto into a poem and then that poem into song. Or translate a song into another song. This kind of composing is a relational generativity—recycling and recomposing. For the past few years I've been working on a choral recomposition of Karl Marx and Friedrich Engels's *Manifesto for the Communist Party*. The piece is a way to sound out an alternative anti-capitalist manifesto by re-sounding an existing anti-capitalist manifesto. Maybe you'd like to take a listen: https://soundcloud.com/e-philbrick/choral-marx-movement-six-july.

Note

1. The *Academy of American Poets* defines erasure poetry as "a form of found poetry wherein a poet takes an existing text and erases, blacks out, or otherwise obscures a large portion of the text, creating a wholly new work from what remains." Works

such as Ronal Johnson's *Radi Os* and M. NourbeSe Philip's *Zong!* are named as exemplary texts in the genre.

Works Cited

"Erasure Poetry." *Academy of American Poets.* https://www.poets.org/poetsorg/text/erasure-poetic-form. Accessed 12 September 2018.

Goldman, Danielle. *I Want to Be Ready: Improvised Dance as a Practice of Freedom.* U of Michigan P, 2010.

Johnson, Ronal. *Radi Os.* Flood Editions, 1977.

Philip, M. NourbeSe. *Zong!* Wesleyan UP, 2011.

Articles

Naming What We Feel: Hierarchical Microaggressions and the Relationship between Composition and English Studies

Meaghan Brewer and Kristen di Gennaro

> This article uses a combination of speech act theory and research on microaggressions to analyze statements made by scholars in the fields of literature and creative writing towards their colleagues in composition. We argue that framing these interactions as "hierarchical microaggressions," a term coined by Kathryn Young et al., helps explain compositionists' potentially defensive reactions to seemingly innocuous remarks, and also points towards ways of engaging in constructive communication among English department colleagues about the field of composition.

One author of this article, Meaghan Brewer, attended a session at the 2017 Conference on College Composition and Communication (CCCC) that explored the relationship between composition studies and the Modern Language Association (MLA). Before she entered the panel, she was talking to three prominent scholars in the field of composition in the hallway. When she expressed interest in the session, one of them quipped, "MLA? We don't care about them—they certainly don't care about us!" Another of the composition scholars pointed out that Anne Ruggles Gere would soon be president of MLA, but this did not deter the first composition scholar.

When Meaghan entered the session, the presenters were much more sanguine that there was a place within composition studies for MLA (as well as the reverse). One pointed out that both the MLA Publications Program and *PMLA* have increasing interest in articles and books about composition, characterizing the organization as a whole as "decidedly hospitable" to compositionists (Bleich et al.). However, at least a few audience members were skeptical. One noted the difference in the relationship between national organizations like CCCC and MLA and the more local relationships between composition and literature scholars in English departments. "Those who study literature still consider themselves to be in a better class than those who study writing," the audience member proclaimed. Others felt they had been discriminated against in their home departments because of disciplinary differences, like the fact that the empirical work many compositionists do often takes longer to complete and publish or that co-authored works tend to be more common in composition than in literary studies.

This opening anecdote illustrates that whereas there seems to be a general feeling that composition is more respected among the broader field of English studies than it was three or four decades ago, this respect does not necessarily trickle down (or perhaps it trickles down more slowly) to the individual institutions where many of us are working and interacting with colleagues across fields included in English studies. This combination of progress and slow (or stagnating) progress also might make it more difficult for compositionists to deal with academic slights or snubs when they happen.

Consider, for example, the following conversation between a composition scholar and a literary scholar who had been hired to teach composition. The conversation occurred in the hallway, as the composition scholar was leaving her office, and at the end of the literary scholar's first semester. For the purposes of referring to it later, we label the conversation as "Example 1" and represent it in dialogue form, which the composition scholar reconstructed from memory shortly after it occurred:

Example 1

    Literary scholar (LS): Are you an Americanist by any chance?

    Composition scholar (CS): No.

    LS: Is there anyone around who is an Americanist?

    CS: Maybe [name of Americanist], but it looks like he's gone. You could try [name of another Americanist] around the hall.

    LS: Thanks. What is your field, by the way?

    CS: Composition

    LS: *Yes, but I mean, what do you do?*

    CS: → Composition. It is a field in its own right, you know. Would you expect an Americanist to also be a Medievalist?

    LS: Fair enough.

During this conversation, the literary scholar displays a stunning lack of knowledge of what compositionists do. To him, composition is a class or an administrative position, not a discipline with its own set of research and content knowledge. Although some might attribute this conversation to ignorance (and view the literary scholar here as atypical), we believe it illustrates that composition as a field still does not merit recognition to some in literary studies.

This conversation is one example of the phenomenon we describe and analyze in this paper. During the exchange, the composition scholar was taken aback by the condescension expressed toward the field of composition by the literary scholar. Her reactions (indicated with the symbol →) to the remarks in italicized font show the feelings they elicited. Based on this and additional anecdotes provided later in the article, we place the field of composition, rather than the composition scholar directly, as the object of the literary scholar's disdain or ignorance.

Although English faculty typically pride themselves on their fight against racism, sexism, ableism, and other types of marginalization, they are less aware of how class-based, hierarchical prejudices play into the relationship between composition and literature (Crowley; Hairston; Miller). Framing comments such as those described in this article as hierarchical microaggressions, a term coined by Kathryn Young et al. to describe subtle, everyday insults and snubs occurring in higher education based on status, may help shed some light on the underlying messages and metamessages that English department faculty send to their colleagues in composition. Ultimately, we hope this article leads to constructive communication among the various branches of English studies as well as some solutions for dealing with misconceptions about the field of composition.

This article uses speech act theory in conjunction with research on microaggressions to analyze the speech act described above as well as six more examples. Six of the statements we describe in this article (including the one above) are the result of spontaneous, non-elicited interaction. That is, rather than use surveys or interviews to gather data, as is typical of microaggression studies, we draw on naturally occurring ordinary conversations. These statements either happened to or were witnessed by one of the co-authors of this article, though we should note that they occurred across different institutional contexts. To be specific, the statements were made in traditional English departments (meaning those that house both composition and literature as well as other sub-fields) at three different universities, all large to mid-sized institutions in the Northeast. We note this to avoid stigmatizing any one institution, to maintain greater anonymity, and to suggest the possibility that such statements might occur in many English departments. Because the targets of microaggressions might only identify them as such later, the statements discussed are based on recalled, reconstructed conversations. While we recognize this as a limitation, we note that most research on microaggressions is based either on hypothetical statements that convey the gist of similar statements one might have experienced or on recalled statements or testimony from the targets of microaggressions after the fact (see, for example, Sue et al.; Young et al.). The final example from an article published in the "advice" column of the *Chronicle of Higher Education* supports our suspicion that the hierarchical microaggressions experienced in Examples 1-6 are widespread.

Doing Things with Words

Speech act theory, as described by John Austin and John Searle, works from an important premise from the perspective of microaggressions research: utterances not only communicate information but also *perform actions*. We use speech act theory in our analyses (rather than a method like conversation analysis or critical discourse analysis) because of its focus on both the speech act itself and the listener's response to that speech act. Moreover, because the examples we present are based on recalled, reconstructed conversations and not transcriptions, a method like conversation analysis (which examines and quantifies pauses in conversation, length of discourse units, etc.) would not be feasible. Although critical discourse analysis contains the potential for uncovering power relationships in discourse (and may, consequently, prove useful for analyzing microaggressions), it also often uses transcripts of data which are then coded to produce a more fine-grained analysis than would be possible for the present study.

Speech act theory breaks utterances down into three types of acts, each conveying a type of meaning or "force." The first type, the locutionary act, references the literal meaning of the words in the utterance. The locutionary meaning of the phrase in example 1, *Yes, but I mean, what do you do?* is a request for information about the composition scholar's area of work or study. However, since the composition scholar in Example 1 had already answered the literary scholar's question about her field of study, the intended meaning of the utterance must be different from the literal meaning, revealing a second type of speech act called the illocutionary act. The illocutionary act is often equated with the speech act itself, or what the utterance performs (e.g., a request, an offer, an invitation). It is, therefore, the most central part of a speech act analysis because it illustrates that more is communicated than what is said in the simple locutionary act. In other words, the follow-up question implies that the speech act is more than a simple request for information. Although more than one possible interpretation of the utterance's intended meaning exists, given the context, the second iteration of the question probably includes an assumption that faculty who teach composition must also engage in another (more scholarly?) activity. That is, moving from the utterance's locutionary to its illocutionary meaning turns the question into an assertion: that scholars do not specialize in composition in the way that an Americanist specializes in American literature—one can be an Americanist but not a compositionist.

The difference between the utterance's locutionary and illocutionary meaning also illustrates the importance of context in speech act theory. An illustrative example typical in discussions of microaggressions in the public sphere is the question, "Where are you from?" Whereas in some contexts, the locutionary and illocutionary meaning would have little difference, making this a legitimate request for information, in other contexts, as when someone white asks this of a person of color, the illocutionary meaning could be something more like, "You don't look like an American." In the case of Example 1 above, the context of the English department makes the illocutionary meaning, that composition is peripheral or marginal to what faculty members in an English department do, more apparent.

The third type of meaning associated with an utterance is its perlocutionary meaning or "force," as it refers to the effect of an utterance on the recipient. In our example, the composition scholar reacted to the second question by repeating the same answer she had just provided with the addition of her assertion of composition as a field in its own right. In her arguably defensive response, the composition scholar shows that she was offended by the repeated question, interpreting it as questioning the legitimacy of composition as a scholarly field. The composition scholar's question (*It is a field in its own right, you know. Would you expect an Americanist to also be a Medievalist?*) further demonstrates that she interpreted the utterance as viewing composition as an administrative position or set of courses rather than a field of study. The literary scholar's terse reply (*Fair enough*) shows that he understood the composition scholar's reaction and that her interpretation of his repeated question was accurate.

While a speech act analysis can identify the utterances that elicit negative reactions in this and other conversations and uncover the illocutionary meanings they express, it fails to provide a term for the specific speech acts that composition scholars might find offensive. We needed a label that could capture commonalities among offending utterances. For this we turned to research on microaggressions.

Labeling the Speech Act: Hierarchical Microaggressions

Chester M. Pierce coined the term "microaggression" in the 1970s to label the subtle but widespread insults toward or about African Americans that tend to go unnoticed by other members of society. Over the past forty years, this definition has expanded to become both more detailed and more inclusive. The most well-known scholar of microaggressions, Derald Wing Sue, defines them as "the everyday verbal, nonverbal, and environmental slights, snubs, or insults, whether intentional or unintentional, which communicate hostile, derogatory, or negative messages to target persons based solely upon their marginalized group membership" (*Microaggressions and Marginality* 3). Sue asserts that "while microaggressions are generally discussed from the perspective of race and racism, any marginalized group in our society may become targets" ("More Than Just Race"). David L. Wallace recently added to this expanded conception of microaggressions in a presentation at CCCC 2017, arguing that seeing microaggressions only in terms of race marginalizes other oppressed groups. Advocating for an intersectional analysis of microaggressions, Wallace argues that when we only view microaggressions in terms of race, it keeps us from seeing the whole picture in which other aspects of identity (like class, gender, sexuality) are at play. Research by other scholars supports this expanded focus (Bright and Gambrell; Swim et al.; Young et al.).

We should state clearly that in society at large, composition scholars are not a marginalized group and may even, from the perspective of language and literacy research, be considered an especially privileged one. For example, in his 2016 plenary address at the Council for Writing Program Administrators (CWPA), Asao B. Inoue called for renewed examinations of whiteness in writing program administration and composition's historical role in gatekeeping. Citing Miriam Brody, Laura Micciche notes that composition studies' continued existence is linked to "its relation to dominant cultural machinery" (435). In addition, in universities at large, composition may be viewed as more central and relevant than literature, arguably contributing to the anxiety and lack of security motivating some of the microaggressions we describe. However, as with speech acts, context matters. Among the community of English Department faculty at many colleges and universities, the study of English is interpreted as the study of literature, and composition is simply a preliminary set of courses often taught by instructors trained in literary analysis rather than in writing theory and pedagogy.

Although Sue, Wallace, and other scholars advocate an expanded definition of microaggressions, we appreciate that some readers might feel uncomfortable with our application of this term to compositionists, particularly those who identify as white. In recognition of this potential discomfort and in order to distinguish what we experienced from more insidious racial microaggressions, we borrow the term "hierarchical microaggressions" from Young et al., who conducted a study of microaggressions based on status in higher education. They define hierarchical microaggressions as "everyday slights found in higher education that communicate systemic valuing (or devaluing) of a person because of the institutional [and we would add disciplinary] role held by that person" (62). Young et al. include among these hierarchical microaggressions the devaluing of staff versus faculty and pre-tenure versus post-tenure faculty.

Given the long-standing and well-known marginalization of composition scholars within the field of English, we believe the term hierarchical microaggression aptly labels the speech acts we present, as they "deliver hidden demeaning messages that often lie outside the level of conscious awareness of perpetrators" (Sue, *Microaggressions and Marginality* 4). Because people take on identities based on their careers, academic titles, and the status these positions accrue, hierarchical microaggressions can be hurtful (Micciche 437; Young et al. 68-9). The speech acts we identify include subtle, yet recognizably reductive views or demeaning stereotypes of the field of composition and, consequently, of composition scholars. Finally, while we do not discuss gender explicitly in this article, we also think a case can be made for seeing these statements as hierarchical microaggressions because of the gendered associations with the field of composition, which have been documented by scholars like Eileen Schell and Elizabeth Flynn.

Sue's research classifies microaggressions into three types: microassaults, microinsults, and microinvalidations. Microassaults include conscious expressions of bias or intentional actions against a group based solely on their membership in a marginalized group. We do not believe the microaggressions frequently experienced by composition scholars in English departments are of this type. Indeed, recent research (Lilienfeld; Young et al.) has called into question whether or not microassaults belong in the category of microaggressions at all, given that they represent what Sue et al. describe as "'old fashioned' racism" (274). The other two categories, microinsults and microinvalidations, tend to reveal ingrained attitudes and values and are more descriptive of the speech acts we've encountered. Microinsults include remarks or actions that demean a person's group identity and may even take the form of a compliment, as in the comment "You have a good arm, for a girl." A similar example from composition would be when English faculty members praise full-time composition faculty for doing excellent work, and use this to deny the need for additional hires in composition; they use compliments to justify the view that the composition element of the department should remain small and marginalized.

Microinsults also include environmental features, such as representations of success that stigmatize certain members or exclude them from full membership in the larger group. An example relevant to our discussion is a display found in many English departments dedicated to showcasing faculty members' books but no comparable recognition of other types of successful scholarship. Such a display sends the message that monographs are valued more than peer-reviewed journal articles and that scholars who publish monographs are more praiseworthy than those who do not. What is presented as a way for faculty to exhibit their work marginalizes fields in which articles are more indicative of success.

Finally, microinvalidations are phrases or actions that exclude, negate, or deny the worldviews or experiences of a marginalized group. By ignoring differences of power and privilege, they deny that one group benefits from the status quo. Microinvalidations often occur when a member of a marginalized group calls out the microaggressions of the dominant group and is then made to feel as if she is overly sensitive or "crazy" as a result. Consequently, Sue asserts that microinvalidations are probably "the most insidious, damaging, and harmful form" (*Microaggressions and Marginality* 10).

Bringing research on microaggressions together with speech act theory illustrates that an important characteristic of microaggressions is the difference between their literal (locutionary) meaning and their illocutionary or perlocutionary force. That is, both their covert meanings (illocutionary acts) and their effects on recipients (perlocutionary acts) help reveal the potentially unconscious biases toward the marginalized group targeted by the microaggressions. As the examples we describe will illustrate, this difference often gives the utterer of the microaggression plausible deniability. However, applying both speech act analyses and Sue's framework to composition scholars' experiences allows us to identify, label, and perhaps respond to remarks and actions that are invisible to many speakers but conspicuous and offensive to members of the marginalized group in this context.

Hierarchical Microaggressions and the History of Composition's Relationship to Literary Studies

Many of the hierarchical microaggressions we discuss represent deep-seated prejudices that derive from historical assumptions about composition dating back to when the first composition and literature courses were instituted at Harvard. The symbiotic nature of these two constituents of English is significant because it allows us to see how, historically, literary studies has been able to accomplish the double move of defining itself as "high" and more worthy of serious study than composition, while still using composition to justify its relevance. While literary studies took on the belletristic project of acquainting students with canonical texts to develop taste and aesthetic sensibility, "institutionalized writing-as-composition could be implicitly demeaned as unequal to writing from the advanced elect" (Miller 55). In figure 1, we use terms from Susan Miller's *Textual Carnivals* to represent what we see as a culturally ingrained, hierarchical relationship between composition and literary studies

As Miller argues, the demeaned status of composition derives from the fact that it is often housed within English departments; Crowley further asserts that "the unkindest cuts of all to composition teachers . . . stem from their association with full-time faculty who subscribe to humanism's conflicted attitude toward composition" (120). In 1991 Miller pointed out that the normative identity of a scholar in English studies is a person who studies literature (128). Composition is thus stigmatized, not because of its "intrinsic qualities" but because of its relationship with the "normal" identity of being a scholar of literature (Miller 128).

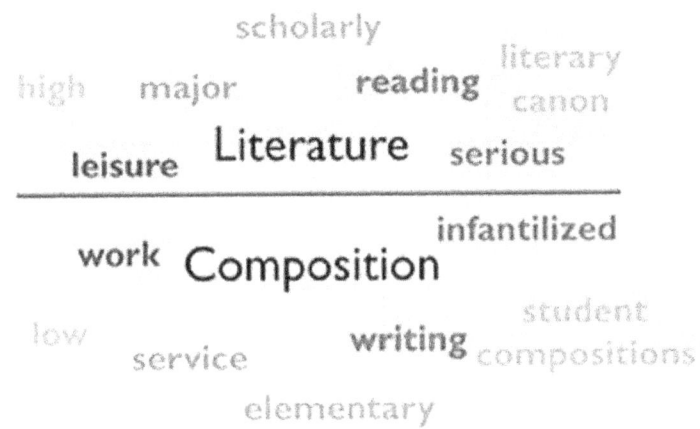

Fig. 1. The Hierarchy between Composition and Literary Studies, based on Susan Miller's *Textual Carnivals*.

Composition scholars and scholarship now undoubtedly receive more respect and have achieved more power in many English Departments and organizations than when Maxine Hairston, Miller, and Crowley wrote in the eighties and nineties. However, as recent scholarship notes, this respect does not always translate into equality. In their 2012 study of English department chairs and writing program administrators' (wpas) perceptions of wpa work and authority within English departments, Shirley K. Rose et al. found that "some conditions that were present in [the] 1989 [study by Gary A. Olson and Joseph M. Moxley that they replicated] still persist and continue to hold writing program directors back from being able to garner sufficient authority to do their work effectively" (45). Borrowing Miller's description of compositionists as "The Sad Women in the Basement," Jane Detweiler et al. argue that even with the progress compositionists have made, gendered hierarchies in English departments persist, so that we are now "madwomen in the mezzanine" (454).

Figure 1 doesn't include other disciplines that are also housed within English departments, including creative writing, which often gets left out of institutional histories like the ones cited above. Tim Mayers argues that because both composition and creative writing have been marginalized in English departments and because they have similarities (particularly their emphasis on textual production rather than interpretation), "creative writers and compositionists together should strive to invert the traditional hierarchy of English studies" in order to shift the focus of English departments to writing (xv). We're intrigued by the possibility of uniting composition with creative writing to upend the focus on interpretation that still "reigns supreme in the vast majority of English departments" (Mayers xv). We don't doubt that creative writing specialists also have to contend with attempts to demean their status in English departments.

However, some of the hierarchical microaggressions we have heard about and experienced also came from creative writers who held problematic, romantic conceptions of the writing process that they have expressed as ways of characterizing their disdain for what they falsely believe to be compositionists' mechanical, grammar-focused views of writing. Moreover, in our current home department, creative writing scholars are gaining increased status because student demand for creative writing courses is higher than for literature courses, a trend towards increasing enrollments in creative writing that Doug Hesse also notes in his article on the relationship between composition and creative writing (32). Unlike composition, creative writing has not been cast into the service role in post-secondary institutions and can thus claim to be engaged in a different, higher project. As Mayers notes, in its early days, creative writing in universities "fought for prestige mainly by capitalizing on notions of the mystical, special, and rare nature of creativity" (Mayers xiii). This notion of creative writing as engaged in "superior, 'artistic' study" is inherent in one of the microaggressions we will be discussing (Miller 6).

Hierarchical Microaggressions in English Departments

To illustrate further the presence of hierarchical microaggressions in the everyday activities of some composition scholars, we include and briefly discuss several interactions that we either witnessed or participated in.

Example 2

During a departmental meeting, English department faculty were discussing the dean's rejection of the department's request for a tenure-track line in literary studies. The dean had added that a request for a composition/rhetoric line would be considered instead. The following dialogue took place after this announcement.

LS: *So they just want to hire someone to teach grammar and spelling?*
CS: → I'm offended at your suggestion that all we do in composition is teach grammar and spelling.
LS: I'm sorry. I didn't mean to offend anyone.

Example 3

During a coffee hour, in which a candidate for a tenure-track position in literary studies met for a casual interaction with faculty and students, a literature faculty member talked about how she used drama as a way of helping students understand and interpret texts. A composition scholar reacted saying that she also used drama in her classes:

>CS: Oh, I've used drama as a pedagogical tool in my classes too.
>LS: [Laughing]: But, CS, *how do you act out grammar?*
>CS: → [Also laughing, points jokingly at the LS] That's a stereotype of composition!

We group Examples 2 and 3 together because they indicate the same reductive view of composition as the discipline that handles the "nuts and bolts" of writing while literary studies is engaged in more scholarly study. The responses to these hierarchical microaggressions, however, differ significantly. Whereas in Example 2, the composition scholar reacts directly to the remark, immediately recognizing and calling it out as offensive, in Example 3, the composition scholar reacts with humor, though her laughter betrays the fact that she is calling out the perlocutionary force of the statement, which is that the literary scholar is stereotyping composition. In this situation, however, the composition scholar uses humor to "make it all right"; given that the context was entertaining a job candidate, she did not want to embarrass herself or the department.

To use the speech act framework described earlier, both hierarchical microaggressions evince a significant difference between their locutionary and illocutionary meaning. As in Example 1, although the locutionary meaning of both position these utterances as questions, in their illocutionary meaning, neither appear to be actual questions. The literary scholar in Example 2 is not simply wondering whether the dean wants the English department to hire someone to teach spelling and grammar, nor is the literary scholar in Example 3 asking the composition scholar to describe or demonstrate how she "acts out grammar." The perlocutionary force of each statement, which is evident in the responses indicating that the compositionists were "offended" and "stereotype[d]," reinforce that these are hierarchical microaggressions.

Example 4

The discussion described in the next example followed a dean's request for the English department to consider narrowing future tenure-track hiring requests to the area of rhetoric and composition. In this exchange, a composition scholar was trying to explain a potential rationale for the dean's request: that the department had a number of faculty whose specializations were literature and creative writing teaching composition, arguably outside their disciplines.

>CS: I think what . . . [the dean] was saying is that just because you teach literature doesn't mean you know how to teach writing.
>LS: *I disagree!*
>CS: → [no reply]

The composition scholar was attempting to clarify that not everyone whose expertise is in literature is also an expert in teaching composition. Interestingly, the composition scholar, perhaps realizing that she, as a non-tenured faculty member, was vulnerable, hid her own belief (literary scholars are not necessarily qualified to teach writing) by attributing it to the dean. Moreover, the composition scholar did not challenge the literary scholar's disagreement, but instead remained silent. This silence is significant in that it indicates that additional hierarchies overlay the one between composition and literary studies. The composition scholar's non-tenured status made it difficult for her to challenge the literary scholar; given that literary scholars constituted a majority of the department and many of them held high status within the department, the composition scholar probably felt that disagreeing would not only lead to an uncomfortable conversation but could also jeopardize her future bid for tenure. This demonstrates that, as one reviewer of this article pointed out, many composition scholars are young and new and must face off against an older guard of literature scholars who are full professors and have significant power within their departments and institutions.

Without a response by the composition scholar inviting the literary scholar to elaborate, the intended target of disagreement might seem ambiguous: Was it the dean (in absentia) or the composition scholar sitting across the table from her? The absence of a rebuttal by the composition scholar provides the answer, as it indicates that she understood the disagreement to be with the content of the statement (attributed to the dean), and not with the composition scholar herself. That the literary scholar did not press the composition scholar to defend the statement further supports this interpretation.

The literary scholar then added that she thought *anyone* trained in literary studies was also equipped to teach writing, suggesting that teaching writing requires no special training beyond what literary scholars already know, and perhaps that literary scholars offer more than composition scholars in that they can teach both literature and writing. Through her disagreement, the literary scholar was not only asserting that literary scholars are naturally qualified to teach composition but also denying that someone trained in composition might be more qualified to do so, making this another example of a microinvalidation of what composition, as a field, offers an English department.

Example 5

The following dialogue took place during an informal conversation between a wpa and a relatively new adjunct faculty member trained in literature but teaching composition courses.

> CS: Based on your background, wouldn't you rather be teaching literature courses instead of composition?

LS: *Of course I'd rather teach literature – wouldn't everyone?*

On the surface, the literary scholar's statement is merely an expression of her preference to teach courses in her own field. However, in its illocutionary meaning we read a reinforcement of the idea that the normative identity in the department is that of a literary scholar. Miller speaks directly to the issues created when those outside of the field have to move between the roles of composition teacher and literary scholar. She argues that "a surplus Ph.D. or a Ph.D. candidate in literature will take one of two paths: openly to choose the unlicensed, subnormal identity associated with composition, . . . or more covertly to provide this teaching on a part-time, ad hoc basis while implicitly retaining a 'normal' ego identity" (133). In the above statement, the adjunct has undeniably chosen the second path and, further, assumes that "everyone" would rather claim this identity, as a literary scholar first and a composition teacher (reluctantly) second, rather than take on the stigma of actually *being* a composition teacher. The "of course" and "wouldn't everyone" parts of this speech act clearly reinforce that the microinsult in this statement lies in its attempt to deny that teaching composition can be a "normal" ego identity. As Miller so aptly puts it, "it is one thing to go the circus each year for entertainment, or even as part of one's . . . duty, and another thing entirely to run off to *join* the circus that composition was constituted to be" (132).

Example 6

Following an exchange during an English department meeting, in which a scholar in creative writing (CWS) characterized the curriculum for the composition courses as "boring" because they did not include literature, another scholar in creative writing made the following statement to a composition scholar who had defended the content of the composition courses:

CWS: I myself wasn't criticizing current composition pedagogy per se, but *maybe he and I, as writers ourselves,* both take the view of English as a "service department" too personally?

The composition scholar's first reaction to the conversation was to accept the creative writing scholar's premise, which was also his way of claiming ethos. As a creative writer, he claimed to be a *writer* who would be especially sensitive to the "reduction" of these courses to service courses. When the composition scholar relayed the comment to a colleague (who is also a composition scholar) to help explain the lack of agreement among factions of the department, as soon as the composition scholar repeated the italicized statement ("maybe he and I, as writers ourselves"), her colleague interrupted with, "Oh, and you're not [a writer]?" In other words, by distinguishing himself and another creative writer as writers, and theorizing that this distinction might be the cause for disagreement with the composition scholar, the creative writer's statement includes the illocutionary meaning and microinvalidation of denying that compositionists are also writers.

The reaction by her colleague left the composition scholar both offended and empowered: offended at the realization that she was not seen as a writer by members of her own department (despite having published many articles in peer-reviewed scholarly journals) and empowered at her colleague's remark reminding her that she is, indeed, a writer. The composition scholar's initial acceptance of the creative writer's statement implying that she was *not* a writer demonstrates the psychological effects hierarchical microaggressions can have, in that they create in their targets feelings of inferiority that sometimes lead the victim of the microaggression to accept the offensive positions of the aggressors.

Example 7

For our final example, we extend the scope from interpersonal communication to a published article. On October 3, 2016, *The Chronicle of Higher Education* (*CHE*) published an article titled "Are We Teaching Composition All Wrong?" by Joseph R. Teller. While the content of the column generated a lively and somewhat heated discussion on the email listserv for writing program administrators (WPA-L), arguably the most contentious aspect of the article was not the criticism of composition instruction expressed by the author, but the positioning of the author as a composition scholar. The article byline describes Teller as a professor of English, and Teller states in the article that he has been teaching writing for ten years. Based on responses to the email list, many composition scholars were surprised at Teller's depiction of composition pedagogy, with several noting his dated view of the privileging of process over product and his misunderstanding of what comprises peer response. Teller concludes with a list of solutions, most of which offer nothing new to composition scholars (i.e., students should start writing early in the semester, not all assignments require peer response or the same number of drafts, and process is merely a means to an end), yet this list is presented as if it were groundbreaking for composition, or at least for those who read *CHE*.

As Nora Bacon notes in a 2015 review essay of Steven Pinker's book, *The Sense of Style*, "when he [Pinker] presents himself as a teacher of writing, he doesn't seem to be aware that the field he's entering is already occupied, or even that it exists as something separate from his own discipline" (299). Teller makes the same mistake as Pinker. By presenting his views as if he were an expert in composition instruction, Teller equates his ten years of experience teaching writing with expertise in the field of composition,[1] thus ignoring or denying the existence of composition as a discipline in its own right. Furthermore, by publishing Teller's column under "advice," the editors of *CHE* are complicit in this microinvalidation, as they perpetuate the view that anyone in an English Department has the training and expertise to give advice on how to teach composition (see Example 5, above). We include this example to illustrate that hierarchical microaggressions against composition as a field are present on both interpersonal and institutional levels, making them all the more difficult to identify and combat.

Table 1 summarizes, labels, and classifies the speech acts and hierarchical microaggressions described in Examples 1-7.

Table 1
Classification of Speech Acts and Hierarchical Microaggressions

Example	Utterance or Action	Speech Act	Type of Hierarchical Microaggression
1	Yes, but I mean, what do you do?	Rejection of composition as a scholarly field	Microinvalidation
2	So they just want someone to teach grammar and spelling.	Reduction of composition's scope	Microinsult
3	But how do you act out grammar?	Reduction of composition's scope	Microinsult
4	I disagree!	Denial that knowing how to teach literature is different from knowing how to teach writing	Microinvalidation
5	Of course I'd rather teach literature – wouldn't everyone?	Assumption that teaching composition is inferior to/less desirable than teaching literature	Microinsult
6	… maybe he and I, *as writers ourselves*, both take the view of English as a "service department" too personally?	Denial that composition scholars are writers	Microinvalidation
7	*Are We Teaching Composition All Wrong?*	Belief that experience equals expertise in composition	Microinvalidation

Table 1 not only helps us identify the speech acts and types of hierarchical microaggressions composition scholars experience but also reveals the misconceptions that literary scholars and creative writers seem to hold about composition as a field and the work composition scholars do. Based on these speech acts, as well as others that our colleagues have reported to us, these misconceptions can be summarized as follows:

1. Composition is not a scholarly field.
2. Composition's scope is limited and boring.
3. Anyone who teaches literature or creative writing is qualified to teach composition.
4. Teaching composition is inferior to teaching literature and creative writing.
5. Teaching composition is equivalent to expertise as a composition scholar.
6. Composition scholars are not writers.
7. English departments are best represented by literary scholars and creative writers.

Not only do these misconceptions denigrate composition as a field, they also reinforce a view that literary scholarship and creative writing are normative for an English department and, as a result, perpetuate the marginalization of composition.

Conclusion: Moving from Hierarchical Microaggressions to Intersectional Explorations

We wrote this article because narratives of progress like the one presented at the CCCC presentation we reference at the beginning, while necessary to assessing and recognizing the gains composition scholars have made, also have the effect of invalidating the feelings of those who continue to experience marginalization at the local level. It is important, therefore, to call attention to the hierarchical microaggressions we have witnessed and experienced as composition scholars, as ways of complicating these narratives of progress and highlighting the work we still have to do. The conversations presented in this article, and the accompanying analyses, provide an explanation for the feelings of marginalization some composition scholars experience but have trouble articulating. That is, using the label of hierarchical microaggressions has enabled us to "name what we feel," to borrow from the title of Linda Adler-Kassner and Elizabeth Wardle's book and the feminist political practice of "naming," in which women share experiences and find ways to articulate common experiences previously assumed to be individual or personal (see Cameron). In evoking "feelings," we are *not* suggesting that the hierarchical microaggressions described here are "all in the heads" of the victims, a criticism that has been frequently levied by members of the conservative right. Indeed, our use of speech act analysis confirms that the feelings we describe and seek to label can be viewed as part of the microaggressions' perlocutionary force, in response to speech as *actions*. Furthermore, the work of neuroscientist Antonio Damasio reminds us that feelings (and emotions, which Damasio theorizes as separate but related to feelings) are not "mere decoration" but rather "expressions of the struggle for balance" (7). And because wpa work is, as Micciche argues, emotional labor, we believe that acknowledging the emotions that microaggressions provoke is an important step in raising consciousness, first in order to label the "problem without a name" (to borrow from Betty Friedan) and second, to begin a dialogue about how to deal with them. Identifying and labeling feelings, in these as in other cases, confirm that the personal is indeed political.

Our first reaction as compositionists when studying these comments was anger. Upon further reflection, however, our findings had the positive effect of validating our feelings of marginalization. Ultimately, we believe our findings can empower composition scholars to respond constructively to the misconceptions our analysis reveals and enlighten all faculty (compositionists included) about the unintended metamessages certain remarks convey. That is, we believe that simply raising awareness of hierarchical microaggressions may motivate composition scholars to pre-empt or respond to comments similar to what we observed. We also believe that composition scholars who direct graduate programs or are in mentoring relationships with future composition faculty should make these students aware of the potential prejudices they might face, particularly if they join the faculty of traditional English departments.

We also found that informing other faculty about composition research proved an effective way of responding without making faculty feel defensive. For example, we challenged statements made by the literary scholar from Example 2 who depicted composition as a field focused on "spelling and grammar" by talking to him about research on the effectiveness (or lack thereof) of drill-type grammar instruction. Another composition scholar shared her research during a faculty colloquium that was well attended by literary scholars and creative writers. When we presented on the topic of microaggressions at conferences, we also gathered other ways of coping with hierarchical microaggressions, such as having colleagues in other fields, even outside of English studies, observe our teaching and then talking to them about the scholarship informing it. A recent meeting in our current home department is evidence of the progress we've made. During the meeting, several literature colleagues recognized that by offering upper-level literature courses as rewards to adjuncts who had met their "service requirement" of teaching composition courses, we were perpetuating inequalities between the fields and stigmatizing composition as a set of "service" courses.

An important limitation of the present study is that it is based predominantly on the observations of two self-identifying white women. In addition to Wallace (cited earlier), Collin Lamont Craig and Staci Maree Perryman-Clark suggest that future research might take a more intersectional view of microaggressions, examining how interactions between gender, race, sexuality, status, and discipline expand upon or complicate this discussion ("Troubling the Boundaries"). For example, do compositionists who are men experience or respond to hierarchical microaggressions differently? Are men or women of color more likely to *also* experience hierarchical microaggressions targeting their fields or areas of study? Such intersectional work may be difficult, but given the marginalization described by faculty of color within academia as well as the fact that writing and wpa work are embodied practices, we believe such research is crucial. Indeed, a recent symposium on "Challenging Whiteness and/in Writing Program Administration and Writing Programs" positions the need for studies on the intersections between race, gender, and wpa work as especially urgent, since discrimination based on a person's institutional role often intersects with racial discrimination (L'Epplattenier et al.).

Many of the pieces in the symposium overtly call out microaggressions that relate to combinations of faculty members' race, gender, and institutional roles. Jasmine Kar Tang and Noro Andriamanalina describe an incident one of them experienced when she told a white, female colleague that she worked for the "Office of Diversity." The colleague responded, "Oh, that's important. The students must have a lot of language issues" (11). In this microinsult, the colleague immediately presumes that diversity must equate with deficit and positions the institutional roles of either Tang or Andriamanalina as managing these deficits. Perryman-Clark describes having her administrative decisions be "read only as agenda-driven race work," having to justify a writing assessment decision to "an inexperienced, first-time TA with little background in composition pedagogy," and even having to deal with the same TA requesting that she be fired, a threat relating to her race, gender, and pre-tenure status ("Revisited" 21). In addition, Craig and Perryman-Clark's narrative of the microaggressions and discrimination they experienced as graduate students at the CWPA conference reminds us to be aware of the ways in which we, as compositionists with access to whiteness, may be microaggressing others ("Troubling the Boundaries"). We hope that bringing research on microaggressions together with speech act theory, as well as other forms of linguistic and/or rhetorical analysis might provide increased insight into the misconceptions that motivate microaggressions and, ultimately, lead to a decrease in their occurrence.

Acknowledgments

We are deeply grateful to Kung-Wan Philip Choong for brainstorming the initial premise of this article with us and to Laura Micciche and the anonymous reviewers for their guidance in shaping the final version.

Notes

1. Like Elizabeth Wardle and J. Blake Scott, we acknowledge that expertise in rhetoric and composition doesn't have to equate to having a graduate degree or coursework in the field (73). However, expertise is different from experience, in that it should consist of what Wardle and Scott refer to as "primary source knowledge" (reading foundational and current research and theory in composition), "interactional expertise" (having "social connection to and interaction with groups conversing about composition"), and/or "contributory expertise" (presenting at conferences, publishing in composition, and/or conducting research/assessment in composition) (78-80).

Works Cited

Adler-Kassner, Linda, and Elizabeth Wardle. *Naming What We Know: Threshold Concepts of Writing Studies*. Utah State UP, 2015.

Austin, John L. *How to Do Things with Words*. Oxford UP, 1962.

Bacon, Nora. "Cross-Disciplinary Approaches to Style." *CCC*, vol. 67, no. 2, 2015, pp. 290-303.

Bleich, David, et al. "Writing Studies at the MLA: The Past and Future of English and Writing Studies." CCCC, 16 Mar. 2017, Portland, OR. Conference Presentation. Chair: Clancy Ratliff, Respondent: Anne Ruggles Gere.

Bright, Anita, and James Gambrell. "Calling In, Not Calling Out: A Critical Race Framework for Nurturing Cross-Cultural Alliances in Teacher Candidates." *Handbook of Research on Promoting Cross-Cultural Competence and Social Justice in Teacher Education*, edited by Jared Keengwe, IGI Global, 2017, pp. 217-35.

Cameron, Deborah. *Feminism and Linguistic Theory*. Palgrave Macmillan, 2002.

Craig, Collin Lamont, and Staci Maree Perryman-Clark. "Troubling the Boundaries: (De)Constructing WPA Identities at the Intersections of Race and Gender." *WPA*, vol. 34, no. 2, 2011, pp. 20-26.

—. "Troubling the Boundaries Revisited: Towards Change as Things Stay the Same." *WPA*, vol. 39, no. 2, 2016, pp. 37-58.

Crowley, Sharon. *Composition in the University: Historical and Polemical Essays*. U of Pittsburgh P, 1998.

Damasio, Antonio. *Looking for Spinoza: Joy, Sorrow, and the Feeling Brain*. Harcourt, 2003.

Detweiler, Jane, et al. "Academic Leadership and Advocacy: On Not Leaning In." *College English*, vol. 79, no. 5, 2017, pp. 451-65.

Flynn, Elizabeth. "Composing as a Woman." *Feminism and Composition: A Critical Sourcebook*, edited by Gesa E. Kirsch et al., Bedford/St. Martin's, 2003, pp. 243-55.

Friedan, Betty. *The Feminine Mystique*. Norton, 2001.

Hairston, Maxine. "The Winds of Change: Thomas Kuhn and the Revolution in the Teaching of Writing." *Landmark Essays on Writing Process*, edited by Sondra Perl, Hermagoras P, 1994, pp. 113-26.

Hesse, Doug. "The Place of Creative Writing in Composition Studies," *CCC*, vol. 62, no. 1, 2010, pp. 31-52.

Inoue, Asao B. "Friday Plenary Address: Racism in Writing Programs and the CWPA." *WPA*, vol. 40, no. 1, 2016, pp. 134-54.

L'Epplattenier, Barbara, et al. "Symposium: Challenging Whiteness and/in Writing Program Administration and Writing Programs." *WPA*, vol. 39, no. 2, 2016, pp. 9-52.

Lilienfeld, Scott O. "Microaggressions: Strong Claims, Inadequate Evidence." *Perspectives on Psychological Science*, vol. 12, no. 1, 2017, pp. 138-69, doi: 10.1177/1745691616659391.

Mayers, Tim. *(Re)Writing Craft: Composition, Creative Writing, and the Future of English Studies*. U of Pittsburgh P, 2005.

Micciche, Laura R. "More than a Feeling: Disappointment and WPA Work." *CCC*, vol. 64, no. 4, 2002, pp. 432-58. doi:10.2307/3250746.

Miller, Susan. *Textual Carnivals: the Politics of Composition*. SIUP, 1991.

Rose, Shirley K, et al. "Directing First-Year Writing: The New Limits of Authority." *CCC*, vol. 65, no. 1, 2013, pp. 43-66.

Schell, Eileen E. *Gypsy Academics and Mother-Teachers: Gender, Contingent Labor, and Writing Instruction*. Boynton/Cook, 1998.

Searle, John R. *Speech Acts: An Essay in the Philosophy of Language*. Cambridge UP, 1969.

Sue, Derald Wing. *Microaggressions and Marginality: Manifestations, Dynamic, and Impact*. Wiley, 2010.

—. "Microaggressions: More than Just Race." *Psychology Today*. 17 Nov. 2010. psychologytoday.com/blog/microaggressions-in-everyday-life/201011/microaggressions-more-just-race.

—, et al. "Racial Microaggressions in Everyday Life: Implications for Clinical Practice." *American Psychologist*, vol. 62, no. 4, 2007, pp. 271-86. doi: 10.1037/0003-066X.62.4.271.

Swim, Janet K., et al. "Everyday Sexism: Evidence for Its Incidence, Nature, and Psychological Impact from Three Daily Diary Studies." *Journal of Social Issues*, vol. 57, no. 1, 2001, pp. 31-53. doi: 10.1111/0022-4537.00200.

Tang, Jasmine Kar, and Noro Andriamanalina "'Rhoda Left Early to Go to Black Lives Matter': Programmatic Support for Graduate Writers of Color." *WPA*, vol. 39, no. 2, 2016, pp. 10-16.

Teller, Joseph R. "Are We Teaching Composition All Wrong? *The Chronicle of Higher Education*, 8 Oct. 2016, chronicle.com/article/Are-We-Teaching-Composition/237969.

Wallace, David L. "A Queer Reading of the Rhetoric of Microaggressions." CCCC, 16 Mar. 2017, Portland, OR. Conference Presentation.

Wardle, Elizabeth, and J. Blake Scott. "Defining and Developing Expertise in a Writing and Rhetoric Department." *WPA*, vol. 39, no. 1, 2015, pp. 72-93, wpacouncil.org/archives/39n1/39n1wardle-scott.pdf.

Young, Kathryn, et al. "Hierarchical Microaggressions in Higher Education." *Journal of Diversity in Higher Education*, vol. 8, no. 1, 2015, pp. 61-71, *ERIC*, doi:10.1037/a0038464.

"Higher" School: Nineteenth-Century High Schools and the Secondary-College Divide

Amy J. Lueck

This article traces the emergence of nineteenth-century U.S. high schools in the landscape of higher education, attending to the gendered, raced, and classed distinctions at play in this development. Exploring differences in the conceptualization and status of high schools in Louisville, Kentucky, for white male, white female, and mixed-gender African American students, this article reminds us of how these institutional types have been situated, socially inflected, and structured in relation to broader political and power structures that transcend explicit pedagogical considerations. As a result, I argue for the recognition of high schools as historically significant sites in the history of college composition instruction.

In *A History of American Higher Education*, educational historian John Thelin reveals much of our common knowledge about the traditions and legacies of educational institutions to be backformations—attempts to shore up contemporary schools, policies, or practices by aligning them with a sense of revered history (xv).[1] That is, the development of colleges and universities as distinct institutions in this country seems smooth and obvious from a certain vantage point because some aspects of the story have been obscured through revisionist histories that have an investment in conveying tradition and longevity. Thelin cites the University of Louisville as an example of a university whose history was subject to such a revision when the city's mayor traced the school's founding beyond the traditionally accepted year of 1842, pushing it back to the 1798 founding date of its institutional forerunner, Jefferson Seminary, in an attempt to "contribute to civic or state pride" (xv). He uses this example to "illustrate that historical writing about higher education is constantly subject to new estimates and reconsideration" (xv).

Though Thelin does not explore the point further, the Seminary is not the only controversial institution in the University of Louisville's past deserving of new estimates and reconsideration: The public high schools in Louisville are also importantly connected to—and perhaps purposefully obscured in relation to—the history of the university as it developed. As I will demonstrate, high schools played a central role in higher education in Louisville. They embraced a collegiate liberal arts mission as well as normal (or teacher) training work, were understood to be providing the highest branches of education for their communities, and had a close (at times even indistinguishable) physical and administrative relationship to the University of Louisville in the antebellum period. An examination of Louisville's high schools illustrates the complex and unstable relationship between many nineteenth-century urban high schools and colleges across the country.

Newly established and still developing their own educational missions, early U.S. high schools had few distinguishing characteristics to define them as a type beyond their position at the upper level of common schooling and their public funding through taxation. Unlike today, the public high school in the mid-nineteenth century was not understood as a preparatory institution for college, even though many high schools did indeed prepare students for college, purposely or incidentally. Instead, antebellum high schools (and normal schools, as well as some academies) were more often framed as an alternative higher education, especially for those who would not pursue the traditional professions for which the antebellum college typically prepared students. After all, one did not need a high school diploma to attend undergraduate colleges (or even medical or law schools), and the average college and high school matriculant were similar in age, often around 14 or 15 but up to their late teens and twenties, following completion of grammar or common school, respectively. Thus, high schools' curricula, pedagogies, missions, and even degrees and credentials overlapped with those of academies, seminaries, normal schools, and colleges—each of which were often what Roger Geiger calls "multipurpose" institutions that provided various kinds of education under one roof (128; see also Leslie).

As numerous educational historians of this time period attest, "The definition of the college experience, as a formal entity distinct from secondary education and from graduate studies, remained unclear" throughout the nineteenth and into the twentieth century (Thelin 97; also see Farnham; Gordon; Hampel). William J. Reese explains the ambiguity that particularly surrounded the idea of "high schools" in the nineteenth century: "Americans throughout the early 1800s wrote approvingly of schools of a 'higher order' that offered 'advanced education' in the 'higher branches' in something often called a 'high' or 'higher school.' High was whatever was not low" (Reese 34). Reese himself uses the phrase "the higher learning" to describe the work of high schools throughout his comprehensive history of *The Origins of the American High School*. Karen Graves, writing about the St. Louis high schools, similarly points out that "'high school' was an ambiguous term in the nineteenth century," noting that it was not until the 1880s that the public high school overtook the academy as the dominant institution of secondary education in the United States—taking on its preparatory status in the process (107). By the end of the century, reformers were attempting to articulate a reliable system of educational leveling in the

U.S., from elementary to secondary to post-secondary institutions, and those efforts established many of our current understandings of academic hierarchies and educational progression across academic levels. Before that articulation of programs in the system though, Marc VanOverbeke points out that some larger high schools "even offered courses and programs that exceeded those available in several colleges" and were actually in some competition with colleges and universities for students (18).

These observations of the confounding morphology of "higher learning" by educational historians suggest the need to reevaluate our assumptions about what it means to study the history of college writing. While it may not be necessary to produce numerous institutional histories of high schools within our field, and while important political differences often do persist between colleges and high schools, we would do well to pay some attention to the ways early high schools can complicate our existing narratives about higher learning and, subsequently, the history of writing instruction in the U.S. As I argue, the historical role of writing in high schools is important not only because of how it may have *influenced* college writing but also because of the ways it *functioned as* college writing in some cases, both pedagogically and politically. Recognizing the differential social value attributed to historical high schools for different gendered and raced student groups is particularly important to our histories of writing and rhetoric because it helps us to engage critically with these terms and designations as we compose our historical narratives and consider their implications for present and future practice.

And yet, the history of high schools remains largely overlooked by our field. We do not write and publish stand-alone histories of high schools, and we neglect them in otherwise comprehensive lists of institution types in almost every volume on nineteenth-century instruction. But as we continue to extend the scope of historical institutions and sites of rhetoric and literacy learning that we examine, the tacit divide between secondary and college writing in our disciplinary self-conception is becoming increasingly untenable. In light of recent feminist recovery efforts, master narratives of rhetorical instruction and delivery in America's colleges have already given way to a strong interest in local, archival histories that elaborate a nuanced rhetorical heritage in this country that increasingly understands such "peripheral" institutional spaces as women's colleges, normal schools, agricultural colleges and historically black colleges and universities (HBCUs) as centrally constitutive of our rhetorical past (see Donahue and Moon; Enoch; Gold; Gold and Hobbs; Ritter). High schools in many ways seem like the next logical sites to study to diversify our historical accounts of writing instruction and practice.

The need for this step towards examining the history of American high schools has been suggested by the work of Lucille M. Schultz in collaboration with Jean Ferguson Carr and Stephen Carr. They have long been attentive to the theories, pedagogies, and practices of the lower schools, particularly through the examination of textbooks. More recently, Henrietta Rix Wood has explored the use of epideictic rhetoric by nineteenth and early twentieth-century school girls. A collection of histories edited by Lori Ostergaard and Wood brings together high schools and normal schools under one historical umbrella: institutions that taught the vast majority of nineteenth- and early twentieth-century writers, both men and women. These texts remind us, as Kelly Ritter puts it in the introduction to *In the Archives of Composition*, that "'writing' does not emerge, fully formed, out of first-year college students (whether at the community college, the four-year comprehensive, or the research university, private or public). Writing happens in secondary schools, and *has* happened in this location in rich and vital ways for nearly two hundred years" (Ostergaard and Wood xi). As implied by Ritter, a great many students and their writing have never emerged on our scene of research at all, though writing and learning has been happening in our schools for a broad span of time. I will argue that high school students deserve our attention not only as *high school students* or *future college students,* as others have argued, but also as learners and practitioners of writing who powerfully challenge the historical high school-college divide itself.

To make this case, I present a brief case study of the Louisville schools, focusing on how, in their own time, the schools' pedagogies and their institutional titles invited productive uncertainty about their role and status in the landscape of higher learning. The unreliability of these institutional designations—high school or college—deserves more attention. While historians can (and do) make necessary distinctions between institution types in the course of their own research, my call is to attend to the interpretive (and political) process of making such distinctions. I make two observations in this regard: First, the institutional titles have been adaptable to different educational contexts. Second, those official designations have always been reflective of the interests of those in power, even as actual students and teachers have used rhetoric and literacy to work within and against those structures. Hence, I begin by establishing the white men's high school as a chartered liberal arts college with an unequivocal (if short-lived) position within the university. I then turn to a consideration of the white women's and mixed-gender African Americans' high schools in the same city. These schools put the status of the men's high school in relief: They evidence how non-dominant populations gained access to meaningful higher learning opportunities, pedagogically comparable to at least some colleges of the time, while the fact that *their* high schools were never proposed as colleges also reveals the differential cultural and political value that characterized the education of women and people of color. This development had less to do with the identity of the *high school* than with the identity of the *students* therein. The stakes of accepting these institutional designations at face value should be clear.

In presenting this case study of Louisville high schools, then, I gesture also to the many other schools that challenge the historical reliability of the secondary and college designations. Take, for example, Baltimore's Central High School, which transformed into Baltimore City College, or the Philadelphia Central High School that conferred bachelors' degrees (and continues to do so to this day). Each of these white male high schools benefited from the uncertain nature of the "higher" school in relation to a college, while their female and non-white counterparts remained subordinated and contained. In the case of Philadelphia, until 1860 women were provided only a normal (teacher training) education, expressly *not* intended to provide advanced academic study as the prospect of such "higher schooling" for women remained controversial.

In light of these and other examples, I present Louisville as what proponents of microhistory would call an "exceptional normal"—a case whose value lies "not in its uniqueness, but in its exemplariness" (Lepore 133; see also McComiskey). Especially in the face of seemingly "new" challenges to the high school-college distinction posed by dual enrollment and similar programs, there is a need to examine more closely the historical nature of the high school-college relationship. While this relationship invites potential new sites for historical research and inquiry in our field, it also initiates an interrogation of what we have taken to be the defining features of college writing instruction in our past and present.

Higher Schooling in Louisville: Male High School

Like many across the country, Louisville's public high schools began with a general interest in expanded public schooling around midcentury, though the schools' relationship to existing educational models was as yet unclear. A brief overview of the early history of Louisville's Male High School illustrates the ambiguity of its institutional designations. Established in 1792 as the Jefferson Seminary, the high school was renamed Louisville College in 1842, "under the powers granted to the City of Louisville to establish a High School," demonstrating the close relation between several institutional titles (seminary, college, and high school) (*Public School Laws* 20-21). The college was renamed University of Louisville in 1846, and an "Academical Department" was established with reciprocal privileges for academic and medical students. In 1856, the Academical Department was renamed Male High School, though it was still located on the university campus and continued to be referred to also as the Academical Department.

The curriculum of Male High School in its earliest years aspired to cover the traditional collegiate subjects, though (like many high schools and colleges) they were limited by funding and staffing issues. As in many colleges, the curriculum during the school's first year was heavily weighted towards the classical subjects, with all 79 students studying mathematics, 65 studying ancient languages, and 37 studying modern languages (*Annual Report* [1857] 17). But already in that first year of operations, the school leaders were expressing interest in curricular reform. Reporting on behalf of the Committee of Examination and Control in 1857, a representative praised the school and averred that those citizens who had "stood aloof" of the other public schools are now "earnestly urging the claims of their sons to the educational advantages" of the high school; yet, he goes on to say, "the Committee cannot but lament the imperfect system of collegiate education as yet afforded," without a "Professorship of Belles Lettres, or as it is styled, 'Rhetoric and English Literature'" (ibid).

William N. McDonald, who held a Master's degree from the University of Virginia, was accordingly hired as professor of rhetoric and English literature the following year, and textbooks selected for that year reflect a new emphasis on rhetoric and elocution, primarily in the first years of study, using George P. Quackenbos' *Advanced Course of Composition and Rhetoric* and Epes Sargent's *Standard Speaker* in the first year, along with assigned declamations in the first two years. Though they reflect the impoverished tradition of rhetorical theory in American colleges bemoaned in the foundational work of Albert Kitzhaber, James Berlin, Robert Connors, Sharon Crowley, among others, these textbooks were nonetheless very common collegiate fare. In addition, students used Robert Gordon Latham's *A Handbook of English Language* in the upper two years of study, which is a volume marketed "for the use of students of the universities and the higher classes of schools," comprised of one half history and analysis of the English language and one half exhaustive catalogue of grammar, syntax, and orthography rules, suggesting the ascendance of current-traditional approaches to writing instruction traced by historians of rhetoric and composition.

The superintendent of the school board, reporting on the students' exam performances, noted that "there was a demonstration of an attainment in each, of extraordinary excellence" such as "would be difficult to parallel—it could not have been surpassed" (*Annual Report* [1859] 25). While these remarks undoubtedly smack of adulation and hyperbole, they are also telling insofar as they reveal the expectations of the school board: that students and professors will reach the "highest" levels of performance and study in their fields. Though the students' examination papers in rhetoric and composition, which are said to be appended to the school board report, have been lost to history, the expectations of the school's leaders (as well as the textbooks used) tell us much about what they understood the function and status of the high school coursework to be: a fully elaborated liberal arts education.

By 1859, the rhetorical instruction at Male had been further extended in this direction. While still featuring Quackenbos' *Advanced Course of Composition and Rhetoric* in the first two years of study, along with Sargent's *Standard Speaker* and declamations, the upper years of rhetorical studies became even more clearly collegiate, with students studying George Campbell's *Rhetoric* and Lord Henry Kames' *Elements of Criticism* in their junior year and Richard Whateley's *Rhetoric* and *Logic* in their senior year. According to the Committee on the High School, students' examination performances the following year, which included questions about rhetoric and elements of criticism, provided "evidence not only of a thorough acquaintance with their text-books, but a comprehensive knowledge of the subjects. They also evinced an independent and philosophical accuracy of thought, a purity of taste, and an elevation of moral sentiment rarely found among students of the most celebrated *colleges* in the country" (*Annual Report* [1860] 28; emphasis added).

And, indeed, 1860 is the year that the school became a college. While retaining the name of Male High School, it was determined by law that Male High School "shall be in fact and in law a College . . . [and] shall have power to confer any and all degrees that may be lawfully conferred by any College or University in the Commonwealth of Kentucky," at which point Male took on the additional moniker of the "University of Public Schools" (*Public School Laws* 43). Serving effectively as an undergraduate college for the university, though eventually moved to its own site separate from the university campus, Male High School conferred bachelors and even masters' degrees on its students until 1912, and the work of students during the degree-granting period from 1860-1912 is reported to have compared favorably with the leading colleges of the day ("300 Male Grads"). Even if not comparable to the *leading* colleges, it is doubtless that the school's work compared to a great number of lower ranked colleges across the country.

If this account of institutional title changes and curricular transformations seems confusing, that is the point: The boundaries between these institutions and the terms used to name them were unstable as the face of higher learning in the city was being worked out. At times a high school, university department, or college, what is now known as Male High School (which exists as a co-educational high school today) was not clearly distinguished from *collegiate* or *liberal* education, which it embraced as its mission and which it provided in connection to the University of Louisville for a time. In fact, when Male High School was separated from the university system in 1860, the University of Louisville functioned exclusively as a professional school for law and medicine (Federal Writers' Project 19). Emerging accreditation requirements pushed for the revival of an academic department in 1907 in order for the University of Louisville to be considered a comprehensive university (Yater 53). In this odd way, then, the defining feature of the University of Louisville qua university was, for a time at least, the men's public high school.

Pedagogically Similar, Politically Different: Female High School

The history of Louisville's Female High School runs parallel to Male's, beginning with an 1851 charter that designates a school tax for the "support of the Public Schools and High School for females of said city, and the University of Louisville" (*Public School Laws* 20-21). As indicated by the language of this charter, plans to establish a female high school were circulating prior to any specific mention of a male high school but in tandem with developments of the "academical department" of the University of Louisville that would become Male High School, suggesting its alignment with that collegiate project (ibid). From the language of the charter itself to the operation of those schools in subsequent decades, Louisville highlights the unclear status and function of the early high school in the landscape of nineteenth-century higher learning. But that lack of clarity meant something different for women than for men: It meant that the city's young women were getting their advanced collegiate education at a public institution with the name of *high school*, not college or university. While always designated a high school, though, Female's institutional position and status is complicated by its own advanced curriculum and the fact that it was at several points in its history posited as a normal, or teacher training, school for the city and even the state.

Though not as advanced as the curriculum of Male in its early years (and also omitting that most collegiate of subjects, Greek), the curriculum at Female was nonetheless serious and ambitious. From 1859-1861, students studied Latin and French, mathematics, geography, history, English, and rhetoric and composition across a three-year course of study. In rhetoric and composition, they used Greene's *Analysis of English* in the first and third years, and Quackenbos's *Advanced Course in Rhetoric and Composition* in the second year, along with weekly composition exercises across all three years. Quackenbos's text, as discussed earlier, was commonly used in colleges, even though it has been criticized by modern scholars of rhetoric and composition for being reflective of a "less theorized" nineteenth-century rhetorical tradition (Berlin; Connors; Crowley; Kitzhaber). Greene's text is more complicated to unpack. Insofar as the instruction of English grammar became the purview of elementary schools, Greene's text has been remembered as foundational to the development of grammar instruction at the elementary level; and yet, in its own time, *Analysis of Grammar* was in use at Michigan's Hillsdale College and other colleges that were using English grammar in place of ancient languages for mental discipline at the higher levels. Thus, the various uses of this text speak not only to the "low standards" of colleges but also to the frequent overlap between different schools, their texts, and their curricula in a time of changing educational philosophies ("Formal English" 255).

It is also important to consider how these texts might have been used in different contexts. Though we cannot capture much about pedagogy and rigor in the use of these texts (particularly given the limited archival records of these schools), the studies at Female were praised as "solid, rather than showy" by the 1859 board of examiners—a claim certainly intended to contrast then-current characterizations of women's higher education as ornamental or superficial, which was a criticism often leveled at women's education in the South (*Annual Report* [1859] 24). Elaborating on this same theme in a speech the following year, Principal Holyoke of Female High School expressed the high aspirations he had for his students, writing

> We aim to do our part in making honorable, intelligent, high-minded women. . . . We wish them to become accurate thinkers and reasoners. . . . We wish them to be able to communicate the knowledge they have gained, and we instruct them in the great principles of language by means of a thorough instruction in the Latin and French, by constant practice in impromptu compositions, and by giving the simpler principles of Rhetoric. . . . Above all this, however, we labor to make them independent in thought and action. We endeavor to cultivate the individual character of each, and not bring all down to one dead level. (*Annual Report* [1860] 11)

These "high-minded," independent women are akin to the "female scholars" in St. Louis high schools recovered by historian Karen Graves (xii). In both Louisville and St. Louis, the educational atmosphere of the public high school is comparable to women's and coeducational colleges across the South and West. But unlike their college counterparts—who were barred from presenting their own essays at graduation ceremonies even at the most liberal colleges of the time—Female High School students had another benefit: They composed and read original compositions for their public commencement ceremonies, essays that reveal evidence of strong rhetorical instruction and remarkable freedom and variety in topics, ranging from playful meditations on the occasion of graduation to earnest critiques of women's position in society (Lueck; see also Buchanan). Since students were up to 21 years old, they challenge our ideas about age and maturity as markers of high school or college writing. As late as 1905, Emma Woerner (who would later become the first principal of Louisville's Atherton High School for Girls in 1924) was able to enter the

University of Kentucky as a junior, based on her academic accomplishments at Female High School ("History").

In addition to the advanced liberal arts education and rhetorical training, students at Female High School were professionally trained and credentialed as teachers at what was at several points in time the only public normal school in the area. Seniors were trained in teaching theory and methods, and all eight of the first graduating students (and a large majority thereafter) were said to have gone into teaching, their diplomas from Female serving as a privileged credential in district hiring decisions.

The provision of both advanced liberal arts and normal education at Female suggests it has a place in a broadly construed history of higher learning. For historically underprivileged or underserved populations, in particular, access to *higher* schooling was not only quite significant but also not always usefully distinguished from access to college in terms of either form or function within the community. That is, students in high schools and colleges learned a similar curriculum, and attending higher schooling was a privilege that conferred occupational benefits comparable to college attendance at a time when neither was a required credential.

And yet, it is also for these populations that it becomes most clear why a "college" designation has been so powerful: It is no coincidence that women's and African Americans' high schools were *not* conflated with colleges, as high schools for white men were. Instead, the boundaries around the term "college" were heavily policed by state legislatures and conservative social critics alike. As Christie Anne Farnham explains in her study of southern women's colleges, some women's schools across the South specifically avoided the term "college"—opting for "collegiate" or other variations—to avoid the additional public and governmental scrutiny attendant to colleges. Such scrutiny included both ongoing social criticism about the appropriateness of college for women and the necessity of having a charter passed in state legislatures for the granting of college degrees (18). Farnham goes on to argue that the flexible naming conventions and the "incremental process" of expanding course offerings at women's academies to include college subjects led to important gains in the expansion of higher education for women.

This incremental process was necessary even within the high school itself. Female High School serves as an example in light of its ever-expanding course of study: The school began with a limited curriculum that comprised only two years of study, then extended to three years, then added a preparatory department, until it finally became a four-year course of study, like that offered by the Male High School. As Principal Holyoke explained in 1860: "We have thus accomplished something, but each year the mark is set higher, and both teachers and pupils look upon each succeeding year as but a step towards a constantly receding summit" (*Annual Report* [1860] 11).

The "A Grade" and High School Course at Central Colored School

Access to anything resembling a public high school was a feat in itself for African American communities in the South, and it was through a similar progression that African American students of Louisville attained access to public high schools. After the much-delayed public schools for the lower grades were established in 1870, an "A Grade" was added to the Central Colored School in 1876. The "A Grade" was a one-year course for the education of prospective teachers who, as was commonly believed, required at least one more year of education than their pupils.

The central importance of teacher training as a sponsor of higher learning opportunities for both women and African Americans should not be overlooked, nor should the challenge that normal schools have posed to institutional designations. As both Female High School and Colored High School featured teacher training as a central aspect of their operation and even their *raison d'être*, the distinction between high schools and normal schools is less than clear. Recent recoveries of normal schools in our discipline have already invited us to reconsider the role of these schools in our histories, but the case of Louisville's African American schools further reveal them to be an almost exclusive pathway to higher learning for black students in the segregated South. As historian J. Blaine Hudson explains, "The state's determination to preserve the color line by staffing its segregated Black schools with Black teachers prompted the development of limited public higher educational opportunities for African Americans" (113). Though limited, these opportunities for higher education, including the "A Grade" and high school, were not insignificant.

The writing curriculum recorded in this "A Grade" in the annual report for 1880-81 features English and History as one combined subject, taught with the use of Noble Butler's *Practical and Critical Grammar*; Greene's *Analysis of English*, accompanied by exercises in composition; and reading aloud, reciting or speaking selections in prose and poetry. Butler's text is produced by the city's own notable educator, Noble Butler, by a printing press in the city. Greene's is recognizable as one of the texts in use at Female in the 1860 school year. By the next year, changes were made across the course listings. In particular, the English and history course was replaced by three separate courses of study, marked as follows: John Seely Hart's *A Manual of Composition and Rhetoric*, English Literature, and John J. Anderson's *General History*.[2] Courses on spelling and defining were added, as well as weekly lectures on the theory and practice of teaching.

Hart's *A Manual of Composition and Rhetoric* is notable as the text that introduced personal writing to composition classrooms, according to Robert Connors' *Composition-Rhetoric*—though Schultz contends that other textbooks did so earlier in the century (Connors 156; Schultz 156). The text is also notable as the earliest example of what Carr, Carr, and Schultz call (drawing on Connors) a "composition-rhetoric": texts that "orient their account of rhetorical principles toward a direct intervention in student writing" and "selectively adopt some practices of composition books" (66, 68). That is, composition-rhetorics like Hart's were not philosophical treatises on rhetoric but instead combined theory and practice, which was a common approach to rhetorical instruction in the last quarter of the century.

Because of its status as a composition-rhetoric, Hart's text has been a lightning rod for disagreement among scholars of nineteenth-century writing and rhetoric textbooks. Specifically, Carr, Carr, and Schultz disagree with Connors about the audience that Hart's text addresses. Connors' claims that, from 1865-1890, composition-rhetoric texts "were relegated to secondary school texts, while college texts again became treatises" (Connors qtd. in Carr, Carr, and Schultz 68n33). But Carr, Carr, and Schultz consider composition-rhetorics to be intended for college audiences or a combined high school and college audience (68). So, are composition-rhetorics for high school students or college students? My findings help to explain this ongoing confusion about texts like Hart's: The attempt to distinguish between high school and college rhetorical traditions has always been confounded by the uncertain relationship between these two educational sites before the turn of the century. Indeed, the distinctions are further blurred by the introduction of something like an "A Grade" into the educational landscape.

In 1882, the "A Grade" at last was replaced by a proper high school curriculum, though the course of study still comprised only three years in contrast to the four-year course at the all-white Male and Female High Schools. Nonetheless, the establishment of the city's first public high school for African Americans, called Colored High School (later Central High School, which name it retains today), was a point of pride for the Black community and students who had long fought for it. The school provided an advanced education and normal school training for its graduates, and the curriculum advanced each year.

The student speeches at the early commencement ceremonies of this school provide insights into the writing and rhetorical instruction of students, each one of whom presented during the ceremony, many reading original pieces of prose and poetry. In the early years of the "A Grade," in particular, graduations featured a range of genres, including a narrative poem, a humorous stump speech, and historical orations and essays such as one on Frederick Douglass as "the hero of the colored race, the world over," on "Our Next Door Neighbor, Mexico," and other historical figures and topics ("Commencements"; "Commencement Day"). These topics appeared alongside those more current-traditional themes such as "A Rolling Stone Gathers No Moss," "Life Is What We Make It," and "Progress" ("Colored Children"; "Commencement Day"). Several students spoke on themes of oratory or rhetoric, showing metacognitive engagement with their own rhetorical education and the notion of themselves as students and writers.

In fact, rhetorical and political education was the focus of this school to such an extent that the principal was criticized in 1893 for overemphasizing subjects like rhetoric and political economy to the detriment of basic studies in geography and mathematics, needed to pass the teacher examination. Not coincidentally, then, the leaders of this school were noted educational and political leaders in the city, such as Principal Albert E. Meyzeek, second principal of Colored High School (1893-1896), who was counted among the "more militant proponents of the activist civil rights thrust of W. E. B. DuBois" (Hudson 112). Though access to public college for African Americans in Louisville would be delayed for nearly another half century, it is thanks to these leaders that Louisville's African American students were learning (and teaching) writing in public and private institutions of higher learning since at least the 1870s.

Attempts to develop other public and private institutions for African Americans in Louisville reflect this same dedication as well as the same trend of confounding institutional morphology. There was a normal school established by the Freedmen's Bureau and the American Missionary Association as early as 1868, which later came under control of the local school board. A private normal school was established in 1879 (that would later become Simmons University), and another private institution was established just outside the city in 1890. But Hudson notes that "true higher education opportunities" for African Americans in Kentucky were available only through the State University in Frankfort (which grew from a state normal school established in 1886) and the coeducational Berea College (114). To further complicate matters, though, with the passage of the Day Law in 1908, school leaders of Berea College established a segregated African American branch of the college, which became "recognized as one of the premier *secondary* institutions for African Americans in the South" (Hudson 114; emphasis added). When the racially segregated Louisville Municipal College was at last established in 1931 as a branch of the University of Louisville, it was among the first nine municipal institutions of higher education established for African Americans in the U.S. by that time, the first six of which were all normal schools and the other two of which were part of the regular public school system, "housed in the same buildings with the public schools and under the control of the local Boards of Education" (qtd. in Hudson 120). The question, then, is how do we "count" Kentucky's previous six normal schools, the two junior colleges housed within the public schools, or the Louisville "A Grade" or high school when we turn our attention to "college" writing? What are these terminological short-hands missing? By not paying attention to politics behind these institutional titles, we may be inadvertently perpetuating the racism and sexism that informed them.

Implications: New Terms of Engagement for College Writing

This history of Louisville's "higher" schools is necessarily abridged, but the story that emerges here begins to push against rhetoric and composition's commonly accepted narratives about the development and practice of U.S. higher education by insisting on the inclusion of at least some high schools as sites of advanced literacy practices and progressive pedagogy on par with, sometimes forerunner to, and at other times quite literally equated with college composition and rhetoric instruction. Whether specific schools were or were not ever considered colleges, they all raise the question of what—and more pointedly, who—has constituted and defined histories of writing.

From the perspective of rhetoric and composition as a field, the history of Louisville's high schools pushes us to question current institutional designations and terms that we have taken for granted and to rethink our disciplinary histories and the origins they posit. High schools were not just preparatory institutions, perennially inadequate to the task, as they came to be commonly understood by the turn of the twentieth century. In fact, many were institutions of higher learning in their own right and represent an alternative tradition that is worth recovering. Though the histories of high schools and colleges ultimately follow different trajectories, it is important to draw on both to recover some of the messiness and overlap that existed at this moment in history and to highlight the stakes of this project for ongoing conversations about the shape, meaning, and purpose of writing instruction in the U.S. In this recovery, we need more meaningful connections between our field and the fields of education and history, where the methods and claims may differ, but where important work about rhetorical education is undoubtedly occurring. The research on historical high schools that comes from education, which I have cited throughout this piece, refreshes and challenges our disciplinary perspectives and assumptions.

We have much to gain from cross-disciplinary work, and I offer this piece as a beginning from which I hope will arise further archival research on student writing, classroom practices, and the uses of education across diverse institutional contexts. My book project, *A Shared History: Writing in the High School, College, and University 1856-1886,* responds to and extends this call.

As I elaborate there, such historical work influences our approaches to major questions within our discipline today. In particular, this historical inquiry has bearing on one of the most pressing questions facing our discipline: the role and status of dual-enrollment programs that are blurring the divide between high school and college. I suggest that a shift in historical perspective can help—and that collapsing traditional distinctions between secondary and college writing might, paradoxically, enable us to develop more useful partnerships in their place. We might recognize that the seemingly clear divide between high school and college has never, in fact, prevailed. From there, we can focus our energies on understanding how best to negotiate that fluidity and advocate for teaching and learning across this ostensible divide in our present historical moment. I hope that this history supports these efforts, and that subsequent histories of high school and college connections will help us to better understand both: What has made these sites of writing instruction distinct, and what they have had (and continue to have) in common.

Notes

1. For their invaluable feedback, I am indebted to the anonymous reviewers of this article and those who commented on previous drafts.

2. The courses of study at the high schools were frequently designated by the textbook in use to teach that subject. Here, rhetoric and composition and history are both designated by a specific textbook; it is not clear what students read for English literature.

Works Cited

Annual Report of the Board of Trustees of the University and Public Schools to the General Council of the City of Louisville, for the Year Ending July 1, 1855. Hull & Brother, 1855. Louisville Free Public Library, Louisville, KY.

Annual Report of the Board of Trustees of the University and Public Schools to the General Council of the City of Louisville, for the Year Ending July 1, 1857. Morton & Griswold, 1857. U of Chicago, Chicago, IL.

Annual Report of the Board of Trustees, of the University and Public Schools, of the City of Louisville, for the Year Ending June 30, 1859. Munger, Settle & Co, 1859. U of Kentucky, Lexington, KY.

Annual Report of the Board of Trustees of the Male High School, Female High School, and Public Schools of Louisville, to the General Council of the City of Louisville, for the Scholastic Year of 1859-'60. Bradley & Gilbert, 1860. Microfilm. Archives and Records Center, Jefferson County Public Schools, Louisville, KY.

Berlin, James A. *Writing Instruction in Nineteenth-Century American Colleges.* Carbondale: SIUP, 1984.

Buchanan, Lindal. *Regendering Delivery: The Fifth Canon and Antebellum Women Rhetors.* SIUP, 2005.

Carr, Jean Ferguson, Stephen L. Carr, and Lucille M. Schultz. *Archives of Instruction: Rhetorics, Readers, Composition Books in the United States.* SIUP, 2005.

"Colored Children." *Courier-Journal* 15 June 1884, p. 5.

"Commencement Day: A Brilliant Audience." *Courier-Journal* 11 June 1886, p. 6.

"Commencements: The Graduating Exercises of the Colored High School." *Courier-Journal* 16 June 1883, p. 6.

Connors, Robert J. *Composition-Rhetoric: Backgrounds, Theory and Pedagogy.* U of Pittsburgh P, 1997.

Crowley, Sharon. *Composition in the University: Historical and Polemical Essays.* U of Pittsburgh P, 1998.

Davies, Margery W. *Woman's Place is at the Typewriter.* Temple UP, 1982.

Donahue, Patricia, and Gretchen Flesher Moon, editors. *Local Histories: Reading the Archives of Composition.* U of Pittsburgh P, 2007.

Enoch, Jessica. *Refiguring Rhetorical Education: Women Teaching African American, Native American, and Chicano/a Students, 1865-1911.* SIUP, 2008.

Farnham, Christie Anne. *The Education of the Southern Belle: Higher Education and Student Socialization in the Antebellum South.* New York UP, 1994.

Federal Writers' Project of the Work Projects Administration for the State of Kentucky. *A Centennial History of the University of Louisville.* Louisville, Kentucky: The University of Louisville, 1939.

Fitzgerald, Kathryn. "A Rediscovered Tradition: European Pedagogy and Composition in Nineteenth-Century Midwestern Normal Schools." *CCC*, vol. 53, no. 2, 2001, pp. 224-50.

"Formal English Grammar as a Discipline." *Teachers College Record*, vol. XIV, no. 4, 1913, pp. 251-343.

Geiger, Roger L. "The Era of Multipurpose Colleges in American Higher Education, 1850-1890." *The American College in the Nineteenth Century,* edited by Roger L. Geiger, Vanderbilt UP, 2000, pp. 127-52.

Gold, David. *Rhetoric at the Margins: Revising the History of Writing Instruction in American Colleges, 1873-1947.* SIUP, 2008.

Gold, David, and Catherine Hobbs. *Educating the New Southern Woman: Speech, Writing, and Race at the Public Woman's College, 1884-1945.* SIUP, 2013.

Gordon, Lynn. *Gender and Higher Education in the Progressive Era.* Yale UP, 1990.

Graves, Karen. *Girls' Schooling during the Progressive Era: From Female Scholar to Domesticated Citizen.* Garland Publishing, 1998.

Hampel, Robert L. "Blurring the Boundary Between High School and College: The Long View." *Phi Delta Kappan*, vol. 99, no. 3, 2017, pp. 8-12.

"History." *Atherton High School.* Kentucky Department of Education. 15 March 2015. http://schools.jefferson.kyschools.us/high/atherton/history.html.

Hudson, J. Blaine. "The Establishment of Louisville Municipal College: A Study in Racial Conflict and Compromise." *The Journal of Negro Education*, vol. 64, no. 2, 1995, pp. 111-23.

Kitzhaber, Albert. *Rhetoric in American Colleges, 1850-1900.* Southern Methodist UP, 1990.

Latham, Robert G. *A Handbook of the English Language*. Taylor, Walton, and Maberly, 1851. *Google Books*. 15 Sept 2016. https://books.google.com/books?id=ZGwCAAAAQAAJ&printsec=frontcover&source=gbs_ge_summary_r&cad=0#v=onepage&q&f=false.

Lepore, Jill. "Historians Who Love Too Much: Reflections on Microhistory and Biography." *Journal of American History*, vol. 88, no. 1, 2001, pp. 129-46.

Leslie, W. Bruce. "Where Have All the Academies Gone?" *History of Education Quarterly*, vol. 41, no. 2, pp. 262-70.

Lueck, Amy J. "'High School Girls': Women's Higher Education at the Louisville Female High School." *Ohio Valley History*, vol. 17, no. 3, 2017, pp. 44-62.

—. "'A Maturity of Thought Very Rare in Young Girls': Women's Public Engagement in Nineteenth-Century High School Commencement Essays." *Rhetoric Review*, vol. 34, no. 2, 2015, pp. 129-46.

—. *A Shared History: Writing in the High School, College, and University 1856-1886*. SIUP, 2019.

McComiskey, Bruce. *Microhistories of Composition*. UP of Colorado, 2016.

Ostergaard, Lori, and Henrietta Rix Wood. *In the Archives of Composition: Writing and Rhetoric in High Schools and Normal Schools*. U of Pittsburgh P, 2015.

Public School Laws of the City of Louisville, A Compilation of the Acts of the Legislature and Laws Establishing and Governing the Male High School, the Female High School and the Public Schools of the City of Louisville, Ky (1882). Microfilm. Archives and Records Center, Jefferson County Public Schools, Louisville, KY.

Reese, William James. *The Origins of the American High School*. Yale UP, 1995.

Ritter, Kelly. *To Know Her Own History: Writing at the Woman's College, 1943-1963*. U of Pittsburgh P, 2012.

Schultz, Lucille M. *The Young Composers: Composition's Beginnings in Nineteenth-Century Schools*. SIUP, 1999.

Thelin, John. *A History of American Higher Education*. Johns Hopkins UP, 2011.

"300 Male High Grads Become U. of L. Alumni" *Alumni Bulletin* (July 1998). U of Louisville Archives and Special Collections, Louisville, KY.

VanOverbeke, Mark A. *The Standardization of American Schooling: Linking Secondary and Higher Education, 1870-1910*. Palgrave Macmillan, 2008.

Wood, Henrietta Rix. *Praising Girls: The Rhetoric of Young Women, 1895-1930*. SIUP, 2016.

Yater, George H. *Two Hundred Years at the Falls of the Ohio: A History of Louisville and Jefferson County*. The Filson Club, 1987.

Translational Learning: Surfacing Multilingual Repertoires

Ryan McCarty

This article presents the experiences of six bilingual Spanish-English students transitioning from high school to college, highlighting the ways they theorize translation and its relationship to writing and learning. As increased attention to theories of translingualism has established translation as deeply embedded in writing processes, and awareness of the multilingual makeup of college classrooms has further dispelled the "myth of linguistic homogeneity," we are poised to see writing in ways that align more closely to how our students experience language on a daily basis. Student reflections on writing and translation featured in this article contribute to a growing understanding of what I call *translational learning*: a process that allows students to develop awareness of differences in languages across contexts, contributes to metalinguistic awareness that allows them to engage with these differences, and builds a broad linguistic repertoire that allows for greater rhetorical dexterity.

"Well I think, you have an idea that it would be hard to actually translate the same words from English, like if I'm describing oppression, I really don't know how to say that in Spanish, so I would actually use another word, like describe it in another way like 'oh somebody being forced to do something in a unjust way'. So I would say that in Spanish but I would use that instead of the actual word. So it would be a harder translation. You can't say the same things that you put on your paper in English to your parents in Spanish cause they will probably not understand it and it won't really translate the same way."

—Mickey (2015)

"It just kind of makes it easier because I think of it in a kind of different perspective. If, speaking in Spanish it's like we'll use – something in Spanish, I guess like I live in a Spanish household so my mom, my grandmother, my father all speak Spanish, so they would use something that you would usually see in your household like what your parents do that could always relate to something in math, science, or any of the classes. And then explaining that it's like 'oh ok now I get it'. So I guess it wouldn't really be Spanish itself but like things that a normal Spanish family would do, I guess."

—Bernice (2015)

These reflections on language and learning, taken from interviews for a larger study of my former students[1] as they prepared to graduate from high school in the Bronx, illustrate some of the problems and possibilities facing multilingual students. How to go home and talk in one language about learning done in another? How to bring knowledge from other languages and contexts to bear on academic work in English? And—most importantly, as I will argue—how to draw on this process of translating back and forth to develop rich understandings across contexts?

Navigation between languages across contexts offers an interesting dialogue with the ongoing development of theories of translingualism, a framework that often questions the validity of thinking about languages as discrete entities as these students might tend to. As articulated by Bruce Horner, Min-Zhan Lu, Jacqueline Jones Royster, and John Trimbur, the translingual paradigm recognizes difference not as a problem but as an innate reality of language. Instead of taxonomizing these differences, Horner and co-authors, as well as other theorists of translingual dispositions (Lee and Jenks 319-24) or orientations (Canagarajah, "Negotiating" 40-41), ask why and how an individual uses language and to what effects in what contexts. Indeed, researchers argue that since "languages and language practices not only differ but fluctuate and interact, pursuit of mastery of any single identified set of such practices is inappropriate insofar as it leads language learners to a false sense of the stability of such practices and the finite character of language learning" (Horner et al. 307). From a translingual view, then, both interviewees quoted above are offering interesting reflections on their languaging processes, though theorists might ultimately see these discussions as problematic because of their emphasis on difficulty and views that languages function as fixed markers of different contexts.

However, Mickey and Bernice's comments reflect their experiences moving between contexts that they *perceive* as more or less monolingual, even as they themselves are engaging with the situations in complex and dynamic ways. Mickey presents his translations in terms of the problem of what to do with knowledge once it is acquired, particularly if it must be modified in order to be useful or communicable. For him, language difference presents a problem, one that is productive insofar as it encourages him to develop awareness of the affordances of resources from across his repertoire. Similarly, Bernice focuses on the ways that her translations illuminate the interaction between academic concepts and correlated understandings in the home. Differences are matters of practice, with understandings developing out of the language of the home and the activities that are structured by that language. Both recognize a relationship between prior learning and the development of new concepts; that is, they recognize that there are many contexts in which phenomena are experienced and many ways those phenomena are talked about. All contexts seem equally valid for contributing to Mickey and Bernice's understandings of the world, so their tasks as individuals who have broad linguistic repertoires drawn from a range of experiences involves choosing language that is best suited to understanding the context at hand and mobilizing the most rhetorically effective choices, given audience and situation.

In this way, Mickey and Bernice seem to understand their own language use in terms of critical movement between and across all of the resources and practices in their repertoires. Translingual views of codemeshing as an enactment of individuals' full repertoires emphasize exactly this sort of critical understanding of the differences between practices in contexts. In a notable instance, Suresh Canagarajah describes the pluralization of standard written English (SWE) through codemeshing as a process of drawing attention to multiple ways of knowing and articulating. He argues: "As [codemeshers] shuttle between languages, they develop a keen sensitivity to the differences and similarities of language resources. In fact, codemeshers often develop a more critical awareness of SWE and its potential as they shuttle between diverse norms" ("Practice" 126). That is, the strategic incorporation of resources from across students' repertoires draws their awareness to the ways that languages mean differently and to the range of associations that each choice brings.

But what these two participants, and others in the study discussed below, describe are situations in which they are aware of the need to engage in practices they associate with a particular language and context, an exigency that often forces them to think about the meaning they made in one context, the relationship of those words and understandings in another context, and the negotiations they will have to make in order to be effective. Translinguals, as theorists argue and these participants' comments remind us, often appear to attempt approximations of monolingualism, even as they draw productive insights from the process of shifting between languages. Like the Jamaican Creole-speaking students described by Vivette Milson-Whyte, the students in the present study often seem to "decline invitations to code-mesh or disregard translingualism because these students live/operate in situations where languages are still treated as discrete systems" (121). Therefore, building on the themes raised by participants in this study, I would like to draw attention to the ways in which participants discuss their movements between the language practices they encounter in different contexts and their reflections on how those movements develop their abilities to be more nuanced thinkers and communicators. While participants' discussions of language use across contexts resonate with translingual theories that emphasize critical awareness developed through negotiations across languages, as students, these participants seldom see explicit code-meshing or overt language manipulation as key to their navigation between contexts. Therefore, this movement is discussed instead as translation.

But what exactly does *translation* mean in such cases? In many common conceptions, rooted in monolingual language ideologies, translation entails a substitution of words in one language for equivalents in another, with the most effective translations being the ones that closely recreate meaning unchanged in the new language (Cronin 63-67, 124-25). However, theorists of translation (e.g., Cronin; Pennycook; Venuti;), and interviewees in this study, understand translation as a practice that makes a difference: in forms, meanings, and effects on audiences. As Lawrence Venuti reminds, translators "can never entirely avoid the loss that the translation process enforces on the source text, on its meanings and structures, figures and traditions. And translators cannot obviate the gain in their translating, the construction of different meanings, structures, figures, and traditions" (37). For participants in this study, awareness of changes to meaning that occur when translating across languages and contexts is strong, developing through students' lived experiences navigating school, family, neighborhood, friend, and career relationships. Study participants' understanding of what can and cannot be directly transferred from one context to another is also strong, especially as they note the difficulties of talking about school with family members at home and the paucity of opportunities for incorporating knowledges from home in their academic lives. Still, navigating these losses often leads to the kinds of gains Venuti alludes to as well: a heightened understanding of translation practices sheds light on how different languages construe experiences and convey them to audiences, as well as a more general understanding of how language changes to suit contexts.

What the reflections described in this article suggest is that an expanded view of translation, one in which students recognize that a change in words is a change in meaning as well as phrasing, produces a distinct form of knowledge, what I call translational learning. Such learning stems from recognition of the functional differences between possible language uses across situations and is solidified as learners develop the metalinguistic awareness necessary to talk about these differences. Ultimately, awareness of language differences leads to greater rhetorical dexterity, as students expand their communicative repertoires in ways that help them both conform to and, when they choose, subvert the language expectations of given situations. This learning process helps to solidify students' authority over their own development as writers, even when they seem to be conforming to monologic norms in their writing. Standardized academic English can be a goal without denigrating other languages and ways of knowing because learning through translation enriches one's sense of language generally. Knowing and communicating across contexts encourages students to develop all of their languages, recognizing one language not as a means of communicating the knowledges of another but as a source with its own distinct epistemologies.

In this article, I describe the context of my study of writers who learn through and across languages, its impetus, and the processes by which study participants helped me to understand their conceptions of translation and learning, which I put in dialogue with themes emergent in translingual theories of writing. Next, I provide examples of talk about three aspects of translational learning: awareness of functional differences in languages, development of metalinguistic understandings, and construction of a broad communicative repertoire to draw on across situations. As much of my discussion in this section describes reflective practices developed by individuals in their roles as students, I conclude by situating my discussion of translational learning in practices of reflection common to writing classrooms, suggesting ways that students illustrate possibilities to revise and expand upon current practice. Two appendices provide background information about participants and further reflections on methods of interviewing and coding.

Methods

The Study

My argument is based on interviews with six former students, collected as part of an ongoing longitudinal study of two consecutive cohorts of Spanish/English bilingual students moving from high school through college. The first cohort consisted of five participants, while the second cohort consisted of six, though at the time this piece was written only one member of the second cohort completed enough interviews to analyze. Therefore, the six individuals discussed here represent the full first cohort plus one representative of the second cohort. As more data is collected from both cohorts, further analysis and discussion will follow.

All six of the students discussed here graduated from a small Bronx high school in New York City. Five went immediately to college, and one decided at the last minute to delay enrolling. Of the five who began college immediately, three did so within the City University of New York (CUNY) system and one began in a State University of New York (SUNY) school but transferred back to a CUNY school in his second year. One enrolled in a small Catholic college in upstate New York. Most participants' families were from the Dominican Republic, where they were born, had lived, or frequently visited. Alejandra's family moved to the Bronx from Mexico, though she reported experiences with learning and language similar to other members of the cohort. All identified with the Bronx as their home community but maintained their identities, respectively, as Dominican or Mexican as well (see appendix A for profiles of each participant).

Participants were selected as a matter of convenience, an accident of circumstances and timing. I had taught all of them during their early years of high school, and kept in touch via email after I left the school, sometimes helping with writing or suggesting books to read, other times sharing pictures or stories about my son, who was born while I was their teacher. As I moved to a PhD program outside of the city, some often checked in with me, either to hear about what graduate school was like or to tell me about something exciting they had read or written or experienced. When they began to prepare for graduation, I exchanged emails with several students as they reflected on high school and their expectations for college, writing several recommendations and offering advice when they asked. The depth of their insights and their eagerness to talk about their own experiences as multilingual students was not surprising—my daily experiences as their teacher had illuminated their rich reflective capabilities and astute political savvy in relation to questions about language and identity—but I began to wonder if these critical tendencies would carry over into fyw courses. My experiences across a range of fyw programs led me to worry that such rich resources would simply go untapped.

Recognizing the ongoing need to dispel the "myth of linguistic homogeneity" that Paul Matsuda critiqued over a decade ago, I set out to document these students' conceptualizations of their language and writing, and how those ideas developed throughout their college years ("The Myth" 638). I sought IRB approval for a study to follow students from graduation through college, interviewing them once a year and collecting samples of their writing.[2] I emailed students who had kept in contact and who were already 18 years old, describing my project and asking if they were interested in participating in the study. The informal nature of this recruitment process and the potential selection bias is inescapable given my ongoing teacherly relationship with these individuals; however, this relationship also helps to mitigate problematic aspects of my own researcher positionality. As a white former high school teacher with a passing fluency in Spanish, I have represented (or currently represent) multiple nodes of power and am likely to misunderstand realities of my multilingual students—indeed, as I describe below, it was their corrections of my misreadings that led to this study's focus on translation. However, because of our past relationships, I was able to comfortably admit my own gaps in understanding and my former students were willing to correct my misconceptions. Still imperfect, this dynamic nevertheless allowed me to further deconstruct misunderstandings stemming from my own exposure to "raciolinguistic ideologies" that equate racialized bodies with language practices that are inherently different than those of dominant groups and presume that certain difficulties will arise as a result of this difference (Flores and Rosa 150-51). That is, I was able to identify ways that my dominant position continues to generate incorrect premises and limiting conclusions, a reflective stance that teachers and researchers would all likely benefit from practicing.

Interviews and Analysis

In the summer of their high school graduations, students agreed to be interviewed. Initial interviews were face-to-face during the week of graduation. This timing was mainly a matter of convenience, motivated by the fact that I was in the Bronx to attend graduation. Follow-up interviews were conducted via phone and Skype, usually during the weeks immediately following the end of a semester in spring and early summer. Participants consented to the use of email conversations as data, which sometimes provide a more in-the-moment view of student experiences than do retrospective interviews.[3] Interviews, approximately one hour, were audio recorded, transcribed, and coded. Emails have been selectively coded, leaving out personal details (conversations about baseball, significant others, politics and current events unrelated to courses or education, etc). Coding followed two threads. One focused on theoretical concepts I brought to the study, drawn from literature on multilingual students and college writing (Leki; Roberge, Losey, and Wald; Ruecker) and writing development more broadly (Beaufort; Sommers and Saltz; Thaiss and Zawacki). My codebook included grammar instruction, deficit frames, home literacies, feedback, writing assignments, and subject/disciplinary differences. The other coding thread was developed through a listening process and categorization described by Joseph A. Maxwell (104-108) and Robert Emerson, Rachel Fretz, and Linda Shaw (142-44). As I listened to interview responses, I became increasingly aware that important themes were not addressed by my codes. This was reinforced as I listened to recordings, transcribed them, and began the focused coding process drawing on the sources above. Several types of translation activities became apparent: translation troubles, translating for others, thinking about translation, and learning from translation. This range of types led me to revise questions for future interviews, but this revision also took place in the semi-structured space of our conversations as I realized that I was asking the wrong sorts of questions.

As Sonia Nieto points out, attending to such moments is important insofar as they can draw a researcher's attention to places where students are helping us to re-theorize the work of our classrooms and, more broadly, the ways we understand writing development for multilingual students. She recalls how the most important parts of interviews often are brought up by student-participants, not through explicit questions in an interview protocol (396-97). If students—especially those who are often marginalized by English-only practices and racialized deficit frames—are the focus of research and teaching, then it is critical that we allow our terms and understandings to dialogue with how these students experience writing and language development. Such a dialogue is especially important given the prevalence of white monolinguals in the field. As a researcher who is neither Latino nor someone who was raised in a multilingual home, I was, through these conversations, better able to understand how my own theoretical dispositions had undervalued practices that are central for these students (see appendix B for more reflections on interviewing and coding).

Three Aspects of Translational Learning

In these interviews, translation became a central focus. For participants, reflecting on learning increasingly complex ideas and on expressing views in writing was always related to thinking across languages and, as they moved from late high school into early college, students consistently found themselves thinking *about* languages. In interviews, they described themselves becoming more acutely aware of specific language differences, both between Spanish and English and between different varieties of English. While they had obviously been long aware of the ways that language changed from home to school and from classrooms to hallways, in this phase of their lives, they also began articulating an awareness of the effect that these differences had on meaning making across contexts. Several discussed the process of making meaning with these differences in mind, thinking in metalinguistic terms about how they were writing and communicating. Finally, in some cases students also began to deploy new understandings about language to broaden their own linguistic repertoires, not just to identify and articulate language difference but to use that knowledge to develop greater rhetorical dexterity. For each person, the act of translating while learning was commonplace.

In the analyses that follow, I present three related ways that study participants talk about developing an ability to learn through translation. While appearing to form a linear narrative in which an individual might first develop awareness of different meaning-making resources across languages, then acquire a metalanguage to taxonomize and describe those differences, and finally apply such understandings in the construction of a broader rhetorical repertoire, there is no reason to assume such a pattern holds for all learners, or even for these six individuals. People might develop a rich repertoire that is devoted to audience awareness without ever thinking much about metalinguistics or the nuances of differing meaning-making resources of a particular language, just as they can develop metalinguistic awareness without becoming aware of how language differences foster distinctly different meanings across contexts. The three categories I describe—developing awareness, acquiring a metalanguage, and engaging in highly dexterous rhetorical moves across languages—represent approaches to learning that are impelled by students' navigations across languages as they draw from and across all their knowledges and resources. Instead of a linear progression, then, I suggest that what these students' theorizations of their own learning illustrate is how daily translations, or movement between a range of languages and ways of knowing, reflect rich abilities, always already in development.

Developing Awareness of Language Difference

The question of how translation produces new knowledge requires us to attend to how one might begin to see that languages mean differently, with awareness of that difference being a goal of learning. To learn from translating is not a matter of learning some things from English and others from Spanish. Participants were, of course, long aware of the differences between the Spanish of home and the English of school. They could learn in one language from parents and another in school, but it was not until later that they developed a sense that these differences entailed more than simple rules about what to speak where. Meaning making differed across contexts; concepts changed along with shifts in language.

The most direct way research participants discussed developing this awareness was when they described a process of translation that allows them to examine what they know in one context, put it in dialogue with what they know in other contexts, and understand more in the act of doing so. For example, Manny, following his first year of community college, observes:

> With two languages I'm able to know more because in English, you know, I watch Spanish media and also watch English media, and they have different news for certain channels. So because I have two languages I can gather more information and also the different viewpoints from a variety of people. I can get a clearer understanding of what it is about.

Manny speaks of two languages that are inherently separate and of how fortunate he feels to be able to move back and forth between them, allowing him to "know more" than either monolingual Spanish-speakers at home or similarly monolingual English speakers at school. But the causality that he lays out is important: it's *because* he has two languages that he can gather not just more information but also more ways of processing that information.

His sense that those perspectives are linked to different ideas, even different ways of understanding facts, suggests an emerging understanding that there are distinct ways of knowing associated with the contexts in which he speaks either Spanish or English. He also suggests that his ability to learn from both of these contexts can lead to a productive practice of translating between them. He notes that he can get a "clearer understanding" from comparing media in Spanish and English, illustrating the extent to which thinking about the differences he encounters when flipping through the channels is itself a knowledge-making experience.

Other participants' growing awareness of language difference centered even more strongly on the relationship between a particular context's language and related concepts. Bernice's reflections on the ways that her parents help her talk through difficulties, described above, illustrate her awareness that she learns to understand school concepts not simply by talking about them at home in Spanish but also by finding related analogies in her family life that can be brought to bear when thinking about academic work. Her emphasis that "it wouldn't really be Spanish itself but like things that a normal Spanish family would *do*" (her intonational stress) highlights her embodied understandings; it is her reflection on practices at home in Spanish that Bernice translates to insights about school concepts in English.

It is not that Bernice was unaware that concepts from school could relate to outside practices, but that her experiences translating between English and Spanish allowed her to best recognize these connections. Just after high school, she describes herself as a somewhat passive student who "tried to participate, but it was more of the listen to what others were saying to try to understand." The practices that led to learning were much different than those she describes at home, where she engaged in practices that led to insights about concepts she struggled to understand through the language and ways of knowing of school. Bernice valued the intellectual challenges she encountered in school, but not as a replacement for her other ways of knowing. Instead, finding ways to draw insights from across her languages and knowledges became an important practice for her, as doing so developed her sense of the different meaning-making potentials of each. As Steven Alvarez notes, such interactive work between family and school contexts is common in multilingual families, where education is deeply valued but monolingual academic norms force both parents and students to develop strategies for drawing on the rich resources of the home. Alvarez's research highlights the importance of a broker who frequently acts as a "mediating participant who establishes or destabilizes the link of communication among communicants," but Bernice and Alejandra's cases illustrate ways that these students can also develop as their own brokers, learning how to navigate across languages and knowledges through conversations both at home and in school (43).[4]

For both of these students, translating between Spanish and English revealed how the two languages conveyed and constructed meaning differently, with Bernice also expressing an emerging sense that these differences themselves, not just the different content typically expressed in each language, can be leveraged against each other when learning. However, study participants also expressed critical understandings of language difference, drawn from the process of translating. While reflecting on the English-only practices of her high school during the summer after graduation, Alejandra suggests that moving from one language and context to another allows her to see holes in the perspectives she was encouraged to embrace in certain contexts:

> In English, I feel like we're taught and we learn to speak a certain way. The words are stronger and somehow aggressive, just the sound of the words, and for example if we're talking about a topic in English class, if it seems ok and you agree to it but then you go home and you think about it and you think about your background and stuff then you're like 'no, wait why did I ever think that was ok it's not ok.'

Relating the "aggressive" tendencies of English to her own willingness to adopt views endorsed in English-speaking contexts, Alejandra echoes Bernice's spatial description of the relationship between language and context. The talking, thinking, and doing common to one context lead her to certain conclusions, which do not always align with her conclusions as a result of talking, thinking, and doing in another context. In particular, she described a survey in her senior year English class asking if the school provided sufficient extra-curricular opportunities. She agreed that it did. At home with her mother, speaking in Spanish, she found herself remembering how much she loved drawing and music, which she regretted giving up because of a lack of emphasis on the arts in school. She blamed this inconsistency in her own perspectives on the different understandings of the world encouraged by differences in contexts and the languages used in them. She notes that the words used in particular contexts "influence what you're thinking or how you're feeling, versus in the Spanish-speaking community and how they feel because you know their opinions and what they think is right or wrong versus the English-dominant community." Alejandra's reflections powerfully illustrate the extent to which not only words and meanings but also whole epistemologies change when translating. What began as a sense that English words inherently convey aggression shifted to a critique of how school languages and contexts worked together to limit her ability to draw on her full range of insights and abilities. Like Bernice, these reflections led Alejandra to develop a commitment to thinking about translating between contexts in order to construct more nuanced and critical understandings of how her learning was deeply rooted in the language and practices of those contexts.

Developing Metalinguistic Awareness

Through translation, participants reported that they also came to better understand the formal features of both Spanish and English, developing awareness of the ways that language functioned at the linguistic level, usually in terms of learning grammar and usage, and usually during struggles to understand different ways to write "correctly." In this sense, my participants' development of language awareness is consistent with traditional definitions of metalanguage, which describe systems for understanding language as an object of inquiry. To develop metalinguistic awareness is to recognize how to describe the functions of language in use. For many theorists, particularly those in educational psychology, metalinguistic understandings are part of a broader category of metacognition, which encompasses awareness of the ways that all processes of thought and activity function (Gombert 5-8). My sense of metalinguistics is similarly broad, including all talk about language and its functions. Admittedly, understanding metalinguistic awareness in this wide scope does not provide the in-depth specificity associated with "the language of schooling" (Schleppegrell 3-5), nor direct classroom practices that allow students to identify linguistic patterns in particular academic settings (see, for two excellent examples, de Oliveira; Siczek and Bennet). Instead, metalinguistic awareness develops an understanding that words and meanings change across languages, in this case in ways that affect how to structure language for a particular context.

In a typical example of early metalinguistic talk, Nino responded to my question about whether he could look at his writing and see moments when he was thinking through translations by saying that he could at times, particularly during his usual processes of drafting responses to fyc writing assignments written in English. Specifically, he noted that he becomes aware of his thinking across languages when proofreading, saying: "Since some of the words are switched, the sentence structure is different between Spanish and English, some of the things I wanted to say end up being backward." Unlike the descriptions above of participants developing awareness of differences across languages, with a focus on both the resources of the language (the words, the contexts they index, the cultural associations) and the meanings created, metalinguistic talk like Nino's focuses on the structure of particular languages and the impact on how those languages are used. Though the observation is a fairly simple one, there are important nascent possibilities in his understanding that his writing takes a certain structure in one language and another structure in other languages, especially insofar as Nino is linking these differences to a growing awareness that he is drawing on a range of knowledges when speaking or writing, even if he is unconscious of these differences until he is proofreading. The "backward" sentences serve as a reminder to himself, allowing Nino to recognize nuances in his process of moving between languages.

In more developed instances of students using translation to construct metalinguistic understandings, explicit focus on learning grammatical rules often spans languages, leveraging one against another when possible. Describing his first year of college, when he focused heavily on improving the grammar and mechanics of his writing, Manny illustrates a growing awareness of not only the formal differences in Spanish and English but also the ways that he can draw insights from across these two languages when writing:

> They do have their similarities, English and Spanish, except for Spanish the conjugations are more complicated. They are really concise and also they have so many different rules that I have to know. So English and Spanish sometimes there are conjugations where I can rely on English, like when it comes to subjunctive, that is very similar to English so I understand that's how I need to write. But then for certain conjugations possibly, in English, I won't rely as much in Spanish. I have to kind of understand the two languages' conjugations, words, what is correct. So from time to time I have, if it's English you have to rely things in Spanish, so then I can understand what I'm writing.

Manny's development of grammatical language to discuss overlap between uses of the subjunctive mood in Spanish and English is interesting insofar as it is a very concrete example of his overall goal to develop an efficient way to understand how both languages are structured. He recognizes the effectiveness of building metalinguistic knowledge in one language, then translating to another language, a practice that is likely familiar to many learners who develop grammatical concepts in a new language, only to find that they illuminate the grammar of their native language as well.

However, his final points are important for illustrating how metalinguistic awareness can help translational learners draw on the full range of their languages and knowledges. After noting that he often learns grammatical concepts by comparing two languages, Manny goes on to note the ways that he uses this range of concepts in learning and writing. For him, thinking about what he does in one language in terms of what he does in another is a key way to "understand what [he's] writing." Manny's interest in mastering the grammatical structures of both languages—a mastery that he pursues by learning terms, recognizing them in context, and consciously using them—enables him to think about his writing across languages, developing greater proficiency in both of them simultaneously.

Building a Broad Repertoire for Greater Rhetorical Dexterity

Many interviewees highlighted the ways that translating between languages helped them to understand the different meanings and forms of both English and Spanish. A smaller number seemed to be learning to deploy understandings learned through translations to develop hybrid rhetorical strategies, making them more effective learners and communicators in general. These individuals might be considered to be developing greater rhetorical attunement or translingual dispositions, insofar as they seem to fulfill Rebecca Lorimer Leonard's description of individuals developing "rhetorical attunement," moving beyond simply knowing about differences in language resources and beginning to show "where these resources come from, how writers put them to use, or how they play out in specific moments of communication" (231). In this way, Mickey's reflections on his difficulties talking about oppression with his parents in Spanish, discussed above, point toward his growing understanding of how to successfully (or unsuccessfully) shape resources and practices in particular contexts. His recognition that speaking in definitions carries less persuasive weight than ideologically heavy terms like *oppression* illustrates one way that translation is helping him to fine-tune his repertoire, albeit through recognitions of his own missteps and difficulties in translation.

However, participants also voiced views that were less deficit-oriented when discussing how drawing on their full repertoires could encourage learning and convey meaning more effectively. Compared to others in the study, Rivera, in an interview shortly after graduation, articulated a theory of language mixing that closely resembles approaches to translingual communication that privilege code-meshing and other visible signs of linguistic difference. Recognizing the range of resources in his repertoire and drawing on them accordingly was intimately tied-up with Rivera's understanding of language use as a social interaction between individuals, one that is always readjusting to fit the needs of the situation. He explained: "For me I think language is more like a cheat code y'know what I'm saying? Like different meanings but for different places." You need a different cheat code because everyone would have their own ways.

The "cheat code" of language, then, is a way to get things done in a particular context, while playing a particular game.[5] Importantly though, these codes won't work when the game is changed. When I asked, he denied that this was a matter of switching languages from one person to another, suggesting instead that codes changed for every person in every situation. He offered a concrete example:

> When trying to teach or help other classmates I would use that English and Spanish mixed together. Like my best friend didn't understand a couple things in English, and I ended up explaining it to him in Spanish and English and you know he got it. And I feel like that right there is an amazing thing for a human being to get because you're learning something from both languages and you mix it together then you got it.

At first, Rivera seems to present Spanish and English as separate tools that do separate jobs, with each serving as an equal substitute for the other. But the instrumentalism slips away in the final sentence, where he points out that learning comes from both languages and culminates in the mixture. His description of the process entails first learning in one language, then another, then mixing them together to actually grasp meaning. Importantly, his emphasis on the ways that he has used this practice to help others learn doubly illustrates the effectiveness of translational learning. Navigating between languages when developing an understanding of content provides a way to learn via a hybrid incorporation of knowledges and phrasing, but it also provides a glimpse into the ways that Rivera is drawing on a developing understanding of audience and purpose when helping his friend learn. What is an effective individual strategy for learning is thus transferred to social interactions, making Rivera a more effective communicator because of his recognition of the ways that translation is productive of insights that are greater than the sum of the two languages alone.

Students' recognitions of the productivity of translation did not always lead to code-mixed language production like Rivera's, though. Others focused on ways that translating between school and home helped them develop ideas and rhetorical approaches to writing, since such translations made explicit processes of rephrasing and of comparing when language changes with context. For participants, translational learning was not about producing utterances that represented their full range of language practices, nor was it about creating the kind of fetishized images of linguistic difference that Matsuda argues is at the heart of much translingual writing ("The Lure" 480). Instead, participants emphasized that considering all the possible choices in their repertoire led to a more reflective and nuanced production of Spanish *and* English texts, illustrating that by seeing the overlaps, distinctions, and epistemological shifts resulting from translation, students could be better language users according to the monolingual standards by which they are often judged.

This point is made by Nino, a first-year college student in the CUNY system, as he discusses the back and forth translations between English and Spanish that help him generate ideas for writing. Often, he reflected, these translations were similar to the drafting and revision process. Like Mickey, Nino's thinking and writing processes are highly influenced by conversations with his mother, both while he is in high school and in his first year of college. Early on, he tried to provide more word-for-word translations, especially while discussing his senior year research on the economics of a living wage, a topic his mother was also interested in. However, he was unsatisfied with his translations and the conversation did not feel particularly convincing. Instead, he began thinking of his translations in terms of broader concepts that he could then articulate in a more natural way while speaking with his mother. He describes this translational project in terms of lessons he learned while giving speeches in early college:

> It's like, let's say you're doing a speech—and I did this in college too—so the way that I would practice my speech, we couldn't really read the whole notes so I would basically just remember the big points of it and then say it all out a bunch of times and each time it would come out different and sometimes you just get used to saying it, so the right words just come out at the same time.

For Nino, the process of communicating knowledge in a certain context goes hand in hand with developing a dexterous ability to speak (and eventually write) that knowledge in a number of ways, based loosely on an understanding of what he identifies as the most important concepts or points. He likens this process to conversations with his mother while he thinks about the content of his classes and prepares for writing: "So basically me translating into Spanish is basically remembering the big point of the topic I'm trying to say and just saying it all over from Spanish to English to Spanish to English, you get better at wording it just by practicing it by translating and saying it." Trying out ideas in one language and then another, revising wordings and understandings each time, produces more accurate expressions of the points Nino is trying to make and draws on the full range of resources in his repertoire. Like Manny's sense that thinking about grammar across both Spanish and English allows him to understand what he is writing in a given context, Nino observes that when he develops his discussion of key concepts in both English and Spanish, he gets better at wording overall, thereby enhancing his ability to be more articulate across contexts.

Nino sees the main benefit of translating back and forth as helping him develop better speaking and writing in his college classes. His awareness of language difference and his ability to draw on a wide range of resources in his writing process led him to the production of what he felt to be more nuanced and insightful writing in academic English, with few, if any, easily detectable markers of his translational learning left on the page. This kind of rhetorical dexterity is important insofar as it aligns with an often under-emphasized feature of translingual theories of writing: the question of agency when viewing translingual practices as a *process* of creating texts that seem to conform to norms associated with standard academic Englishes and those that seem to deviate from those norms (Lu and Horner 600-601).

For Nino, it was exactly this kind of *practice* of drawing on productive understandings of translation that allowed him to shape and reshape language and knowledge across contexts to create more effective college writing in English. The rhetorical dexterity that he developed was not simply a functional one, providing him with a wider range of phrasings to consider putting on the page, but a much more reflective awareness that allowed him to imagine alternate ways of phrasing *and knowing*. This awareness helped him to both deepen his understandings of the content he was writing about and understand why he was making the choices he made. Such critical understanding allows for the kind of rich learning that Lu and Horner, along with other theorists of translingualism, have suggested to be important for thinking about and with multilingual students.

Implications: Reflection and Making Translation Visible

These cases illustrate the extent to which multilingual students often engage in complex negotiations across a range of languages and diverse knowledges, doing so to eventually produce texts that satisfy monolingual requirements. That is, as in formulations offered by translingual scholars, students negotiate across a range of resources to be more successful in particular contexts; however, the insights that they develop while moving across languages—indeed, the negotiations themselves—often go unnoticed. The problem, then, is how the productive nature of such translations could be made visible and thus be more effectively built upon. How could Manny's metalinguistic negotiations be leveraged to more fully engage him in seeing the relationship between grammars across languages and larger rhetorical patterns, helping him to link his interest in sentence-level features with global writing issues? How could explicit reflection on knowledge-making practices in Bernice's home help to develop critical consciousness about the ways that knowledge production functions in and across academic disciplines? How could Rivera's sense that code-meshing can help clarify misunderstandings for multilingual students be developed into a more fully rhetorical understanding of the ways that he could use resources from across his own repertoire?

Though there are certainly many approaches to answering these sorts of questions, one approach might involve a simple adaptation of common reflective practices in our classrooms, with an eye toward the productive potential of such adaptations. Indeed, such reworking is long overdue. Reflections that link personal motivations with writing processes are common enough in first-year writing courses, but when asked to write such reflections, participants in this study were never asked to put their multilingual experiences at the center of their writing. As Nino put it in one of our many email exchanges, his first English class was "a bunch of practice essays that forced us to look deep within ourselves," but when I asked if any of the writing assignments encouraged him to draw on his full repertoire of languages and knowledges, the answer was a firm no. This answer was universal across all six of these participants, suggesting that at least some instructors are still not yet modifying established best practices to account for the multilingual realities of their classrooms.

As a very manageable adaptation, instructors could ask for drafts that put language and translation at the center of reflection on moments of what Kathleen Yancey has called "reflection-in-action" that occur during "the process of reviewing and projecting and revising, which takes place within a composing event" ("Reflection" 200). Noting when they are framing something differently than they might in other language contexts or identifying particular choices they would reconsider if the audience shifted would have helped Nino and Manny surface their developing metalinguistic understandings. A practical approach to this might build on Naomi Silver's description of students using self-reflective marginal comments to monitor difficulties and successes during their writing process. Silver describes a student who inserts such a note "when he is having trouble (or when he finds something that works for him), then he is prompted at those moments to name what the problem is, and this act of naming and describing may help him better understand why he is running into trouble," maybe even developing a solution out of such patterns of reflection (4). Making similar reflective notes when he recognizes moments of grammatical overlap or difference, with a summative reflection on these comments at the end, could help Manny to systematize his understanding of certain formulations. Asking a student like Manny to use such reflective notes to make his sentence-level concerns central to his writing process might lead to the kinds of increased engagement that Silver attributes to development of agentive metacognitive abilities.

Reflection-in-action can also help students who are shifting between languages and ways of knowing to reframe deficit-oriented discussions of difficulty, highlighting the productive potential of translations. For Nino, such reflection-in-action practices might contribute to a fuller understanding of the importance of "accidental" grammatical formulations like those he describes in his note about the "backwards phrasing" that sometimes happens when he moves between languages. Such moments draw attention to the fact that his choices are not the only ones possible, that his thinking could be influenced by a range of languages and understandings. His writing carries a visible sign of his language negotiations—what Venuti refers to as "translational remainders"—which illustrate the gains and losses that translators cannot hope to fully obviate when moving between languages (37-41). The productive nature of translation could be richly surfaced by asking students to identify such moments and then reflect on their relationships to phrasing and knowing in other contexts. What was Nino writing about at the moments in which he sees signs of other languages in his writing? How might those other ways of knowing be influencing his thinking here, or how could they be brought to bear in this task?

Mickey could similarly benefit from bringing reflective notes into his writing processes, helping him to identify the key terms and concepts in his arguments, the ways that he is using them for the task at hand, and the ways he will have to shift his approach when discussing these ideas in other contexts. For a student who is deeply committed to thinking about taking academic understandings to a broader audience, making reflective notes on his ideas in development would not only allow him to identify central concepts in his writing but also help to keep other ways of phrasing and knowing in constant dialogue during the drafting process. Thus, what first seem to be difficulties encountered while navigating between languages and contexts become productive opportunities to help students maintain an awareness of the relationship between those different resources.

Beyond these in-the-moment approaches to reflection, instructors could also ask students to focus on the productive insights drawn from translations in other common assignments like definition-based essays or comparative analyses. Bruce Horner and Lauren Tetreault highlight the translingual possibilities of assignments that ask students to delve into the range of meaning-making potential that comes with considering how to, for instance, find a French translation for *education*. While a cognate exists, they describe one student who preferred *formation* because of her sense that it conveyed ideas of being trained and shaped through the process of schooling (20-22). For Mickey, a similar assignment, though paired with earlier writing assignments, might have allowed him to reflect on the negotiations he made while thinking and writing about differing ways to present *oppression* across languages and contexts. Such an assignment would entail what Yancey calls "constructive reflection," which asks students to present "a cumulative multi-selved, multi-voiced identity, which takes place between and among composing events" (200). That is, Mickey could be asked to see his writing about oppression in class and his conversations with his family as related composing events, developing awareness of the ways in which his multi-voiced selves are tied up in and produce new meanings through viewing these texts as such. Considering his interest in helping other multilingual students understand materials in class, Rivera could engage in similar kinds of constructive reflections by describing and assessing how he explains concepts. Importantly, such reflection might ultimately ask him to go beyond his sense that, for different audiences, English, Spanish, or a code-meshing of both might be clearer or easier to understand. Instead, such a reflection might allow him to deepen his sense of why a particular choice works better, for what kinds of concepts, in which genres, and for what purposes.

Such reflective work is important because, while participants in this study tended strongly toward a belief in the need to produce texts that appeared to adhere to strict monolingual views of English, erasing signs of multilingualism from their writing, they were themselves deeply interested in understanding how to navigate across languages and contexts as a result of their translation experiences. While not the only ways to do so, language and context-focused reflective assignments that ask students to consider all aspects of writing and knowledge production as potential sites of translation could help them to deepen their ability to draw insights from their experiences across languages. Ultimately, by bringing acts of translation to the center of students' thinking about writing, such reflections might help such students develop their abilities to transcend the monolingual limits imposed on their language use, making translation visible in the form of active critical reflection on all the translational activities they engage in and all the rich choices their languages can afford them.

Acknowledgments

Many thanks to the numerous people whose comments contributed to this piece: Laura Micciche and the two *Composition Studies* reviewers, as well as Anne Ruggles Gere, Casey Otemuyiwa, Naitnaphit Limlamai, Sidonie Smith, and my classmates in her writing course. Above all, thank you to my student participants, who have been blowing my mind since they were kids and continue to do so every time we talk. All errors or shortcomings are, of course, my own.

Notes

1. Deciding how to refer to the subjects of my research presented me with some difficulty. They are participants first and foremost, co-constructing meaning with me, as I hope my methods section and appendix make clear, but they are also discussing their insights mainly in their roles as students, as their reflections on translation almost always refer in one way or another to learning in school settings. They also acted as interviewees, dialoguing with me within the space of the interview itself.

Because it is useful to think about how identities like *student, research participant*, and *interviewee* might interact, I have made an attempt to distinguish between these roles. Like language though, these identities are fluid and interrelated.

2. The IRB at my university exempted this initial study, as well as my request to continue my research with the next cohort of former students graduating the following year. See appendix A for student participant details. Although interviews sometimes addressed specific writing samples submitted by participants, systematic coding of these samples has not yet begun; this article will limit its focus to discussions in interviews and other correspondence.

3. In *Agents of Integration*, Rebecca Nowacek makes a similar point in her critiques of some transfer research methodologies, noting that they depend solely on recall after the fact. While the email conversations help to avoid this methodological problem, asking students to have samples of writing in front of them during interviews also helps to mitigate recall difficulties by concretizing student discussions of writing and translation.

4. Marjorie Orellana documents the literal translations that students often perform on behalf of their parents, illustrating the ways that students act as brokers who sometimes must mediate or reframe information. Like in Alvarez's study, Orellana's research illuminates a range of learning potential in these translations. While students in the current study reported often translating for parents, they were less convinced that they had to negotiate or modify meanings in these cases.

5. Interestingly, the "cheat code" metaphor is also used by a student in Shannon Carter's study of basic writers, *The Way Literacy Lives*. It would be useful in the future to investigate how metaphors intertwine with translation, illustrating another way that nuanced differences between contexts might be surfaced and reflected upon by students who are deepening their understandings of how to tweak their language in the most rhetorically savvy ways.

Appendix A: Participant Profiles

Mickey graduated from high school in 2015. Our first interview was face-to-face, conducted that summer before he left the Bronx for a four-year school in the SUNY system upstate. Further correspondence was through email and text message, until Mickey decided to stop participating in the study because of his many time commitments. In his first year of college, Mickey enrolled in a sign language course, which he thought might make him "more useful" as a participant in my research, as he told me in one email. He continued to develop his interests in social and racial justice, declaring a major in an interdisciplinary Black studies program. But because of difficulties living upstate, Mickey transferred back to the city and enrolled in a CUNY school where he has developed an interest in education as a possible politically active career. Currently, Mickey and I have conducted one face-to-face interview in the summer after high school, four chains of email conversations and three extended Twitter message conversations during his college years. He has shared a sign language video but decided not to submit writing samples.

Bernice graduated from high school in 2015, and we conducted a face-to-face interview during the week of her commencement. She left the Bronx to study pre-law at a small private catholic college, which offered her a good financial aid package. In-depth follow-up correspondence has been limited to two email conversations, but she continues to work with high school debate teams as a coach during the summer and is proceeding successfully through her undergraduate years.

Nino graduated from high school in 2015. We emailed extensively during the summer before he started college at a two-year CUNY school where he planned to take classes in computer science. In the summer following his first year of college, I interviewed him via Skype and continued our email correspondence. He has since completed his second year of college, despite some doubts about his future in computer science. By the time of our last series of emails, he had become interested in a career in physical therapy and was investigating schools that could help him move in that direction. He has submitted seven writing samples over the course of four semesters along with brief written reflections.

Manny graduated in 2015 and enrolled in a four-year CUNY school to study criminal justice, with the goal of eventually working for the FBI. Our interviews have all been by telephone, one during the summer after his graduation, and one during the summer after his first year. Our interview and email conversations have been more extensive than other participants, often straying into long asides about baseball, Manny's family's ongoing difficulties with the company that owns the building they live in, and his experiences learning to drive in NYC. Besides maintaining his focus on criminal justice, his course selection and choice of writing topics illustrate his growing interest in religion. He has submitted nine writing samples from high school and his first two years of college, adding short reflections on his purpose and writing process for these assignments.

Rivera graduated in 2015, but at the last minute chose not to enroll in college. In an email at the end of the summer, he explained this choice by expressing doubts that he could avoid some of the mistakes that he felt he had made in high school. However, during our telephone interview two months earlier, he had many ideas about the education he would like to experience, one that respected the range of languages and cultures students bring to the classroom. In our last series of text messages, he reported that he was considering taking classes to expand his auto mechanic skills. He is currently working and considering his options.

Alejandra was the first participant from the second cohort to complete an interview following up on her first year of college. Our two telephone interviews took place during the summer after graduation and immediately following her first year at a four-year CUNY school, where she is studying criminal justice. In emails, she has suggested that she has not gotten much feedback on her writing, except for a few creative pieces, which has sparked an interest in story telling. In our second interview, she noted that these pieces, which drew on her experiences outside of school with family and friends, allowed her to express a bit more of her full voice, even though she had not been encouraged to include any actual Spanish writing. She has submitted writing samples from high school and both semesters of college.

Appendix B: Interviewing and Coding

Interview protocols and analytical categories shifted over the course of this study, based on responses from early participants and my reflections on the important differences between their perspectives and my own when crafting the initial study questions. The most notable example of this was a modification of an initial question, which asked interviewees to talk about the things they could do in language outside of school but couldn't do within the constraints of school English. I asked, "What are some of the differences between the kinds of language you use outside of school and the kinds of language you use in school?" My intention was to give participants a chance to describe their ways with language in different contexts, following up with a question about how this impacted their writing processes. But this question was flawed, as participants often pointed out.

These participants introduced the importance of thinking in terms of translation, but they also provided me with an important reminder that asking about language use in particular contexts is asking about how language is used and with whom. To continue soliciting participants' descriptions of language and use, and following from the patterns suggested in interviews with the first cohort, I revised this question for the second cohort, instead asking, "Do you talk through your ideas with people before and during your writing?" and then following up with individualized questions based on their response. These included questions about whether the conversations were in Spanish or English and what they learned from talking about school work in different contexts and languages. Because of Mickey's description of his trouble navigating insights from his conversations at home when writing for school, I included the follow-up question, "So after talking about your ideas, what do you have to do to get them on the paper?" These kinds of questions replaced the originals when I started interviewing the second cohort of participants. I then inserted them in my follow-up interviews with the first cohort as they began moving through college. In general, taking participants' responses seriously enough to change my questions allowed me to better integrate the insights that emerged during my first round of interviews.

This process of continually revising interview materials is perhaps inevitable in individualized interactions during longitudinal research. Because of issues of timespan and the need for reflexivity on the part of the researcher, shifting questions is a recommended practice in what Herbert J. Rubin and Irene S. Rubin describe as "responsive qualitative interviewing" that stretches over a span of multiple sessions. Rubin and Rubin recommend that "During the pauses between your interviews, you should look over your interviews and see if your questions are inappropriately leading the interviewee to specific answers or if you are avoiding following up in places that warrant additional questioning" (32). Shifting my questions in interviews allowed me to highlight the relationships that informed participants' experiences with language and translation, illuminating lines of inquiry that I had been neglecting in the first iteration of my questions.

Irving Seidman similarly notes that it is important that "over the course of a number of interviews, the interviewer may notice that several participants have highlighted a particular issue, and the interviewer may want to know how other participants would respond to that issue" (92). While I avoided explicitly asking for responses to something that another participant had said, I was conscious of times when revised questions elicited responses that were similar to the previous ones, such as Alejandra's discussion of translating her senior thesis for her parents: "My mom and dad mostly speak Spanish so I would come home and explain it to them but it was difficult because there's these words these facts that sound so astonishing in English and then when I try to say it in Spanish they don't have that big impact on them because those same ones aren't as convincing in Spanish."

Similarly, when preparing for the study, I knew that I would want to learn how students talk about writing issues. I prepared a list of preliminary codes to later disaggregate based on responses. These included discussions of grammar instruction and academic writing. Such etic categories "typically represent the *researcher's* concepts . . . rather than denoting participants' concepts," but they remain important for understanding the relationship of pre-existing theory to the construction and impetus for the study at hand (Maxwell 108, emphasis in the original). In these initial categories, I included a code for translation, but I only imagined it in the most basic sense, reserved for discussions of translating on behalf of their parents, as I knew many students often did. After the first day of interviews, I knew that I had under-estimated the importance of this code and, while writing a memo that evening I already began to note different categories of translation, particularly translating school learning for people at home. Thus, it would be hard to identify my use of participant-generated categories as "open coding" in the sense that Juliet Corbin and Anselm Strauss define it, emphasizing the genesis of codes in the act of reading data (195-204). Instead, codes were developed as a dialogue between my own understandings and those of interviewees.

As Todd Ruecker notes, longitudinal work requires a recursive coding process in order to understand the relationship between data and next steps of research, analysis, and reporting of findings (20). Indeed, Anne Beaufort claims that operational definitions for codes need to be "developed from a theoretical or top-down perspective, and inductively, based on the data, in order for this theory-driven aspect of the coding to be consistent and valid" (218). Being clear about the relationships and divergences between researcher and participant perspectives is a prerequisite for doing longitudinal research. In the case of these participants' talk about translation, we see one example of how the pre-existing etic categories brought to a project by the researcher can be transformed into more emic categories if participants' responses are seriously considered and allowed to influence not the just findings of a study but the trajectory of the study itself.

Works Cited

Alvarez, Steven. *Brokering Tareas: Mexican Immigrant Families Translanguaging Homework Literacies.* SUNY P, 2017.

Beaufort, Anne. *College Writing and Beyond: A New Framework for University Writing Instruction.* UP of Colorado, 2008.

Canagarajah, Suresh. "Negotiating Translingual Literacy: An Enactment." *Research in the Teaching of English* vol. 48, no. 1, 2013, pp. 40-67.

—. *Translingual Practice: Global Englishes and Cosmopolitan Relations.* Routledge, 2012.

Carter, Shannon. *The Way Literacy Lives: Rhetorical Dexterity and Basic Writing Instruction.* SUNY Press, 2009.

Corbin, Juliet, and Anselm Strauss. *Basics of Qualitative Research: Techniques and Procedures for Developing Grounded Theory.* Sage, 2007.

Cronin, Michael. *Translation and Globalization.* Routledge, 2003.

de Oliveira, Luciana C. "Using Systemic-Functional Linguistic Analysis to Explain Expectations of Academic Discourse." *Teaching U.S.-Educated Multilingual Writers,* edited by Mark Roberge, Kay M. Losey, and Margi Wald, U of Michigan P, 2015, 108-31.

Emerson, Robert M., Rachel I. Fretz, and Linda L. Shaw. *Writing Ethnographic Fieldnotes.* U of Chicago P, 2011.

Flores, Nelson, and Jonathan Rosa. "Undoing Appropriateness: Raciolinguistic Ideologies and Language Diversity in Education." *Harvard Educational Review,* vol. 85, no. 2, 2015, pp. 149-71.

Gombert, Jean Emile. *Metalinguistic Development.* U of Chicago P, 1992.

Horner, Bruce, Min-Zhan Lu, Jacqueline Jones Royster, and John Trimbur. "Language Difference in Writing: Toward a Translingual Approach." *College English,* vol. 73, no. 3, 2011, pp. 303-21.

Horner, Bruce, and Laura Tetreault. "Translation as (Global) Writing." *Composition Studies,* vol. 44, no. 1, 2016, pp. 13-30.

Lee, Jerry Won, and Christopher Jenks. "Doing Translingual Dispositions." *CCC,* vol. 68, no. 2, 2016, pp. 317-44.

Leki, Ilona. *Undergraduates in a Second Language: Challenges and Complexities of Academic Literacy Development.* Routledge, 2007.

Leonard, Rebecca Lorimer. "Multilingual Writing as Rhetorical Attunement." *College English,* vol. 76, no. 3, 2014, pp. 227-47.

Lu, Min-Zhan, and Bruce Horner. "Translingual Literacy, Language Difference, and Matters of Agency." *College English,* vol. 75, no. 6, 2013, pp. 582-607.

Matsuda, Paul Kei. "The Lure of Translingual Writing." *PMLA,* vol. 129, no. 3, 2014, pp. 478-83.

—. "The Myth of Linguistic Homogeneity in US College Composition." *College English,* vol. 68, no. 6, 2006, pp. 637-51.

Maxwell, Joseph A. *Qualitative Research Design: An Interactive Approach.* Sage, 2012.

Milson-Whyte, Vivette. "Pedagogical and Socio-Political Implications of Code-Meshing in Classrooms: Some Considerations for a Translingual Orientation to Writing." *Literacy as Translingual Practice: Between Communities and Classrooms,* edited by Suresh Canagarajah, Routledge, 2013, pp. 115-27.

Nieto, Sonia. "Lessons from Students on Creating a Chance to Dream." *Harvard Educational Review,* vol. 64, no. 4, 1994, pp. 392-427.

Nowacek, Rebecca S. *Agents of Integration: Understanding Transfer as a Rhetorical Act.* SIUP, 2011.

Orellana, Marjorie Faulstich. *Translating Childhoods: Immigrant Youth, Language, and Culture.* Rutgers, 2009.

Pennycook, Alastair. "English as a Language Always in Translation." *European Journal of English Studies,* vol. 12, no. 1, 2008, pp. 33-47.

Roberge, Mark, Kay M. Losey, and Margi Wald, editors. *Teaching U.S.-Educated Multilingual Writers.* U of Michigan P, 2015.

Rubin, Herbert J., and Irene S. Rubin. *Qualitative Interviewing: The Art of Hearing Data.* London: Sage, 2011.

Ruecker, Todd. *Transiciones: Pathways of Latinas and Latinos Writing in High School and College.* Utah State UP, 2015.

Schleppegrell, Mary. *The Language of Schooling: A Functional Linguistics Perspective.* Routledge, 2004.

Seidman, Irving. *Interviewing as Qualitative Research: A Guide for Researchers in Education and the Social Sciences.* Teachers College Press, 2013.

Siczek, Megan, and Gena Bennett. "Students as 'Language Detectives': Teaching Lexico-Grammatical Features of Academic Language." *Teaching U.S.-Educated Multilingual Writers*, edited by Mark Roberge, Kay M. Losey, and Margi Wald, U of Michigan P, 2015, pp. 132-53.

Silver, Naomi. "Reflective Pedagogies and the Metacognitive Turn in College Teaching." *Using Reflection and Metacognition to Improve Student Learning: Across the Disciplines, Across the Academy*, edited by Mathew Kaplan, Naomi Silver, Danielle LaVaque-Mantey, and Deborah Meizlish, Stylus Publishing, 2013, pp. 1-17.

Sommers, Nancy, and Laura Saltz. "The Novice as Expert: Writing the Freshman Year." *CCC*, vol. 56, no. 1, 2004, pp. 124-49.

Thaiss, Chris, and Terry Myers Zawacki. *Engaged Writers and Dynamic Disciplines*. Boynton/Cook, 2006.

Venuti, Lawrence. *Translation Changes Everything: Theory and Practice*. Routledge, 2013.

Yancey, Kathleen Blake. *Reflection in the Writing Classroom*. Utah State UP, 1998.

Inhabiting Ordinary Sentences

Peter Wayne Moe

In this article, I present a collection of student sentences to explore what it means to, and how a writer might, inhabit a sentence. Such inhabitation is a matter of ethos, style, and composition—a matter of a writer located grammatically within a discourse. Relying on student sentences, I challenge sentence-appreciation books and websites that look only to the work of the masters as models for prose. I claim we can learn something from ordinary sentences written by ordinary writers. Acknowledging this noteworthy ordinary-ness, the collection of student sentences presented in this article asks that we consider the reader's role in locating a writer's ethos. It asks that we examine place at the sentence level, expand ethos beyond character alone, trust readers to pick up a writer's understated cues, and, most of all, attend to what ordinary sentences do on the page.

"You're always building an inhabitation in your prose,
A place from which you speak to the reader."

—Verlyn Klinkenborg (2012)

I have come across many teachers who use inhabitation to describe a writer's relationship to the sentence. David Bartholomae speaks of writers needing "a kind of form they can inhabit in order to get work done" (qtd. in Boe and Schroeder 264); Stanley Fish claims sentences "organize the world into manageable, and in some sense, artificial, units that can then be inhabited and manipulated" (7); Peter Elbow writes, "All too often people write ineffectually because they don't fully 'own' or 'inhabit' their words" (237). Back in 1966 Louis Milic complained about using metaphors to describe style (124; see also Tufte 2; Williams and Colomb 17), but I find the metaphor of inhabitation compelling nonetheless for its suggestion that a writer might dwell within a sentence, reside there—the sentence a structure that makes the writer's work possible.

In the epigraph Verlyn Klinkenborg calls inhabitation "a place from which you speak to the reader" (83). Klinkenborg understands the writer as situated within and speaking from a discursive space, ideas that resonate with the etymology of ethos. Arthur Miller explains that "the basic denotation [of ethos] is *not* character, but '*an accustomed place*' and in the plural may refer to the '*haunts or abodes* of animals'; it may also refer to '*the abodes of men*'" (310; see also Halloran 60; Hyde xiii). The earliest uses of ethos—going back to Homer and Hesiod (Hyde xvi)—concern place. Nedra Reynolds calls such inhabitation "ethos as location." As she says, writers "inscribe *who* they are by showing *where* they are" ("Ethos" 325).

Recent composition theorists have been exploring the relationship between place and writing (Applegarth; Bacha; Christoph; Keller and Weisser; Rivers; Vandenberg, Hum, and Clary-Lemon; Weisser and Dobrin). In 2014, *College Composition and Communication* devoted issues 66.1 and 66.2 to "Locations of Writing," for which editor Kathleen Yancey asked, "Where do we write? And what difference, if any, does the location of our writing make? How does our location influence what we write and how we share our writing? And what of our own located-ness?" (5). Yancey's last question—about our own located-ness—evokes ethos as location and challenges the idea that ethos is a product of deliberate choice exclusively. This is because "cultural, linguistic, and psychic forces that are beyond a rhetor's control affect what he or she is able to say" (Christoph 665). Reynolds explains: "Writers' identities . . . are constructed by space and the spatial: a writer's subject positions are determined by the space of the body, her geographical location, her shifting intellectual positions, her distance or closeness to others, to texts, to events" ("Ethos" 335-36). Ethos is the product of relationships that the writer might not be aware of even as she is situated within them.

And what of the sentence? What role might it—this most fundamental unit of writing—play in our discussions of place? Klinkenborg reminds us, "Your job as a writer is making sentences" (13). Yet, somewhat surprisingly, in the aforementioned scholarship looking at how writers locate themselves, grammar is noticeably absent. For instance, note that Reynolds makes no mention of the sentences themselves in her understanding of inhabitation:

> Writers inhabit their texts by spending hours of time within them; they know where everything is or have memories of building it. . . . Turning pages, or hitting the page up and page down keys, using the "find" and "go to" commands to get to specific (remembered) parts, or using a post-it note or penciled checkmark—these are a writer's acts of dwelling. Writers inhabit a text when they can still remember "where they were," physically, emotionally, and intellectually, while writing it. (*Geographies* 167)

I add that writers inhabit a text, too, grammatically, syntactically, stylistically. Consider another etymology, that of *elocutio*, the Latin for style. It comes from the prefix *e-* meaning "out of" and a variation of *locus*, meaning "place" (Holmberg 137). Style is language coming out of a place. It is discourse located. This etymology points to the relationship between language and a physical place (I think of accents, of colloquialisms), but we can expand location beyond physical places to include the rhetorical situation, the ways language locates a writer in relation to other people, other ideas, other discourses.[1]

The inhabited sentence is something a writer composes, composition itself deriving from the Latin prefix *com-* meaning "together" and the verb *ponere* meaning "to place." Composition is the act of placing things together, in relation, one word, phrase, idea alongside others. It is the act of making sentences, and composition locates the writer via language from a particular place, a place built and inhabited by the writer. Because this place is contextually bound, we must not think of the inhabited sentence as static. I grant that "inhabited" suggests stability, a solid structure, something set in stone, but it would be a mistake to read "inhabited" as so firmly established. Inhabitation is in flux because it is made of relationships that are always changing. (Such dynamism is seen, for instance, in Reynolds's "writer's acts of dwelling." In the passage quoted above, her gerunds—*spending, building, turning, hitting, using, writing*—nouns though they are, suggest movement, action.) And if ethos concerns relationships cultural, social, and grammatical, then a writer can inhabit a sentence a variety of ways. This is why a single sentence can produce multiple readings.

And so, when Laura Micciche writes that "word choice and sentence structure are an expression of the way we attend to the words of others, the way we position ourselves in relation to others" (719), I read her in light of ethos, of style, of composition. She is talking about the inhabited sentence, about the rhetorical work sentences do to position writers within a particular discursive space. Because I am curious what this inhabited sentence looks like in practice, in what follows I offer a non-exhaustive collection of ways that writers inhabit sentences. The collection gathers familiar moves all writers make within a sentence (punctuating a sentence, for instance, or making a parenthetical aside), yet these moves are not often read as rhetorical in the sense of how they locate a writer. By attending to the overlooked rhetoricity of the seemingly mundane grammar of everyday prose, this collection asks that we—readers and writers, teachers and students—attend to the rhetorical work of ordinary sentences.

A Method for Reading Sentences

In Gerald Graff and Cathy Birkenstein's *They Say / I Say: The Moves that Matter in Academic Writing*, a writer locates herself against the words of others via metatext. Graff and Birkenstein present metatext as a gesture of goodwill, a means to "guide readers through the twists and turns of your argument" (111).[2] Klinkenborg objects. Metatext, he says, assumes the reader "is essentially passive and in need of constant herding" (25). He writes that transitions "take the reader's head between their hands and force her to look where they want her to" (118), and instead of such overbearing (and, at times, violent) syntax, Klinkenborg teaches writers to "imagine a reader you can trust" (139).

In the collection that follows, I do just that. Because metatext can digress into "overused, meaningless words and phrases" (Klinkenborg 118; see also Sale 61), I look to the subtler ways a writer might inhabit a sentence. To their credit, Graff and Birkenstein do note that "Once you get used to using [the templates], you can even dispense with them altogether, for the rhetorical moves they model will be at your fingertips in an unconscious, instinctive way" (11). I want to use this dispensing of metatext not as the end of a curriculum (as it is for Graff and Birkenstein) but as its starting point. I work from the assumption that a writer can get by without heavy-handed metatext, that a reader can pick up metatextual cues without those cues in neon lighting. Many of the sentences I gather are variations of "they say / I say." I don't dispute the importance of that rhetorical move, though these sentences enact it gently, quietly. Useful as Graff and Birkenstein's templates are, they are not particularly graceful.

Trusting the reader means not only moving away from overbearing metatext but also handing the text over to the reader and asking the reader to co-construct its meaning. When Klinkenborg writes, "You're always building an inhabitation in your prose," he's using "you" in the singular to refer to the writer (83). For my purposes, I'd like to read this *you* as plural to consider what it might look like for the reader, as well as the writer, to create habitation. A writer may deliberately choose to situate herself in relation to a passage she's quoting in a particular way, but then she hands the text over to the reader, who reads it and situates the writer in relation to that passage and in relation to the reader as well. The writer locates herself even as the reader (hours, days, weeks, months, years later) locates the writer—and maybe not in the same place the writer had intended.[3]

Because of this messy co-creation, the moves the sentences of this collection make are not reliably repeatable or transferrable from one piece of writing to another. The sentences I gather must be discussed in relation to other sentences. A sentence never stands alone. It is never written or read alone. To offer this collection, then, so that writers can go and do likewise would miss the point. Rather, I offer an account of how a writer might locate herself (perhaps unwittingly—intention is beside the point, especially when the reader contributes to an act of location) and how a reader might have a hand in that process. I am working toward a theory of the inhabited sentence, one that depends upon an ethos of location, one co-constructed by writer and reader. This collection—which gathers familiar moves all writers make—is necessarily and unavoidably incomplete. It gestures toward the many possibilities for how a writer might inhabit a sentence, offering a few such instances as an invitation to find and invent others.

The writers whose sentences I use are all students from fyc courses at the University of Pittsburgh and Seattle Pacific University. I use their work with permission, and I look to it because it is ordinary. Their sentences are not ordinary in the sense of a grocery list or a diary entry but ordinary in that they are written by ordinary writers—not presidents, not Pulitzer Prize winners, not *New Yorker* staff writers. These sentences are written by students for ordinary, everyday circumstances: classroom assignments. This is an ordinary context, one we are all familiar with and encounter day after day, week after week, year after year, as both teacher and student. And these sentences are ordinary in the sense that they make ordinary moves, like using an adverb. I am not gathering a list of figures of speech (e.g., Lanham) but looking to sentences that often do little more than place together subject and predicate. This is not to say that there is nothing remarkable in ordinary sentences. Ordinary is not a disparaging term. Attention to the ordinary calls for a new understanding of ethos and style, one that recognizes how even seemingly boring, inconsequential sentences—ordinary ones—locate the writer in language.[4]

So too, I look to student sentences in an effort to "contest the distinction between 'real' writers and 'student' writers" (Lu 447). I read these students as writers, considering what their sentences might teach us about writing, about rhetoric, about style. I look to their writing not only for how it speaks to the overlooked rhetoricity of ordinary sentences but also because student sentences rarely, if ever, appear in style guides or sentence-appreciation websites and books. (If student sentences do appear there, they are often given as examples of error.) The general absence of student sentences in these, the most common genres our students encounter when dealing with grammar and syntax instruction, makes a subdued but clear argument—students cannot write good sentences—an argument that begets, and is perpetuated by, the argument's own method: looking for good sentences in Joan Didion, Martin Luther King, Jr., Ernest Hemingway, William Faulkner, Jane Austen, Gertrude Stein, Virginia Woolf, former presidents, and the like. As Geoffrey Sirc says of textbooks that treat their selections as museum pieces, "[T]he curated shows always seem to feature the same artists" (3). Plucking ideal sentences by masters is flawed on (at least) three counts: It prizes sentences that appear in certain settings over others (the literary and political over the pedagogical), it claims we can learn about style from the masters only, and it assumes "good" sentences are those with flair while overlooking the value of the ordinary. I make no claims for the sentences I gather to be great or even good, no claims that they belong in the Sentence Museum. I'm skeptical of such labels, and I'm interested, instead, in the work carried out by ordinary plain sentences any writer could write, sentences we have perhaps written ourselves in some form or another.

My method is inherently biased. I have chosen sentences that illustrate how ordinary writers can inhabit sentences, and how they can do so with rhetorical force. Such bias is unavoidable—I am, after all, a reader reading—and it creates a tension: The moment I select a sentence for analysis, it ceases to be ordinary and becomes noteworthy. Acknowledging this noteworthy ordinariness, this collection of student sentences asks that we consider the reader's role in locating a writer's ethos. It asks that we examine place at the sentence-level, that we expand ethos beyond character alone, that we trust readers to pick up a writer's understated cues, and, most of all, that we attend to what ordinary sentences do on the page.

The Collection

Subjects and Predicates

In many sentences, a subject acts upon an object, and a writer's decision whether to be the subject or object of a sentence is a matter of composition, of placing things in relation to each other. William Robinson claims, "[W]riters must make their most important decisions before they get to the verb, when they decide what to put in the topic portion of the sentence, which is where the subject is, and, by implication, what they will reserve for the comment part, which is where the verb is" (442). In the following, the decision of what goes in the subject position and what goes in the predicate position becomes indicative of this student's changing relationship with Gloria Anzaldúa's work. He's writing in response to her essay, "How to Tame a Wild Tongue," in which Anzaldúa moves between English and multiple varieties of Spanish.

> As I read through her article and encountered the areas where she switches from English to Spanish and back again, I found myself becoming frustrated. I understood what she was trying to do but it was upsetting that I couldn't entirely follow. Through this technique Anzaldúa showed me a small fraction of the frustration that she has had to deal with on a daily basis.

In the first two sentences, "I" is the subject, but there's a shift in the third: "I" becomes "me." Anzaldúa now controls the sentence. At the most stripped down, the sentences proceed like this: I read, I found, I understood, I couldn't follow, Anzaldúa showed me. The student enters Anzaldúa's prose, becomes disoriented, recognizes and names his frustrations, and then relegates himself to the object of the third sentence, allowing Anzaldúa to act upon him. His subjects and predicates trace that movement, locating him in relation to her. David Bartholomae writes, "For me, nothing happens, or could happen, until I imagine myself within a discourse—a kind of textual conversation / confrontation with people whose work matters to me and whose work, then, makes my own work possible" ("Against" 21). This conversation / confrontation happens through grammar, through how subjects and objects are situated in relation to each other. Only once Anzaldúa finds her way into this student's sentences—first as object, then as subject—can his work begin.

"And" and "But"

The following is excerpted from a paper in which the student tells of preparing to speak up in a class discussion following the 2016 election. Her classmates and professor had voted Democratic. She writes:

> After about 45 minutes of sitting there just listening to them tear down every Republican, I finally got enough courage to raise my hand. I knew I had the option of sitting there silently as well, but I could not do that any longer.

There's a turn with her use of "but," a distinct moment when the narrative changes direction. There is, as Klinkenborg calls it, "the feel of reversal taking place" (119). There's also a "they say / I say" here, and the "but" clause sets the stage for the writer to now speak.

Contrast this use of "but" with the use of "and" in the following student analysis of how Mary Louise Pratt defines a "contact zone." The student writes:

> By showing you what a contact zone can look like through the narrative of her son's encounter with baseball, she allows you to build up your own definition of her term. In her case, this move is the best, because once she finally does give you the academic definition, it is much easier to understand than it would have been without the story of her son and his baseball experiences. This isn't the only time that Pratt uses this particular technique. Her whole speech is composed this way, and it is through this strategic layout that she solves the problem she created for herself.

The problem Pratt has created for herself, according to this student, is making up a term (contact zone) and using it in her title, which necessitates that Pratt define it. This problem of definition opened the student's essay. I note her use of "and" in her final sentence. It connects Pratt's use of examples to "the problem she has created for herself." That "and" is a road sign. Coming at the end of a paragraph, this "and" cues a statement of significance about what Pratt is doing.

Stanley Fish suggests the conjunction propels prose, writing that "'but' and 'and' are the words that carry the experience forward, the first signaling a thought going in a new direction, the second saying 'and, oh, this has just occurred to me'" (62). In the student sentences above, "but" acts just as Fish says, but "and" does something different. The student is not piling on more ideas. She uses "and" to end the discussion. Her "and" reads as "in conclusion" without being so heavy-handed. It is an "and" of locative ethos, a subtle way for a writer to locate herself within the trajectory of her argument.

The Pivot

Like "but" in the above, the following passage reveals a hinge in a piece of writing. I had asked students to set their reading of a poem against someone else's, and this writer selected Robert Frost's "Stopping by Woods on a Snowy Evening" and a blogger's interpretation of it:

> One analysis I took interest in was that of Yahoo blogger Bridget Delaney, who viewed the poem in a more spiritual context. Where she saw God I saw danger.

From here, the paper continues with the student's reading of Frost set up by "Where she saw God I saw danger." This sentence pivots from the blogger's reading of Frost to the student's. It is a veiled "they say / I say," one that organizes the student's work in relation to Frost, his poem, the blogger, the blogger's reading of Frost, the student's own reading of Frost, as well as to readers—Frost's, the blogger's, and the student's. Not bad for seven words.

Punctuation

Punctuation is often described as having two functions: to mark the grammatical units of a sentence, and / or to give guidance on its delivery (when to pause, when to slow down, how to inflect the voice, etc.). So too, punctuation locates the writer. Consider how the next student punctuates his sentence. This comes midway through an essay addressing why the public is unable to make sense of offensive art. After giving a few examples of seemingly incomprehensible modern art (art he later defends), he writes,

> As counterintuitive as they are, these types of art—the "anti novels," the "noise music," the "pictures your five-year-old could draw"—have become more and more prevalent in modern times; the efforts are often, unsurprisingly, met with bewilderment or disdain.

The punctuation here enables the student to put together a sentence that, despite its length and layers of qualification, is easy to read, both silently and aloud. The first comma locates this rise in modern art against public expectation; it's "counterintuitive." The em dashes allow for a clarification about what types of art he is concerned with. The quotation marks invite skeptics of modern art into the sentence, mocking these skeptics even as they are quoted. The semicolon sets up a pause—not as long a pause as a period would create—that tells us what follows next will comment upon what's been said. Commas set off "unsurprisingly," a word that, given the rest of the essay's criticism of the public's inability to engage the arts, reads as sarcastic. The punctuation enables him to set controversial art, the public's reaction to it, his own reading of it, and his critique of the public all into a single sentence. There's an agility, an authority even, as the student maneuvers around his subject while commenting on it, his punctuation making possible his movement within this syntactic space.

The Parenthetical Aside

The following is the opening paragraph from a student writing about her relationship with her roommate.

> Among the over 3,000 students and faculty at Seattle Pacific University, it would have been incredibly naïve for me to assume that a perfect relationship would form between myself and everyone I encountered. I did, however, hope (and perhaps falsely assume) that my roommate and I would be best friends from the first day. This was not the case.

Notice how the sentences narrow. The first sentence is 34 words, the second 21, the third five, and by the time the student has reached that third sentence, there is a clear sense that her expectations have been dashed. Her decreasing sentence length (a locative device in itself) gives weight, even urgency, to that third sentence, especially when following the parenthetical in the second sentence. Of the aside, Bartholomae believes, "If we taught the parenthesis with the same vigor as a nation that we teach the topic sentence, we'd have a whole different world; our children would be different. They'd be able to say something in their funny voice as well as their serious voice, or think of a qualification while they were thinking of the assertion" (qtd. in Boe and Schroeder 20). In the passage above, the parenthetical allows the student to speak back to herself, to question what she's already said in the opening sentence. The parentheses open up space for commentary on what has already been said, the student pausing to reflect upon, and push back against, the self who speaks in the opening sentence. She locates herself against herself. The writer can have a foot in one spot, another elsewhere. The parenthetical allows for tension between multiple locations and multiple identities within a sentence, the aside offering another perspective, a corrective even, to the sentence proper. The sentence is not as tidy and clean and together a space as it might first appear.

Adverbs and Prepositions

In addition to denoting manner, frequency, and degree, adverbs speak to the when and the where. Because rhetoric is about context, and adverbs provide context, adverbs are the metatext of rhetoric.[5] The following passage was written by the student quoted earlier who wrote about the election:

> Often times we talk about race, gender and identity and my professor is always willing to share her opinions on these issues. After the election, she firmly expressed her political views to our class.

Note the student's use of "always" in the first sentence, an adverb that, by telling readers how regularly the professor shares her opinions, helps to contextualize the discussion that follows. This adverb defines a rhetorical situation, as does the adverbial "often times" opening the sentence. Both establish the scene of the student's narrative. At this point, readers know this class frequently discusses controversial topics.

Prepositions do a similar work. By situating nouns and noun phrases within a sentence, they place together ideas and events and people and things within a rhetorical setting. The prepositional phrase "After the election" situates class discussions within a particular setting: the morning of November 9, 2016. The prepositional phrases "about race, gender and identity," "on these issues," and "to our class" further contextualize the sentences. They become pillars of this student's inhabitation, the student locating herself amid them. These sentences could be pared of their adverbs and prepositional phrases and would remain grammatically sound—

> We talk and my professor is willing to share her opinions. She expressed her political views.

—but everything is lost. The sentences are decontextualized, devoid of urgency, devoid of relevance, devoid of exigency. They are no longer set within a place, no longer inhabited, the student no longer situated within debates about the place of politics in the classroom.

The Parenthetical Citation

The parenthetical citation signals where and how and when the writer will engage the words of another writer, and it locates the reader in relation to that ongoing conversation. In this sense, the parenthetical citation can be read as adverbial (in the sense discussed above) as it provides context for a larger discussion taking place outside the bounds of the paper at hand. The writer uses citations to reconstruct that conversation, enter into it, inhabit it, and locate herself therein.

The following two sentences are drawn from a student paper also about Pratt's "Arts of the Contact Zone." She uses Pratt to analyze an experience in one of her other courses that term:

> When Pratt describes herself leading these discussions in her own classroom, she says, "Along with rage, incomprehension, and pain, there were exhilarating moments of wonder and revelation, mutual understanding, and new wisdom—the joys of the contact zone" (Pratt 39). In my University Foundations class, there were many moments of tension after our professor would speak and then the student would ask yet another question, and I could tell from the occasional sighs from the rest of the class that they wanted a simple agreement and to move out of the contact zone to a less controversial topic.

The first sentence establishes the idea the student will respond to, and the citation pins that idea on the second-to-last page of Pratt's article. With this citation, the student locates herself in relation not to Pratt's entire argument but to a specific moment within it. The citation grounds readers, giving us something to grasp onto from Pratt, an idea the student will build upon as her essay continues. So too, the citation points the reader to the student's works cited page, which is the first thing I look to when I pick up any piece of writing, an effort to situate the text I am about to read against what I have already (and have not yet) read (see Dobrin 54-55).

I would be remiss if I did not note some of the other locative moves this student makes. Her second sentence has the adverbial prepositional phrase "[i]n my University Foundations class," which situates Pratt's ideas within a particular classroom. There's the conjunction "and" joining the two halves of the second sentence; that "and" propels the ideas forward (rather than bringing the discussion to a close as it did in the student sentence discussed earlier). The citation, the works cited page, the prepositional phrase, the conjunction—these work together to locate this student alongside Pratt and other texts, within a particular classroom setting, within the trajectory of this student's larger claims concerning contact zones. The student has inhabited this space, working within it while moving her argument forward.

Appropriation

In the paragraph above, the student takes on Pratt's phrasing. About a course she taught at Stanford that intentionally dwelled within the contact zone, Pratt writes, "there were exhilarating moments of wonder" (39). The student writes in response, "there were many moments of tension." The student speaks back to Pratt using Pratt's own syntax. Such appropriation also shows up in titles. Working with Pratt's definition of a contact zone as a space where "cultures meet, clash, and grapple with each other" (34) and talking about her politically tense classroom as a contact zone, one student titled her piece "The Clashroom," and another, the student who wrote on offensive art, titled his essay "Using Contact Zones to Understand the Modern Arts." In class, we had been reading Pratt alongside Richard Miller's "Fault Lines in the Contact Zone," and students, seeing how Miller uses his own title to situate himself against Pratt, imitated Miller's locative ethos. These titles that reference Pratt can be read as a nod to Miller also; as Bartholomae writes, "Even when the footnotes aren't there, there are footnotes" ("Everything" 78). Through appropriation, writers take on the syntax of others, inhabiting their sentences, making those sentences their own. Because all writers inherit language, it is only through appropriation that a writer can be at home within that language, dwell within its sentences, its ways of thinking, speaking, writing, and being.

The Rhetorical Work of Ordinary Sentences

In *How to Write a Sentence*, Fish admits, "Some appreciate fine art; others appreciate fine wines. I appreciate fine sentences" (3). He continues, likening the best syntactic performances to athletic feats: amazing touchdowns, dunks, and catches: "The response is always, 'Wasn't that amazing?' . . . And always the admiration is a rueful recognition that you couldn't do it yourself even though you also have two hands and feet" (3). But Fish says you can do it, and you can do it through imitation of the best sentences. So, from John Updike's "It was in the books while it was still in the sky" (which describes Ted Williams's homerun in his final at-bat at Fenway), we get Fish's imitations: "She was enrolled at Harvard before she was conceived." "He had won the match before the first serve." "They were celebrating while the other team was still at bat" (10). Fish has no illusions that these are good sentences; instead, he's imitating because imitation is a means of analysis, and through imitation, we might learn to read and write sentences better.

This is all well and good, and it is standard-fare sentence-level pedagogy. Fish focuses on the prose of the best writers, as do many textbooks and sentence-appreciation books and websites too. But I fear that a pedagogy built on imitating the likes of Updike turns reading into a treasure hunt for rhetorical figures of speech, those figures becoming the be-all and end-all of sentence-level instruction. Such a pedagogical approach to grammar and style also overlooks the work our students' (and our own) sentences do. A focus on only the "sentences that take our breath away" (Fish 3) ignores the ordinary sentences that are the steady inhale and exhale of prose. The ordinary makes possible the extraordinary. While it is important for a writer to know how a sentence like Updike's works, more so, a writer needs to understand the rhetorical work all her other sentences do. Those other sentences—the worker sentences—enable a writer to speak from a location, to place words and ideas and people in relation to each other. They carry out the workaday prose of a writer, and they make it possible to inhabit a sentence. It's not that a writer cannot inhabit more stylized prose, but that such prose is often what governs the attention of both reader and writer, even as the understated sentences are doing equally as important rhetorical work. Inhabitation acknowledges that sentences are always situated in relation to other sentences, other clauses, other phrases, always situated amid the ordinary and extraordinary. A sentence is discourse located—so even though Fish does, we should not talk about Updike's sentence without looking at what surrounds it.[6]

The challenge, then, is helping students come to see how their ordinary sentences locate them as writers within the world, to help them see those sentences as inhabited, as (to use Miller's language) a haunt, an abode. When students write reductively about the texts they read, when they fail to consider ideas counter to their claim, when they quote only passages that support their argument or when they choose not to quote the texts they write about—these are problems of location, problems of how and where a writer situates herself, problems that manifest themselves in the student's sentences. To the student whose paper only quotes parts of text that support his argument, for instance, the teacher can ask that his revision account for the rest of that text. Such a suggestion seems obvious, ordinary even, but to carry it out well necessitates the student return to the text, reread it, discern where he stands in relation to it, and then find a way to bring those ideas into his own sentences. The student must rework his sentences down to the very syntax holding them together; he must think through the rhetorical implications of whether "I" or "Anzaldúa" ought to be the subject of his next sentence. He must locate himself in relation to the text at hand and, in response, revise his claim. Such revision positioned alongside other writers' words is, I suggest, the job of the academy, and it happens through the ordinary acts of putting together subject and predicate.

There is a rhetorical density to ordinary sentences, and for that reason, we would be better served attending to the work of sentences like those I have gathered here than the flashy sentences that dominate sentence-level instruction. It is easy to find a figure of speech and marvel at it; it is much harder to look at a plain sentence and discern its role within the paragraph, page, and paper. But if rhetoric is about context, if writing is about setting ideas in relation to each other, if style is about language coming out of a place, if ethos is about inhabiting that space, then understanding the role "and" plays in a sentence is more important than being able to identify President Lincoln's use of epistrophe in "of the people, by the people, for the people." By focusing on the ordinary, we see the rhetorical work our sentences do, and we see, too, how a writer might inhabit them.

Acknowledgments

I thank David Bartholomae and Traynor Hansen, as well as editor Laura Micciche and *Composition Studies* reviewers Eric Hayot and Christopher Carter, for their very helpful comments on drafts of this article. Thanks also to my colleagues at the Seattle Pacific University Faculty Writing Retreat.

Notes

1. For more on inhabitation, location, readers, and writers, see Moe, "Of Chiasms and Composition."

2. It's not uncommon to talk about metatext as goodwill. In *Rhetorical Grammar*, Martha Kolln and Loretta Gray claim, "[M]etadiscourse markers send messages to the reader from and about the writer. They say, in effect, 'I'm helping you out here, trying to make your job of reading and understanding easier'" (132). See also Joseph Harris, in *Rewriting: How to Do Things with Texts*: "Metatext lets you speak directly to your readers, to say to them, in effect, *Here's why I'm approaching this subject this way*. . . . [Metatext] help[s] your readers understand your text from your point of view" (90-91). So too, E. B. White, in his introduction to *The Elements of Style*: "Will [Strunk] felt that the reader was in serious trouble most of the time, floundering in a swamp, and that it was the duty of anyone attempting to write English to drain this swamp quickly and get the reader up on dry ground, or at least to throw him a rope" (xviii, qtd. in King 124). For more on metatext and academic writing, see Beerits; Lancaster; Thonney.

3. My focus in this piece is just on how a writer inhabits a sentence. For a discussion of how readers inhabit a text, see Reynolds *Geographies* 162-68.

4. Jennifor Sinor claims, "We can define ordinary writing as a text that is not literary, is not noticed, and one that should have been discarded but that instead somehow remains" (184), which seems an apropriate description of student writing.

5. The adverbs I'm talking about, of course, are different than the commonly disdained -ly adverb. See, for instance, King (124-28), Strunk and White (75), and Zinsser (68-69).

6. For more on the work of ordinary sentences and Updike's sentence in particular, see Moe, "Scorebooks and Commonplace Books."

Works Cited

Anonymous Students. Unpublished Papers. University of Pittsburgh and Seattle Pacific University, 2012-2016.

Anzaldúa, Gloria. "How to Tame a Wild Tongue." *Borderlands: La Frontera: The New Mestiza*, Spinsters/Aunt Lute Book Company, 1987, pp. 53-64.

Applegarth, Risa. "Genre, Location, and Mary Austin's *Ethos*." *Rhetoric Society Quarterly*, vol. 41, no. 1, 2011, pp. 41-63.

Bacha, Jeffrey A. "The Physical Mundane as Topos: Walking/Dwelling/Using as Rhetorical Invention." *CCC*, vol. 68, no. 2, 2016, pp. 266-91.

Bartholomae, David. "Against the Grain." *Writers on Writing*, edited by Tom Waldrep, Random House, 1985, pp. 19-29.

—. "Everything Was Going Quite Smoothly until I Stumbled on a Footnote." *Writing on the Edge*, vol. 20, no. 1, 2009, pp. 73-84.

Beerits, Laura. "Understanding I: The Rhetorical Variety of Self-References in College Literature Papers." *CCC*, vol. 67, no. 4, 2016, pp. 550-75.

Boe, John, and Eric Schroeder. "Stop Being So Coherent: An Interview with David Bartholomae." *Writing on the Edge*, vol. 10, no. 1, 1998/1999, pp. 9-28.

Christoph, Julie Nelson. "Reconceiving Ethos in Relation to the Personal: Strategies of Placement in Pioneer Women's Writing." *College English*, vol. 64, no. 6, 2002, pp. 660-79.

Delaney, Bridget I. "Analysis of Robert Frost's 'Stopping by Woods on a Snowy Evening.'" *Yahoo! Voices*, 25 July 2010. *Internet Archive Wayback Machine*, web.archive.org/web/20130127203353/http://voices.yahoo.com/analysis-robert-frosts-stopping-woods-snowy-6445730.html.

Dobrin, Sidney. "A Problem with Writing (about) 'Alternative' Discourse." *ALT DIS: Alternative Discourses and the Academy*, edited by Christopher Schroeder, Helen Fox, and Patricia Bizzell, Boynton/Cook, 2002, pp. 45-56.

Elbow, Peter. *Vernacular Eloquence: What Speech Can Bring to Writing*. Oxford UP, 2012.

Fish, Stanley. *How to Write a Sentence and How to Read One*. HarperCollins, 2011.

Frost, Robert. "Stopping by Woods on a Snowy Evening." *Poetry Foundation*, poetryfoundation.org/poems/42891/stopping-by-woods-on-a-snowy-evening.

Graff, Gerald, and Cathy Birkenstein. *They Say/I Say: The Moves that Matter in Academic Writing*. 2006. 3rd edition, Norton, 2014.

Halloran, S. Michael. "Aristotle's Concept of Ethos, or if not His Somebody Else's." *Rhetoric Review*, vol. 1, no. 1, 1982, pp. 58-63.

Harris, Joseph. *Rewriting: How to Do Things with Texts*. Utah State UP, 2006.

Holmberg, Carl B. "Some Available Conceptions of Rhetorical Practice." *Rhetoric Society Quarterly*, vol. 10, no. 3, 1980, pp. 135-42.

Hyde, Michael J. "Introduction: Rhetorically, We Dwell." *The Ethos of Rhetoric*, edited by Michael J. Hyde, U of South Carolina P, 2005, pp. xiii-xxviii.

Keller, Christopher J., and Christian R. Weisser. *The Locations of Composition*. SUNY P, 2007.

King, Stephen. *On Writing: A Memoir of the Craft*. 2000. 10th anniversary edition, Scribner, 2010.

Klinkenborg, Verlyn. *Several Short Sentences about Writing*. Knopf, 2012.

Kolln, Martha, and Loretta Gray. *Rhetorical Grammar: Grammatical Choices, Rhetorical Effects*. 1991. 7th edition, Pearson, 2013.

Lancaster, Zak. "Do Academics Really Write This Way? A Corpus Investigation of Moves and Templates in 'They Say/I Say.'" *CCC*, vol. 67, no. 3, 2016, pp. 437-64.

Lanham, Richard A. *A Handlist of Rhetorical Terms*. 1968. 2nd edition, U of California P, 1991.

Lu, Min-Zhan. "Professing Multiculturalism: The Politics of Style in the Contact Zone." *CCC*, vol. 45, no. 4, 1994, pp. 442-58.

Micciche, Laura R. "Making a Case for Rhetorical Grammar." *CCC*, vol. 55, no. 4, 2004, pp. 716-37.

Milic, Louis T. "Metaphysics in the Criticism of Style." *CCC*, vol. 17, no. 3, 1966, pp. 124-29.

Miller, Arthur B. "Aristotle on Habit (εθος) and Character (ηθος): Implications for the Rhetoric." *Speech Monographs*, vol. 41, no. 4, 1974, pp. 309-16.

Miller, Richard E. "Fault Lines in the Contact Zone." *College English*, vol. 56, no. 4, 1994, pp. 389-408.

Moe, Peter Wayne. "Of Chiasms and Composition, or, The Whale, Part II." *Reader: Essays in Reader-Oriented Theory, Criticism, and Pedagogy*, vol. 65/66, 2013/2014, pp. 88-107.

—. "Scorebooks and Commonplace Books." *The Millions*, 27 Mar. 2015, themillions.com/2015/03/scorebooks-and-commonplace-books.html.

Pratt, Mary Louise. "Arts of the Contact Zone." *Profession*, 1991, pp. 33-40.

Reynolds, Nedra. "Ethos as Location: New Sites for Understanding Discursive Authority." *Rhetoric Review*, vol. 11, no. 2, spring 1993, pp. 325-38.

—. *Geographies of Writing: Inhabiting Places and Encountering Difference*. SIUP, 2004.

Rivers, Nathaniel A. "Geocomposition in Public Rhetoric and Writing Pedagogy." *CCC*, vol. 67, no. 4, 2016, pp. 576-606.

Robinson, William S. "Sentence Focus, Cohesion, and the Active and Passive Voices." *Teaching English in the Two-Year College*, vol. 27, no. 4, 2000, pp. 440-45.

Sale, Roger. *On Writing*. Random House, 1970.

Sinor, Jennifer. *The Extraordinary Work of Ordinary Writing: Annie Ray's Diary*. U of Iowa P, 2002,

Sirc, Geoffrey. *English Composition as a Happening*. Utah State UP, 2002.

Strunk, William, Jr., and E. B. White. *The Elements of Style*. 1959. 50th anniversary edition, Pearson, 2009.

Thonney, Teresa. "'In This Article, I Argue': An Analysis of Metatext in Research Article Introductions." *Teaching English in the Two-Year College*, vol. 43, no. 4, 2016, pp. 411-22.

Tufte, Virginia, with the assistance of Garrett Stewart. *Grammar as Style*. Holt, Rinehart and Winston, 1971.

Vandenberg, Peter, Sue Hum, and Jennifer Clary-Lemon. *Relations, Locations, Positions: Composition Theory for Writing Teachers.* NCTE, 2006.

Weisser, Christian R., and Sidney I. Dobrin, editors. *Ecocomposition: Theoretical and Pedagogical Approaches.* SUNY P, 2001.

White, E. B. "Introduction." Strunk and White, pp. xiii-xviii.

Williams, Joseph M., and Gregory G. Colomb. *Style: Toward Clarity and Grace.* 1981. U of Chicago P, 1995.

Yancey, Kathleen. "From the Editor: Locations of Writing." *CCC,* vol. 66, no. 1, 2014, pp. 5-11.

Zinsser, William. *On Writing Well: The Classic Guide to Writing Nonfiction.* 1976. 30th anniversary edition, HarperCollins, 2006.

Learning about Learning: Composition's Renewed Engagement with Cognition

Ann M. Penrose and Gwendolynne C. Reid

Because so much of composition's core pedagogy takes a reflective learning model for granted, we consider a cognitive perspective essential in preparing new composition teachers. Here we describe how such a perspective informs our work with graduate teaching assistants. First, we model how discussion of current pedagogical topics can be situated in a cognitive frame, calling attention in particular to the critical role of metacognitive awareness in curricular models such as writing about writing (WAW) and in pedagogical practices such as multimodal composing. Then we describe an activity designed to help Graduate Teaching Assistants (GTAs) explore implications of a cognitive perspective for their own pedagogical decision-making. Working from data collected from GTA cohorts over a 10-year period, we examine learning style preferences and variability in the GTA population in comparison with published data on undergraduates from various institutions and disciplines. We use these data to examine cognitive variability in writing classrooms and to illustrate a deliberate instructional focus on learning and metacognitive awareness. Our goal throughout is to help GTAs understand the cognitive core that grounds so much of the discipline's pedagogical practice.

Our disciplinary narrative locates composition's interest in cognition in the 1970-80s when Linda Flower and John R. Hayes introduced their model of writing as a goal-directed process and Andrea Lunsford and Barry Kroll invoked theories of cognitive development to elucidate basic writers' difficulties. The "cognitive revolution" sparked enthusiasm in the research community with its promise of data-based theory and methods for exploring writing processes and was embraced by teachers eager to discover specific strategies to support student writers. But, the narrative continues, reception was mixed and interest waned over the next decade or so. As a field, we worried that in focusing on students as cognitive beings—as individual, active decision-makers—we would fail to understand them as social beings, as culturally and politically situated (Bizzell, "Cognition"). And we were wary that a focus on developmental stages and psychological traits could lead to unwarranted assumptions about what individual students can and cannot do, alert to the dangers of what Mike Rose rightly characterized as cognitive reductionism.

The years since have seen considerable exploration of social, cultural and material contexts for composition and the role of individual agency in those contexts. Today's disciplinary narrative embraces an integrated concept of situated cognition much evolved from the bifurcated perspectives of forty years ago. Cognition has reemerged as a viable focus as contemporary compositionists seek to articulate and to understand today's pedagogical challenges. Indeed, learning theory is enjoying a resurgence in our disciplinary conversation: the concept of metacognition is embraced as an essential "habit of mind" in the 2011 Framework for Success in Postsecondary Writing (CWPA et al.); figures prominently in the rationale for teaching for transfer approaches (Yancey et al.), including the curricular focus on WAW (Downs and Wardle); and grounds pedagogical innovations espoused under the headings of disability studies and universal design (McAlexander). Other disciplinary discussions invoke cognitive principles more implicitly—for example, in considering the role of self-regulation in online pedagogies (Rendahl and Breuch; West et al.), in offering directed self-placement as a mechanism for helping students choose instructional environments supportive of their learning strengths and styles (Lewiecki-Wilson et al. "Rhetoric"; Royer and Gilles), and in championing multimodal composition as a response to learning style diversity (New London Group; Palmeri, *Remixing*). In effect, this widespread engagement with cognition has come to constitute a coherent theoretical base for much of the discipline in practice. As we explore below, each of these disparate professional conversations emphasizes the critical value for learners of understanding how learning happens—that is, of developing the metacognitive awareness that enables individual learners to reflect on what they are doing, to consider alternatives, and to direct their own learning.

Because so much of composition pedagogy takes this reflective learning model for granted, we consider a cognitive perspective essential in preparing new composition teachers. In this piece we describe how such a perspective informs our work with GTAs. First, we model how discussion of current pedagogical topics can be usefully situated in a cognitive frame. When we introduce GTAs to curricular models such as WAW and teaching for transfer, for example, or pedagogical issues such as multimodal literacy and universal design, we call attention to common assumptions about cognition implicit in these disciplinary discussions, in particular the critical role of metacognitive awareness. The significance of the cognitive perspective becomes especially clear when we explore the controversial topic of learning style with these new teachers, as we illustrate in the second part of our discussion. There we describe an activity designed to help GTAs explore implications of a cognitive perspective for their own pedagogical decision-making. Working from data collected from GTA cohorts over a 10-year period, we examine learning style preferences and variability in the GTA population in comparison with published data on undergraduates from various institutions and disciplines. We highlight the danger of cognitive reductionism in the learning style approach and underscore the critical role of metacognitive awareness in resisting such simplifications. We thus use these data to examine cognitive variability in writing classrooms and to illustrate a deliberate instructional focus on learning and metacognitive awareness. Our goal throughout is to help GTAs understand the cognitive principles that ground so much of the discipline's pedagogical practice.

Exploring Cognition in Current Pedagogies

The recent recognition of "Writing Is (Also Always) a Cognitive Activity" as a disciplinary threshold concept (Adler-Kassner and Wardle) identifies cognitivism as integral to composition's current professional knowledge base. We would not, however, characterize this interest as a turn *back* to cognitivism in the disciplinary narrative. We agree with Dylan Dryer that the current engagement with cognitive theory represents a convergence of attention to the cognitive aspects of composing (the "neurological turn") with attention to insights derived from the social turn (74). We share Dryer's optimism that this convergence of sensitivities has the potential to be as transformative as the cognitive and social turns from which it has evolved (71). The characterization of writing as a cognitive activity in Linda Adler-Kassner and Elizabeth Wardle's crowd-sourced compilation, alongside assertions about writing's social and rhetorical nature and role in "enact[ing] and creat[ing] identities and ideologies" (Scott 48), underscores the fact that we have been engaged with cognitive and social perspectives all along. Though much of our disciplinary discussion is theoretical and political—reflecting on who, what and why we teach and with what constraints and consequences—we often turn to the cognitive when we address the practical concerns of pedagogy, that is, our governing decisions about curriculum design and our daily decisions about how to teach. As a profession, for example, we want to understand how access to technology mediates social privilege—and we also want to understand how students learn online. We want to validate students' varied interests and life experiences—and we also want to understand the varied learning habits they have developed. We want to cultivate literacy knowledge that will serve students well in contexts beyond our classrooms—so we want to understand what it takes for such knowledge to transfer. In sum, we cannot enact the ethical and social values of our profession without careful attention to how students learn.

Writing about Writing

As a composition pedagogy that has quickly gained traction, WAW is an approach that many GTAs are likely to be exposed to during their training. It is also an approach that embodies the convergence of the cognitive and social sensibilities Dryer describes. In proposing the WAW model, Elizabeth Wardle and Doug Downs draw upon literature in activity theory that challenges the common division between individual cognition and social, material contexts, instead seeing the mind as part of the world and developed through interaction with it (Downs and Wardle; Wardle, "Understanding 'Transfer'"). While much of WAW is grounded in the social—in context, community, situation—it is just as grounded in the cognitive and in how this mind-in-the-world develops, and particularly in how it transfers learning across contexts. When introducing GTAs to WAW, then, drawing their attention to the cognitive principles underpinning it can help these new instructors make purposeful and coherent pedagogical choices. In fact, highlighting the cognitive dimension of WAW may be the most productive way to introduce this approach to many GTAs, particularly those whose disciplinary specialties lie outside of rhetoric and composition and for whom the argument that WAW allows them to teach about their area of expertise may not resonate. GTAs from diverse disciplines may find these basic cognitive concepts more familiar than some of the other specialized theories and methodologies WAW draws on, such as activity theory and ethnography.

The cognitive core of WAW is perhaps most visible to GTAs in Wardle's observation that "*meta-awareness about writing, language, and rhetorical strategies in FYC may be the most important ability our courses can cultivate*" (Wardle, "Understanding 'Transfer'" 82). This principle informs Downs and Wardle's "Teaching about Writing," where they cite the transfer-related literature, which finds that "self-reflection, explicit abstraction of principles, and alertness to one's context" encourage transfer of knowledge between contexts (576). Attention to meta-awareness also appears in Wardle's "Mutt Genres," where she adds the notion of "mindfulness" to the list of pedagogical practices that encourage transfer (Wardle 771). The instructor preface to *Writing about Writing* also reinforces these pedagogical practices, citing psychologists David Perkins and Gavriel Salomon's work on transfer and outlining how, in order to foster transfer, students need to (1) explicitly create general principles based on their own experience and learning; (2) be self-reflective, so that they keep track of what they are thinking and learning as they do it; and (3) be mindful, that is, alert to their surroundings and to what they are doing rather than just doing things automatically and unconsciously (Wardle and Downs vi). Learning to implement the WAW curriculum productively, then, requires awareness that the curriculum rests on a theory of cognition that sees the ability to think about (writing-related) thinking as central to the success of the fyc teaching and learning enterprise. While not all GTAs consider themselves writing scholars, most of them have meta-awareness about writing and language, and can gain confidence and purpose from recognizing the cognitive goals and strategies behind the WAW curriculum.

Teaching for Transfer

Similarly, introducing GTAs to Kathleen Yancey, Liane Robertson and Kara Taczak's teaching for transfer (TFT) curriculum entails introducing them to cognitive theory and the importance of reflective awareness for learning, as TFT draws even more explicitly on these foundations for its methods and rationale. Like Wardle and Downs and most other proponents of transfer in the composition literature (Anson; Beaufort; Nelms and Dively), Yancey et al. base their approach on principles of transfer articulated by Perkins and Salomon ("Teaching"; "Transfer"). The TFT curriculum is grounded in the assumption that once we understand conditions for the transfer of learning, we can create such conditions in our teaching. That is, we can design curriculum to support students' ability to select, adapt, and repurpose their prior knowledge and skill to address the exigencies of new contexts. Yancey et al. aim to do this by incorporating reflective activities and introducing key concepts that "help students describe and theorize writing" (57), including rhetorical elements such as audience, genre, and exigence as well as writing processes (e.g., reflection, composing, circulation). Students research and write about these concepts; use them to describe their own writing goals, choices and rationales as they complete a series of assignments; and reflect explicitly on how their new knowledge will transfer to future writing situations. The ultimate goal is for students to build their own theories of writing to serve as "a framework of writing knowledge and practice they'll take with them when the course is over" (57-58).

To help GTAs recognize the critical role of metacognition in supporting this process, we can examine Yancey et al.'s reliance on the National Research Council's (NRC) *How People Learn* (Bransford, Brown, and Cocking), and specifically their attention to the NRC's emphasis on integrating metacognitive instruction with discipline-based content. In asserting that different learning activities require different kinds of monitoring, Bransford et al. note that "[in] history, for example, the student might be asking himself, 'who wrote this document, and how does that affect the interpretation of events,' whereas in physics the student might be monitoring her understanding of the underlying physical principle at work" (21). This concept of situated metacognition provides the principal rationale for TFT's dual focus on disciplinary content and reflection.

Multimodal Approaches to Teaching and Learning

Unlike WAW and TFT, pedagogies that introduce GTAs to multimodal composition pedagogy are less likely to include a discussion of the cognitive, namely because the social and rhetorical rationales for multimodality are so compelling, including those related to contemporary media ecologies. This pedagogy, too, however, reflects a cognitive theory of learning. The New London Group's "Pedagogy of Multiliteracies," which has influenced composition pedagogy, in fact ties its rationale to the notion of learner variability—that different learners learn best using different modes—and stresses "the use of metalanguages, languages of reflective generalization that describe the form, content, and function of the discourses of practice" as part of this pedagogy (86). As in the TFT curriculum, the frequent assignment of reflective statements alongside multimodal projects in composition classrooms is a practice with cognitive underpinnings that GTAs benefit from noticing, particularly since these are often framed as opportunities for students to develop transferable insights from their multimodal experiences. Jody Shipka's vision of multimodal composition pedagogy focuses attention not on learning specific modes, genres, or discourses, but instead on learning "rhetorical sensitivity" (89), which requires students to define their rhetorical tasks for themselves. The Statement of Goals and Choices that Shipka asks students to submit with their work cultivates rhetorical awareness by coaching students to elaborate on what they were trying to accomplish, the choices they made, and why they made those choices (113-14). While some instructors may focus on the statement's usefulness as an assessment tool, others believe that GTAs benefit from exploration of the cognitive theory behind the assignment, which includes the assumption that metacognition about rhetorical choices leads to learning. GTAs will also recognize this cognitive theory in Jason Palmeri's description of the numerous ways reflection has been and can be integrated into multimodal pedagogies, with the goal of students becoming "flexible" composers who "can move from participating in directed multimodal activities to making informed, reflective choices about which auditory, visual, and alphabetic strategies will be most helpful to them" (*Remixing* 150).

And indeed, as GTAs are sensitized to the cognitive dimension, they will notice that most of the pedagogies that have recently expanded what we understand as composition still adhere to the same learning theory driving much of composition practice, focusing less on the achievement of particular technical or discursive skills and more on the cultivation of meta-awareness about a range of phenomena related to communication, modality, and mediation that will facilitate future rhetorical adaptation and lifelong rhetorical learning. Although the social and rhetorical arguments for pedagogies informed by multimodality are generally foregrounded, the metacognitive is a palpable preoccupation not far from center stage. Ideally, helping GTAs recognize this cognitive base can mitigate both a skills mindset and anxiety related to perceived gaps in expertise.

Disability Studies and Universal Design for Learning

GTAs sensitized to paying attention to theories of learning will recognize some important affinities between multimodal pedagogies and those informed by disability studies. Palmeri, in fact, has pointed this out, citing Patricia Dunn, Peter Smagorinsky, Karen Klein, and Linda Hecker as examples of compositionists "who have been developing multimodal writing pedagogies informed at least in part by cognitive research on learning differences" and "drawing on diverse cognitive research on multiple intelligences,[1] learning styles, and learning disabilities" (*Multimodality* 92). GTAs can benefit from being exposed to the field's longstanding engagement with cognitive diversity through works like Dunn's *Talking, Sketching, Moving*, where Dunn makes the case for a composition pedagogy that provides students with diverse sensory pathways to learn, invent, and revise, asserting that this multimodal approach will give students important "metacognitive distance" on their written work (11).

The approaches stemming from disability studies, however, have recently been enriched by a number of fields, with design standing out among these. GTAs will particularly benefit from exposure to universal design for learning (UDL), an approach that "stresses the importance of addressing different learning needs and styles by offering many pathways to achieve class goals" (Lewiecki-Wilson et al. "Rethinking" 6). UDL seeks to make learning accessible to diverse learners from the start, whether or not they officially meet criteria for accommodation. While ideally this approach would reduce the need for special accommodations, Margaret Price points out that "universal" is an ideal, with educators setting as their goal "a learning environment that is accessible to all learning styles, abilities, and personalities, but acknowledg[ing] that such efforts must always be partial and engaged in a process of continual revision" (87). UDL, in turn, has a strong basis in cognitive theory that GTAs benefit from attending to. Specifically, as Anne Meyer, David Rose, and David Gordon explain, UDL is informed by neuroscience research showing the importance of three key brain networks for learning: the affective, recognition, and strategic (31). These networks correspond directly with the three recently revised UDL principles for teaching:

- Provide multiple means of engagement (the "why" of learning)
- Provide multiple means of representation (the "what" of learning)
- Provide multiple means of action and expression (the "how" of learning) (Meyer et al. 51)

Putting UDL recommendations in the context of this research on cognition helps explain more precisely how common practices GTAs are likely to be introduced to, like active learning strategies, play a role in learning. Neuroscience research also provides additional context for pedagogies that emphasize metacognition and "learning to learn," emphases consistent with UDL's focus on "mastery of learning itself" over learning goals tied to "mastery of knowledge and skills" (48). To encourage mastery of learning, for example, UDL advises learners to reflect on the modes and media they are using, decide whether this was effective for the type of learning they were trying to achieve, and self-correct with new goals and strategies the next time. These reflective practices can encourage what Carol Dweck calls a "growth mindset," which in a writing classroom can work against harmful attitudes toward writing and instead cultivate the expectation of lifelong writing development (qtd. in Meyer et al. 19). Understanding and attending to the cognitive dimension of disability studies and approaches like UDL can give GTAs the concrete grounding they need to enact pedagogies that address students' needs as social beings—needs like inclusivity and equity.

Exploring Cognition in Practice

These disciplinary conversations demonstrate composition's commitment to recognizing students as cognitive agents—as learners engaging with individual composing tasks in specific rhetorical contexts and material circumstances—while simultaneously understanding them as social agents—embedded in and constituting social, cultural, political, institutional imperatives. We want to support multiple means of engagement, representation, and expression in our teaching not just because there may be students in our classrooms with learning disabilities or other special needs, but because we teach human beings in complex social fields and the natural range of variation in human learning is quite broad.

To help GTAs consider the implications of this variation for their own teaching practice, we've experimented with a practical exercise exploring the contested concept of learning style. In this section we describe a unit from our teaching practicum course designed to help new teachers consider their own learning experiences and the assumptions they make about how others learn. Our purpose is to demonstrate that the learning habits we teachers have internalized may be quite different from those our students rely on and that these differences have implications for the kinds of needs we perceive and the kinds of instruction we design. This dimension of student variability is easy to overlook, particularly for new teachers, especially when we consider that many writing teachers were never writing students themselves. In our experience, GTAs who may be pointedly sensitive to diversity of race, class, gender, sexuality, political views, religious beliefs, and even prior writing experience can overlook cognitive variables that may directly influence how students respond to their instruction.

Our GTA cohort includes MA and MFA students pursuing a variety of disciplinary specializations, including literature, linguistics, film studies, rhetoric and composition, and creative writing. They are introduced to composition scholarship in a required composition theory course (where they encounter topics such as those discussed above), and they later take an applied practicum course concurrent with their first semester in the classroom. When we teach the practicum we routinely ask new GTAs to reflect on their learning habits and preferences as part of a broad discussion of student diversity. We have used an online Inventory of Learning Styles (ILS) that prompts respondents to consider their preferences for working alone or with groups, for learning from text or visual displays, for attending to detail or focusing on the "big picture," and so forth (Felder and Soloman, *Index*). The inventory and the model from which it derives were developed by Richard Felder, Hoechst Celanese Professor (now Emeritus) of Chemical Engineering at North Carolina State, in collaboration with colleagues in educational psychology. Felder's exploration of learning style was prompted by his observation that engineering faculty approached tasks differently from engineering students: "[T]he teaching style in most lecture courses tilts heavily toward the small percentage of college students who are at once intuitive, verbal, deductive, reflective and sequential. This imbalance puts a sizeable fraction of the student population at a disadvantage" (Felder 288). Convinced that these contrasting inclinations contribute to high attrition among engineering undergraduates (Felder and Brent), Felder aimed to investigate learning dimensions that he deemed particularly relevant to science education. His model and comparison data have been of particular interest to us because 58% of NC State's fyc students major in engineering or science disciplines.

Felder and Barbara Soloman highlight four dimensions of learning, which you'll recognize as overlapping with other psychological instruments. According to the ILS model, all learners can be

- Active (trying things out) and Reflective (thinking it through)
- Sensing (focused on facts) and Intuitive (focused on ideas and relationships)
- Visual (remembering what they see) and Verbal (learning through written and spoken explanations)
- Sequential (proceeding incrementally through linear steps) and Global (engaging in holistic thinking, large leaps) ("Learning Styles").

In describing these dimensions, Felder and Soloman argue that all learners process information in all of these ways. Ideally we each have a range of strategies to draw upon as learners, adapting our approaches as needed for a given task or situation. Many of us have developed habits or preferences that lean toward one end of a continuum or the other. Some preferences are mild, others more pronounced. Cognitive theory tells us that successful learners move flexibly among options, sometimes drawing upon familiar strategies with little conscious awareness, at other times deliberately choosing among alternative approaches to best address the challenge at hand (Bransford). The effectiveness of our strategy choices is a function of the learning context and the nature of the task we are engaged in, among many other factors (Bransford, Brown and Cocking).

It is important to note that although Felder's ILS is a handy tool for the purposes of our discussion with GTAs, it is not our intent to promote this or any model of learning style or cognitive style. The pedagogical value of such models is a matter of some controversy. Of course we need to recognize different approaches to learning if we are to design instruction to accommodate all learners in our classrooms (e.g., McAlexander), but rigid and decontextualized taxonomies can be dangerously reductive—as Rose cautioned many years ago. Critics of learning style models worry that categorizing learning approaches can lead to implicit valuing of some approaches over others and the temptation to treat flexible strategies and preferences as fixed traits (Coffield et al.), even potentially encouraging associations between specific cognitive abilities and demographic traits (Reynolds). There is indeed support for the construct of cognitive style as an explanatory tool (Kozhevnikov, Evans and Kosslyn), but the sometimes-associated, and commercially promoted, practice of matching instructional strategies to particular learning styles has been largely discredited (Arbuthnott and Krätzig; Cuevas; Rogowsky, Calhoun and Tallal).

Felder and Soloman caution against such misapplications, especially against using the ILS to diagnose individual students or to assess their "suitability or unsuitability for a particular subject, discipline, or profession" (*Index*, n.p.). They offer the ILS as a tool for identifying a variety of learning habits that students bring to their academic work and the potential advantages and disadvantages of these approaches for learning in particular contexts. Consistent with UDL principles, Felder and Soloman advocate varying instruction to support multiple modes of learning and helping students learn to apply both preferred and less preferred strategies. In an exhaustive review of learning style research and related pedagogical practices, Frank Coffield et al. similarly conclude that "knowledge of learning styles can be used to increase the self-awareness of students and tutors about their strengths and weaknesses as learners. In other words, all the advantages claimed for metacognition . . . can be gained by encouraging all learners to become knowledgeable about their own learning and that of others" (38).

We address this controversy directly in our discussion unit, drawing upon our cognitive foundation to help GTAs recognize the danger of reifying their own or their students' assumptions about student abilities. Discussing the hazards of such taxonomies underscores the need to promote the metacognitive awareness that will enable students to take an active role in their learning. We note that students will need to be able to engage with a wide range of learning tasks and situations as they move through college and the world beyond, some of which will not play to their strengths. Echoing the transfer arguments of Wardle, Yancey and others, we argue that implicit in our responsibility to help students develop rhetorical sensitivity and flexibility across a range of genres and contexts is an expectation that we will also help them develop the cognitive awareness and flexibility they need to apply that knowledge and skill.

We begin the discussion by helping GTAs discover ways in which their own learning habits resemble and differ from those of their colleagues. They complete the 44-item online ILS survey, which generates results on the four continua. We have a lively discussion of their results on each dimension, with some GTAs quickly identifying with—sometimes proudly, sometimes sheepishly—one end of a continuum or another. When we combine results from the eight cohorts who have completed the ILS in our program over time, some patterns emerge. Looking at the group as a whole (see table 1), we notice first that results skew heavily on three of the four dimensions. Responses indicate that most of these new teachers are more likely to reflect first before trying things out, tend to be comfortable with abstractions and hypothetical reasoning ("intuitive" learners), and interpret verbal information more readily than visual representations. No one is surprised by these revelations, consistent as they are with stereotypical characterizations of humanities scholars.

Table 1
Learning Style Profile: Graduate Teaching Assistant Preferences on Felder and Soloman's ILS dimensions, 2000-2011 [N=75]

	Active Reflective		Sensing Intuitive		Visual Verbal		Sequential Global	
	Act	Ref	Sen	Int	Vis	Ver	Seq	Glo
NC State English GTAs	29%	71%	27%	73%	39%	61%	49%	51%

Equally interesting, though, is the variability within the GTA population (see table 2), which we call attention to in discussion. Because the ILS contains multiple survey items pertaining to each dimension, the resulting scores reflect the strength or consistency of the respondent's preference across that set of items. Table 2 shows that both ends of each continuum are represented in this population. (For example, a handful of GTAs favor visual learning just as strongly as most others prefer verbal.) It is also clear that most learning preferences are relatively mild. With the exception of the sensing/intuitive scale, respondents are more likely to have a balanced set of alternatives than to strongly favor one pole or the other. Group patterns are still detectable, but they are less pronounced when we take the strength of preference into account. This pattern is consistent with results of other studies that include strength of preference in their analysis (Felder and Spurlin 106), suggesting that a substantial proportion of learners have a fairly balanced repertoire of strategies to draw upon. Many students may simply need to be prompted to use a less preferred approach when appropriate, given opportunities to practice those less-used skills, or reminded that they have well developed alternative strategies at their disposal.

Table 2
Strength of Preference: Graduate Teaching Assistants Indicating Strong or Mild Preference on Felder and Soloman's ILS Dimensions, 2000-2011 [N=92[a]]

Strong/moderate preference (score= 5-11)	Mild/balanced preference (score= 1-3)	Strong/moderate preference (score= 5-11)
9% Active	54%	37% Reflective
11% Sensing	34%	55% Intuitive
15% Visual	46%	39% Verbal
15% Sequential	56%	28% Global

[a] Includes respondents in table 1 plus an additional cohort.

The ILS results become even more interesting when we compare the GTA profiles with those of students like those they teach. The ILS has gained currency among engineering educators, so a fair amount of comparison data is available in that sector. In table 3 we have compiled results from some of the more recent ILS studies of engineering undergraduates.

Table 3

Learning Style Profiles: Comparison Group Preferences on Felder and Soloman's ILS Dimensions[a], 2000-2011

	Active Reflective		Sensing Intuitive		Visual Verbal		Sequential Global		N
	Act	Ref	Sen	Int	Vis	Ver	Seq	Glo	
NC State English GTAs	29%	71%	27%	73%	39%	61%	49%	51%	75
NC State Comp. Science[b]	43%	57%	57%	43%	84%	16%	54%	46%	67
U. Oklahoma Engineering[c]	49%	51%	70%	30%	79%	21%	59%	41%	71
Tulane U Biomed Engr[d]	66%	34%	55%	45%	88%	12%	41%	59%	128
IUPU-Ft. Wayne ElecComp. Engr[e]	66%	34%	78%	22%	89%	11%	64%	36%	313
Ryerson U Elec. Engr[f]	58%	42%	65%	35%	87%	13%	63%	37%	352

[a] Because these studies tend to report only the direction and not the degree of the preference, the data in table 3, as in table 1, include all expressed preferences, from mild to strong.

Sources: [b]Layman et al.; [c]Ashford et al.; [d]Dee et al.; [e]Broberg et al.; [f]Zywno.

On two of the four dimensions, table 3 shows consistent patterns across the undergraduate groups and clear contrasts between those students and the new writing teachers we work with. Our GTAs' preference for intuitive or abstract learning over working with facts and data contrasts with the engineering students' preferences on the sensing/intuitive dimension, and differences on the visual/verbal dimension are even more striking, given the undergraduate engineers' overwhelming preference for visual learning. Research comparing disciplinary groups is rare, but the patterns we have observed resonate with research on cognitive style in other domains, where differences on some dimensions have been observed among professional groups in the arts, science and engineering, and humanities disciplines (Kozhevnikov et al.). Such findings suggest that as teachers with humanities backgrounds, we may differ in the aggregate from students with other disciplinary inclinations—not just in what we know but in how we go about learning it.

At the same time, the absence of clear patterns on other dimensions reminds us that learning preferences are shaped by the myriad factors that shape individuals, including but certainly not limited to disciplinary orientation. Whether students select their disciplinary paths because they align with their natural learning habits, or whether those habits are conditioned by experience in the discipline, is an intriguing question. Fortunately, however, we do not need to resolve this question in order to teach effectively, for our task as educators is to support a diversity of learning habits whatever their origins. Our goal in this discussion unit with GTAs is to consider the variety of strategies that students, as individuals and as members of disciplinary cultures, might bring to their work in our writing courses—and to consider how reflection on these strategies might prepare them to transfer and adapt learning approaches as needed. We are not especially interested in identifying tendencies within particular groups; rather, we want to help new teachers recognize that their own learning preferences and experiences may make it difficult to imagine the kinds of pedagogical support many of their students might need.

We have found the ILS exercise a useful device for helping GTAs think about how students may respond to the learning activities they design. Using the model as a framework, the GTA group considers how different learning habits and in-the-moment choices might interact with standard features of composition pedagogy. We discuss, for example, how students who learn best in isolation might learn to engage successfully in peer review; how we might help "big picture" learners develop the finer-grained focus needed for careful proofreading; how we might vary our presentation of materials to facilitate interpretation for both visual and verbal learners. We note that some students will benefit from elaborate assignment sheets that break a project into linear steps but others will find them less useful—and that it is not just a matter of who takes time to read the assignment but of how they tend to process information. Of course, this discussion helps us understand that some students will need coaching to benefit from group work and others will take to it naturally under the right conditions. These are all issues teachers can address and on which there is ample practical advice in the composition literature. Situating practices such as peer review, assignment sequencing, and collaborative learning in a cognitive frame highlights their common reliance on metacognitive awareness and intentional learning. From this perspective, these practices are no longer simply topics in a sourcebook but instantiations of a coherent philosophy of learning governing the profession's practice.

Acknowledging our own biases for particular learning approaches can also help us recognize that we routinely make value judgments when interpreting student writing behavior. For example, we may assume that a student who fails to proofread is careless, or disrespectful, rather than unaccustomed to noticing fine detail. Likewise, a student who fails to apply advice from one project to the next may be characterized as lazy or incapable, but the real issue may be that the student is unattuned to the common task features that could facilitate transfer. Examining learning processes gives us another set of variables to consider when interpreting student behavior and attitudes and provides a vivid demonstration of the limitations of teaching from personal experience or intuition alone. In brief, we explore these issues with new teachers in order to help them (1) recognize their own default learning strategies and biases, (2) provide another lens through which to interpret student behavior, attitudes, and difficulties, (3) vary instruction to support a broader range of learning approaches, and (4) help students develop the metacognitive awareness needed to manage, adapt, and transfer their learning.

Conclusions

Returning to the disciplinary narrative, the composition profession is revisiting cognition at a time when scholarly and societal developments have added layers of nuance and significance to the discipline's early understanding of writing as socially situated. Understanding discourse conventions as socially constructed and pedagogy as reflective of world-view (Bartholomae; Bizzell "Cognition," "William Perry") gave rise to questions about how writers negotiate individual identities in academic communities (Ashley; Berkenkotter, Huckin and Ackerman; Haas; Sternglass), to reflections on how those communities are themselves situated in local and global cultural dynamics (Kuebrich; Parks and Goldblatt; Wan; Yancey), and to explorations of the differential effects of the interplay of culture and classroom on students of diverse backgrounds and experiences (Alexander and Wallace; Brodkey; Matsuda; Morse et al.; Royster). Concurrently, the evolution of media technologies and networked social spaces has brought new attention to the material contexts of writing and the expanded range of choices individual learners are now afforded (Fraiberg; Pigg; Selfe).

Composition's appeal to cognitive theory at this juncture can be seen as an effort to understand how student writers negotiate the concrete demands of writing in these complex social and material contexts. Explorations of sociocultural diversity have perhaps primed us to recognize that students vary as learners as well, and our disciplinary discourse indicates that our understanding of variability is not limited to diagnoses of disability (Dolmage; Meyer et al.). The professional conversations we describe above demonstrate that the field has embarked on a productive exploration of learning strategies, confident in the knowledge that in so doing we are not reducing but expanding our understanding of students and their potential.

In sum, we see learning about learning as an essential component of a compositionist's training. Despite the bifurcation of cognitive and social perspectives that characterized much of our early disciplinary discussion, assumptions about individual cognition are still very much at the center of our pedagogical decision-making. The discipline's renewed engagement with cognition thus provides a coherent and practical frame for teacher preparation. Whether we introduce learning theory directly or engage in informal discussions as described here, a deliberate focus on learning can help new teachers better understand their students and the pedagogical practices of our field.

Acknowledgments

We greatly appreciate the valuable feedback we received from *CS* reviewers and extend our thanks to Richard Felder for elaborating on his ILS work; to Patricia Portanova, Michael Rifenburg, and Duane Roen for their input on an early version of this paper; and to the many GTAs who have animated our discussions of learning over the years.

Notes

1. It is worth noting that Howard Gardner's theory of multiple intelligences is controversial in its own right. Interested readers might examine Lynn Waterhouse's review, "Multiple Intelligences, the Mozart Effect, and Emotional Intelligence: A Critical Review."

Works Cited

Adler-Kassner, Linda, and Elizabeth Wardle, editors. *Naming What We Know: Threshold Concepts of Writing Studies*. Utah State UP, 2015.

Alexander, Jonathan, and David Wallace. "The Queer Turn in Composition Studies: Reviewing and Assessing an Emerging Scholarship." *CCC*, vol. 61, no. 1, 2009, p. W300.

Anson, Chris M. "Closed Systems and Standardized Writing Tests." *CCC*, vol. 60, no. 1, 2008, pp. 113-28.

Arbuthnott, Katherine D., and Gregory P. Krätzig. "Effective Teaching: Sensory Learning Styles versus General Memory Processes." *Comprehensive Psychology*, vol. 4, no. 2, 2015, pp. 1-9.

Ashford, Terresa S., et al. "A Survey of Learning Styles of Engineering Students." *Proceedings of the Human Factors and Ergonomics Society Annual Meeting*, vol. 47, no. 6, 2003, pp. 870-74.

Ashley, Hannah. "Playing the Game: 'Proficient Working-Class Student Writer's Second Voices.'" *RTE*, 2001, pp. 493-524.

Bartholomae, David. "Inventing the University." *When a Writer Can't Write: Studies in Writer's Block and Other Composing-Process Problems*, edited by Mike Rose, Guilford P, 1985, pp.134-65.

Beaufort, Anne. *College Writing and beyond: A New Framework for University Writing Instruction*. Utah State UP, 2007.

Berkenkotter, Carol, et al. "Conventions, Conversations, and the Writer: Case Study of a Student in a Rhetoric Ph. D. Program." *RTE*, 1988, pp. 9-44.

Bizzell, Patricia. "Cognition, Convention, and Certainty: What We Need to Know About Writing." *Pre/Text*, vol. 3, no. 3, 1982, pp. 213-43.

—. "William Perry and Liberal Education." *College English*, vol. 46, no. 5, 1984, pp. 447-54.

Bransford, John D. *Human Cognition: Learning, Understanding and Remembering.* Wadsworth, 1979.

Bransford, John D., et al., editors. *How People Learn: Brain, Mind, Experience, and School.* Committee on Developments in the Science of Learning, Commission on Behavioral and Social Sciences and Education, National Research Council, 2000.

Broberg, Hal, et al. "Learning Styles of Engineering Technology and Engineering Students: Pedagogical Implications." *Journal of Engineering Technology*, vol. 25, no. 1, 2008, pp. 10-17.

Brodkey, Linda. "On the Subjects of Class and Gender in 'The Literacy Letters.'" *College English*, vol. 51, no. 2, 1989, pp. 125-41.

Coffield, Frank, et al. *Should We Be Using Learning Styles?: What Research Has to Say to Practice,* Learning and Skills Research Centre, 2004, http://www.voced.edu.au/content/ngv12401.

Council of Writing Program Administrators, National Council of Teachers of English, and National Writing Project. *Framework for Success in Postsecondary Writing.* CWPA, NCTE, and NWP, 2011, wpacouncil.org/files/framework-for-success-postsecondary-writing.pdf.

Cuevas, Joshua. "Is Learning Styles-Based Instruction Effective? A Comprehensive Analysis of Recent Research on Learning Styles." *Theory and Research in Education*, vol. 13, no. 3, 2015, pp. 308-33.

Dee, Kay C., et al. "Research Report: Learning Styles of Biomedical Engineering Students." *Annals of Biomedical Engineering*, vol. 30, no. 8, 2002, pp. 1100-06.

Dolmage, Jay. "Mapping Composition: Inviting Disability in the Front Door." *Disability and the Teaching of Writing: A Critical Sourcebook*, edited by Cynthia Lewiecki-Wilson and Brenda Jo Brueggemann, Bedford/St. Martins, 2008, pp. 14-27.

Downs, Douglas, and Elizabeth Wardle. "Teaching about Writing, Righting Misconceptions: (Re)envisioning 'First-Year Composition' as 'Introduction to Writing Studies.'" *CCC*, vol. 58, no. 4, 2007, pp. 552-84.

Dryer, Dylan B. "Writing Is (Also Always) a Cognitive Activity." *Naming What We Know: Threshold Concepts of Writing Studies*, edited by Linda Adler-Kassner and Elizabeth Wardle, Utah State UP, 2015, pp. 71-74.

Dunn, Patricia A. *Talking, Sketching, Moving: Multiple Literacies for Composition.* Heinemann, 2001.

Felder, Richard M. "Reaching the Second Tier: Learning and Teaching Styles in College Science Education." *Journal of College Science Teaching*, vol. 23, no. 5, 1993, pp. 286-90.

Felder, Richard M., and Rebecca Brent. "Understanding Student Differences." *Journal of Engineering Education*, vol. 94, no. 1, 2005, pp. 57-72.

Felder, Richard M., and Barbara A. Soloman. *Index of Learning Styles Questionnaire.* http://www.ncsu.edu/felder-public/ILSpage.html. Accessed 30 Apr. 2013.

—. *Learning Styles and Strategies*. http://www4.ncsu.edu/unity/lockers/users/f/felder/public//ILSdir/styles.htm. Accessed 20 May 2017.

Felder, Richard M., and Joni Spurlin. "Applications, Reliability and Validity of the Index of Learning Styles." *International Journal of Engineering Education*, vol. 21, no. 1, 2005, pp. 103-12.

Flower, Linda, and John R. Hayes. "A Cognitive Process Theory of Writing." *CCC*, vol. 32, no. 4, 1981, pp. 365-87.

Fraiberg, Steven. "Composition 2.0: Toward a Multilingual and Multimodal Framework." *CCC*, vol. 62, 2010, pp. 100-26.

Gardner, Howard. *Frames of Mind: The Theory of Multiple Intelligences*. Basic Books, 1983.

Haas, Christina. "Learning to Read Biology: One Student's Rhetorical Development in College." *Written Communication*, vol. 11, no. 1, 1994, pp. 43-84.

Klein, Karen, and Linda Hecker. "The Write Moves: Cultivating Kinesthetic and Spatial Intelligences in the Writing Process." *Presence of Mind: Writing Beyond the Cognitive Domain*, edited by Alice Brand and Richard Graves, Heinemann, 1994, pp. 89-98.

Kroll, Barry M. "Cognitive Egocentrism and the Problem of Audience Awareness in Written Discourse." *RTE*, vol. 12, no. 3, 1978, pp. 269-81.

Kuebrich, Ben. "'White Guys Who Send My Uncle to Prison': Going Public within Asymmetrical Power." *CCC*, vol. 66, no. 4, 2015, p. 566-90.

Layman, Lucas, et al. "Personality Types, Learning Styles, and an Agile Approach to Software Engineering Education." *SIGCSE Bulletin*, vol. 38, no. 1, Mar. 2006, pp. 428-32.

Lewiecki-Wilson, Cynthia, et al. "Rethinking Practices and Pedagogy: Disability and the Teaching of Writing." *Disability and the Teaching of Writing: A Critical Sourcebook*, edited by Cynthia Lewiecki-Wilson and Brenda Jo Brueggemann, Bedford/St. Martin's, 2008, pp. 1-9.

Lewiecki-Wilson, Cynthia, et al. "Rhetoric and the Writer's Profile: Problematizing Directed Self-Placement." *Assessing Writing*, vol. 7, no. 2, 2000, pp. 165-83.

Lunsford, Andrea A. "Cognitive Development and the Basic Writer." *College English*, vol. 41, no. 1, 1979, pp. 38-46.

Matsuda, Paul Kei. "The Myth of Linguistic Homogeneity in US College Composition." *College English*, vol. 68, no. 6, 2006, pp. 637-51.

McAlexander, Patricia J. "Using Principles of Universal Design in College Composition Courses." *Basic Writing E-Journal*, vol. 5, no. 1, 2004, n.p.

Meyer, Anne, et al. *Universal Design for Learning: Theory and Practice*. CAST Professional Publishing, 2014, http://udltheorypractice.cast.org.

Morse, Tracy Ann, et al. "Representing Disability Rhetorically." *Rhetoric Review*, vol. 22, no. 2, 2003, pp. 154-202.

Nelms, Gerald, and Ronda Leathers Dively. "Perceived Roadblocks to Transferring Knowledge from First-Year Composition to Writing-Intensive Major Courses: A Pilot Study." *WPA*, vol. 31, no. 1-2, 2007, pp. 214-40.

New London Group. "A Pedagogy of Multiliteracies: Designing Social Futures." *Harvard Educational Review*, vol. 66, no. 1, 1996, pp. 60-92.

Palmeri, Jason. *Multimodality and Composition Studies, 1960–Present*. Ohio State University, 2007.

—. *Remixing Composition: A History of Multimodal Writing Pedagogy*. NCTE/CCCC and SIUP, 2012.

Parks, Steve, and Eli Goldblatt. "Writing beyond the Curriculum: Fostering New Collaborations in Literacy." *College English*, vol. 62, no. 5, 2000, pp. 584-606.

Perkins, David N., and Gavriel Salomon. "Teaching for Transfer." *Educational Leadership*, vol. 46, no. 1, 1988, pp. 22-32.

—. "Transfer of Learning." *International Encyclopedia of Education*, 2nd ed., Pergamon P, 1992, pp. 6452-57.

Pigg, Stacey. "Emplacing Mobile Composing Habits: A Study of Academic Writing in Networked Social Spaces." *CCC*, vol. 66, no. 2, 2014, pp. 250-75.

Price, Margaret. *Mad at School: Rhetorics of Mental Disability and Academic Life*. U of Michigan P, 2011.

Rendahl, Merry, and Lee-Ann Kastman Breuch. "Toward a Complexity of Online Learning: Learners in Online First-Year Writing." *Computers and Composition*, vol. 30, no. 4, 2013, pp. 297-314.

Reynolds, Michael. "Learning Styles: A Critique." *Management Learning*, vol. 28, no. 2, June 1997, pp. 115-33.

Rogowsky, Beth A., et al. "Matching Learning Style to Instructional Method: Effects on Comprehension." *Journal of Educational Psychology*, vol. 107, no. 1, 2015, p. 64-78.

Rose, Mike. "Narrowing the Mind and Page: Remedial Writers and Cognitive Reductionism." *CCC*, vol. 39, no. 3, 1988, pp. 267-302.

Royer, Daniel J., and Roger Gilles. "Directed Self-Placement: An Attitude of Orientation." *CCC*, vol. 50, no. 1, 1998, pp. 54-70.

Royster, Jacqueline Jones. "When the First Voice You Hear Is Not Your Own." *CCC*, vol. 47, no. 1, 1996, pp. 29-40.

Scott, Tony. "Writing Enacts and Creates Identities and Ideologies." *Naming What We Know: Threshold Concepts of Writing Studies*, edited by Linda Adler-Kassner and Elizabeth Wardle, Utah State UP, 2015, pp. 48-50.

Selfe, Cynthia L. "The Movement of Air, the Breath of Meaning: Aurality and Multimodal Composing." *CCC*, vol. 60, no. 4, 2009, pp. 616-63.

Shipka, Jody. *Toward a Composition Made Whole*. U of Pittsburgh P, 2011.

Smagorinsky, Peter. *Expressions: Multiple Intelligences in the English Class*. NCTE, 1991.

Sternglass, Marilyn S. *Time to Know Them: A Longitudinal Study of Writing and Learning at the College Level*. Erlbaum, 1997.

Wan, Amy J. "In the Name of Citizenship: The Writing Classroom and the Promise of Citizenship." *College English*, vol. 74, no. 1, 2011, pp. 28-49.

Wardle, Elizabeth. "'Mutt Genres' and the Goal of FYC: Can We Help Students Write the Genres of the University?" *CCC*, vol. 60, no. 4, 2009, pp. 765-89.

—. "Understanding 'Transfer' from FYC: Preliminary Results of a Longitudinal Study." *WPA* vol. 31, no. 1-2, 2007, pp. 65-85.

Wardle, Elizabeth, and Douglas Downs. *Writing about Writing: A College Reader*. 2nd ed., Bedford/St. Martin's, 2014.

Waterhouse, Lynn. "Multiple Intelligences, the Mozart Effect, and Emotional Intelligence: A Critical Review." *Educational Psychologist*, vol. 41, no. 4, 2006, pp. 207-25.

West, William, et al. "How Learning Styles Impact E-Learning: A Case Comparative Study of Undergraduate Students Who Excelled, Passed, or Failed an Online Course in Scientific/Technical Writing." *E-Learning and Digital Media*, vol. 3, no. 4, 2006, pp. 534-43.

Yancey, Kathleen Blake, et al. *Writing across Contexts: Transfer, Composition, and Sites of Writing*. Utah State UP, 2014.

Yancey, Kathleen Blake. *Writing in the 21st Century*. NCTE, 2009.

Zywno, Malgorzata S. "Instructional Technology, Learning Styles and Academic Achievement." *Proceedings of the 2002 ASEE Annual Conference & Exposition*, ASEE, 2002.

Intellectual Risk in the Writing Classroom: Navigating Tensions in Educational Values and Classroom Practice

Alexis Teagarden, Carolyn Commer, Ana Cooke, and Justin Mando

> This study examines the popularity of "intellectual risk-taking," a pedagogical term that typically describes when a student attempts a new way to learn and risks receiving a lower grade or being perceived as less competent by a teacher (Beghetto), risks facing public criticism by peers (Foster), or risks losing a personal belief or coherent sense of social identity (Haswell et al.). We find this term commonly invoked with praise in U.S. higher education, but ambiguously defined. The lack of definition, we argue, can put the goals of institutions, instructors, and students in tension. To demonstrate the possible tensions, we compare perceptions of risk-taking advanced by institutions of higher education and education scholars with those reported by students and composition instructors. Results indicate that students generally regard intellectual risk-taking as positive but are reluctant to take such risks. Similarly, early-career instructors are unsure how to evaluate intellectual risk or align it with other course objectives. However, rather than jettison the concept, we argue a rhetorical approach could better realize the pedagogical benefits of intellectual risk-taking. To this end, we offer a tentative framework for fostering intellectual risk-taking in the writing classroom, which draws on the rhetorical tradition and attends to the tensions identified in our study.

Imagine two final drafts. The first contains a well-written, well-argued essay. The student successfully and safely executes the assigned tasks. Applying your grading criteria, the paper earns an A. The second student, in contrast, takes a risk. Maybe the research is more robust or the argument more novel. Maybe the student purposefully challenges academic conventions. Evidence abounds that the student went "above and beyond" in some aspect, but the paper overall does not quite work. Some assignment requirements are incomplete, or the argument never fully coheres. When you apply the same grading criteria, this paper earns a low B. And something feels off.

This dilemma arose in our classroom experiences and emerges repeatedly in composition studies scholarship. In *Elements of Alternate Style*, Elizabeth Rankin bemoans her past grading practices, particularly when she "gave As to students whose papers, though mechanically correct, were… well… *boring*" (70). She reports her subsequent course redesign successfully encouraged creative projects, such as "a paper on [Ishmael] Reed's *Mumbo Jumbo* in the form of an FBI file on its 'subversive' author" (68). But she also acknowledges "I am still struggling with what to say about these unconventional papers" (71). How do we as teachers and scholars negotiate this tension—evaluating the skillfully safe against the imperfectly daring?

We see this dilemma as a problem tied to the concept of intellectual risk, a pedagogical term that typically describes when a student attempts a new way to learn and risks receiving a lower grade or being perceived as less competent by a teacher (Beghetto), facing public criticism by peers (Foster), or losing a personal belief or coherent sense of social identity (Haswell et al.). We explore this concept's various definitions and its possible place in writing classrooms by first charting the presence and use of intellectual risk-taking in higher education discourse and research in composition studies. Since previous work has not focused on student and faculty perspectives, we complement existing work by next reporting on a pilot survey of undergraduate student and early-career instructor views of intellectual risk. Drawing together the problems and affordances of different interpretations of intellectual risk, we conclude by advancing a rhetorical approach to intellectual risk-taking and suggest future avenues for research and teaching.

Intellectual Risk-Taking: Definitions in Circulation

When educators invoke the rhetoric of intellectual risk, they often assume its positive value. Yet what constitutes intellectual risk-taking in practice or how it can be fostered remains unclear. In the following sections, we highlight the presence and vagueness of risk-taking within institutional discourse, media reporting, and scholarly literature.

The Public Rhetoric of Risk-Taking in Higher Education

U.S. institutions of higher education celebrate intellectual risk-taking. Of the *U.S. News & World Report* top-ranked liberal arts schools for 2014–2015, 18 of 20 affiliate themselves with intellectual risk-taking in prominent web space and promotional materials. Fourteen of 20 research universities claim intellectual risk as a defining value. The University of Washington's undergraduate research program includes among its values "A safe place for intellectual risk-taking." Harvard welcomes its 2019 class by claiming, in part, "This is the perfect time to take intellectual risks, big and small" (Hu). Such messages pervade the nation's elite colleges and research universities and are increasingly found at a variety of institution types. A goal of Philadelphia University's core curriculum reads "Initiative (intellectual risk-taking)." Florida South-Western's Honors Scholar Program also names intellectual risk as a value.

In short, colleges and universities regularly make intellectual risk-taking an integral part of their public rhetoric and institutional mission.

Media coverage of higher education also foregrounds the term. A review of *The Chronicle of Higher Education* from 1990 through 2015 reveals over 90 articles, letters, and essays about risk-taking in the academy. Most take as axiomatic the essential role of risk in education. Jamshed Bharucha, for instance, asserts "intellectual risk taking" is one of U.S. higher education's distinguishing traits. Those that see higher education in decline argue intellectual risk can save it. "There's a lot of formulaic thinking that's in America's colleges and universities … There's no risk-taking, no risk of knowledge," argues policymaker Clifford Adelman (Hebel). A smaller but significant group challenges the ideal of risk-taking, however. Mallory Young, a professor of French and English, pushes back against calls for risk-taking by explaining the importance of teaching conventions and creating classroom havens. Letters to the editor question whether curricula that promote risk-taking provide students adequate guidance to take risks effectively (e.g., Friel). Noah Roderick asks us to consider students' risk-averse nature as reasonable, arguing that they often finance college through scholarships, whose stringent academic requirements make classroom risks costly when they fail.

Composition Studies and Competing Conceptions of Risk-Taking

Concern about the value of risk-taking in higher education has recently become a point of contention in the field of composition. One view recognizes risk-taking as a means of effecting positive change, exemplified in the 2015 CCCC's theme "Risk and Reward." In her conference call, Joyce Locke Carter asks participants to "reimagine the concept of 'risk' not as something to be mitigated or feared, but rather as something to be sought out" (1). This focus reveals that risk-taking is not just being pushed in university promotional materials—it is becoming a guiding rhetoric for writing programs.

Not everyone is persuaded that emphasizing risk-taking will lead to positive change in higher education. Tony Scott has criticized the CCCC theme, arguing it tacitly accepts "a more explicitly entrepreneurial, and neoliberal, direction" (207), where risk-taking becomes synonymous with "various forms of marketization" (210). The proliferation of terms like "innovation," "risk-taking," and "public engagement," Scott asserts, "flattens scholarship and praxis into unfettered choices and pushes the history of disciplinary expertise, dialectic, and contention that surround terms like 'expressive' and 'current-traditional' to the margins" (211). By uncritically accepting terms like "risk-taking" as ideal or failing to trace the material consequences of these terms, Scott claims, we inadvertently undermine our discipline's own goals.

This divide in views appears sharp, with Carter advocating for risk-taking as an important way to support our field's goals and Scott arguing that risk-taking has the potential to undermine them. We see this divide as a conflict in assumptions about risk-taking; the debate here muddles two conceptions of risk-taking in higher education: *intellectual* risk-taking and *entrepreneurial* risk-taking. By dissociating risk-taking into these different concepts, one can see how Carter attempts to advance the value of *intellectual* risk while Scott questions the allure of *entrepreneurial* risk. This dissociation offers a possible means for clarifying the pedagogical values at stake.

Dissociating Intellectual Risk-Taking from Entrepreneurial Risk-Taking

Scott's critique of the CCCC's theme seems grounded in a reading of risk as entrepreneurial risk-taking, a conception in conflict with how the liberal arts tradition understands intellectual risk-taking. Entrepreneurial risk-taking refers to the type of risk-taking often valorized by venture capitalists and, increasingly, college provosts. In higher education, entrepreneurial risk-taking emphasizes bold financial enterprises, commercializing research, and seeking industry partnership. As Scott explains, this shift focuses on "the 'risks' in program administration that involve branding, marketing, and competition" (211). Entrepreneurial risk tends to be invoked as a politically neutral and positive economic term. It often commends risk-taking in such a vague way that it can make risks of any kind appear desirable. Such an open definition, as our study details below, poses problems in classroom practice and can threaten composition's pedagogical values. We suspect that a primary reason the entrepreneurial sense of risk-taking has gained traction is because it appears to align with the rhetoric that upholds intellectual risk-taking as a foundational value of U.S. higher education.

Intellectual risk, on the other hand, refers to a type of risk-taking valued prominently in the liberal arts. Bruce Kimball summarizes this view as one honoring the importance of students risking being wrong or changing their long-held beliefs in the pursuit of inquiry. Carter's proposal grounds risk in this tradition when she says: "We believe the rewards of trying new things, of putting yourself in someone else's shoes, of thinking critically, outweigh the risks of feeling uncomfortable, of disclosing something personal to fellow writers, of failing" (1). This tradition's influence is also evident in a 2017 edited volume *Risk-Taking in Higher Education*. In the introduction, Ryan Kelty and Bridget Bunten define intellectual risk-taking as "exposing oneself to new and potentially discomforting and challenging ideas, exposing oneself to uncertainty, and questioning one's own and others' assumptions. Further, intellectual risk-taking means exposing oneself to possible failure and being perceived as a less capable individual" (xv). It is this tradition of risk-taking, rather than the entrepreneurial version, that plays a key role in the history of composition scholarship.

Composition Pedagogy and a Tradition of Intellectual Risk-Taking

To develop a grounded sense of how composition studies has defined intellectual risk, we searched the CompPile database for articles using the terms "risk," "risk-taking," and "intellectual risk-taking" in connection with composition or other writing-intensive courses. Discussions of risk most commonly involve studies of students at risk of academic, behavioral, or health problems. After excluding those research lines, we identified two arenas of pedagogy that emphasize intellectual, rather than entrepreneurial, risk-taking. The first highlights the value in challenging accepted ideas or styles, such as when Ken Kantor promotes "skepticism about convention" and "the willingness to be different" (73). Similarly, Janis Haswell, Richard Haswell, and Glenn Blalock discuss the important but difficult work involved when students write about controversial topics or take an unpopular stance; they risk "having convictions unfixed" by being exposed to new ideas (720). Turning to public consequences, Drew Foster considers how students risk being criticized for advancing controversial views.

A second type of intellectual risk-taking focuses more on the cultivation of identity, specifically when writers disclose a personal experience, challenge, or marginalized identity (Monson and Rhodes; Dutro; Berman). Elizabeth Dutro, for example, draws attention to the "vulnerability that is inherent in classrooms, while remaining aware of how privilege and power shape the stakes of those exposures" (199). While both this and the previous type of risk-taking involve the chance of public rejection, here the rejection is of a social identity. By engaging with others through their writing, students confront an existential question. For example, the consequence of students genuinely engaging others' arguments is that other perspectives have the power to change a student's sense of self, which is "a grave risk," James Kastely claims, "since each of us is deeply invested in the understanding of who he or she is" (237). This pedagogy assumes that self-transformation is education's primary aim and such a transformation is a fundamentally social, rhetorical engagement. Common to the types of intellectual risk-taking found in composition scholarship is an emphasis on the value of inquiry (over the entrepreneurial focus on marketization and financial gain), self-discovery, listening, and the capacity for judgment in civic affairs.

One problem we identify in this scholarship is that while risk-taking is invoked as a positive educational ideal, it is rarely defined explicitly. This makes it difficult to support intellectual risk-taking in practice—how exactly can composition teachers help support intellectual risk-taking in their classrooms?

One reason this question remains open might be because prior research often leaves out the perspectives of students and writing instructors in training.

To that end, in what follows we ask: How do early-career writing instructors and students actually define intellectual risk-taking in the context of academic writing? What writing practices do they associate with it? Do they see intellectual risk-taking as an important component of writing assignments? These questions help elucidate the value of intellectual risk-taking and draw out the most urgent concerns about its place in writing classrooms.

On the Ground Study: What Students and Early-Career Instructors Say

To find out what writing practices and concepts students and instructors associate with intellectual risk-taking, we developed an IRB-approved survey. It asked undergraduate students and instructors to define intellectual risk-taking, to describe non-risky writing, and to articulate whether they thought students should take such risks in their writing; we also asked students whether they took risks in their writing and why. In parallel, we asked instructors whether they taught students how to take risks (see appendix for details).

We administered our survey to students and instructors at a private, doctoral-granting university. Instructors included graduate students and adjuncts who were early-career teachers that had received extensive pre-teaching training and participated in a year-long teaching practicum. Students represented sections of three writing-intensive undergraduate service classes: (1) the required first-year English class, which introduces academic argument; (2) a non-major professional and technical writing class; and (3) an introductory class on academic writing for non-native English speakers. Fifty-nine students and fourteen instructors participated; our research team did not complete the survey. At the time of the survey, neither intellectual risk nor personal writing was among the learning objectives for any course.

To provide a comprehensive account of the concepts that students and teachers associate with risk, we used analytic induction (Haas, Takayoshi, and Carr) to develop codes that spanned responses across the four risk-focused questions (Q2 through Q5). After establishing our code list, one pair of researchers separately coded each question and then checked for intercoder agreement; we resolved discrepancies through discussion (Garrison et al.). Our final list of codes is shown in table 1.

Table 1

Intellectual Risk-Taking Association Codes for Students and Instructor Responses

Code	Definition	Representative Excerpts
Writing Conventions	Non-specific "conventions" of academic writing, and/or following or deviating from genre or writing conventions such as organization, formatting/layout, register/formality, and coherence.	"The correct characteristics include standard essay writing skills, that is, a thesis, supporting body and conclusion." "Whatever is the convention of the genre is probably 'safe.'"
Rhetoric/ Argument	Features of argumentation (such as evidence, logic, or argument) and/or persuasion or appeals (ethos, pathos, logos) or persuasiveness specific to an audience.	"Strong evidence, strong argument, and, most importantly, infallible and insightful logical deduction." "Write things that are logical and with which people are likely to agree."
Un/Conventional Ideas	Ideas, viewpoints, or perspectives that are or are not considered safe, conventional, inoffensive. (Distinguishable from Writing Conventions by its focus on ideas rather than observable features of content and form.)	"To me, a 'safe' academic paper is the approach a majority of students take, specifically this means that a safe paper would contain arguments that are widely accepted versus a view that is unconventional." "Students can challenge the conventions of academic writing by taking a point of view that is either unknown or controversial rather than a prominent widely accepted idea."

Code	Definition	Representative Excerpts
Grading/ Evaluation	Grades explicitly, or implied concern with grading/evaluation based on instructor reaction, opinion, or practices.	"As long as they still complete the assignment to the professor's satisfaction, why not? There is nothing to lose except a grade." "The 'correct' way is the way the teacher will grade favorably. The conventional way is to attempt the paper with the intention of getting the highest grade."
Lack of/ Personal Learning Challenge	Challenges associated with students' personal learning, such as one's intellectual capacity, self-imposed challenges, personal shortcomings, self-directed learning choices, or personal knowledge-seeking goals.	"A task that is expected to challenge one's level of intellectual capability." "Taking risks in order to develop your knowledge… maybe even challenging yourself."
Academic Integrity	Acknowledging/integrating sources, citation, plagiarism, and/or misrepresenting others' work or ideas as one's own.	"Always acknowledge the source of the ideas if they are not original. Proper citations would be good." "The risk of copying other writers' ideas."
Objectivity/ Subjectivity	Refers to subjective perspective or input or refers to the need to be objective and/or distance one's subjectivity from information presented in writing.	"No first person or personal input writing." "Present findings as objective as possible."
No answer	An answer left blank.	
No code	Part/entire response was unintelligible, illegible, or off-topic.	

Because our questions were open-ended, many responses articulated multiple conceptions of risk; hence, some responses received multiple codes. Percentages given in our response rate (see table 2) indicate the relative salience of macro-level concepts associated with risk. Because we sought dominant themes rather than responses to specific questions, we counted the number of times codes appeared across all responses rather than reporting individual question response rates. However, we note response rates for Q5 within the discussion below.

Table 2
Percent of Student and Instructor Survey Responses per Association Code*

Code	Student Responses (59 Students)	Instructor Responses (14 Instructors)
Writing Conventions	71%	93%
Rhetoric / Argument	48%	64%
Un/conventional Ideas	48%	79%
Grading/Evaluation	46%	79%
Lack of/ Personal Learning Challenge	34%	N/A
Academic Integrity	34%	0%
Objectivity / Subjectivity	12%	7%
No Answer Given	19%	43%

*Percentages refer to the number of responses that mention the code divided by the total number of responses.

As the results in table 2 indicate, we found distinct differences in how students and teachers conceptualize intellectual risk. Below, we elaborate on the most notable tensions and their relation to institutional and pedagogical discourse.

Intellectual Risk versus Grading/Evaluation

We find it notable, though not surprising, that 46% of student responses and 79% of instructor responses associate intellectual risk-taking with evaluation. Students especially use evaluation to justify their answer to "Should students take intellectual risks? Why or why not?" Just under half of the students answer no to this question and ground answers with evaluation concerns. For example, a common rationale holds that grades in writing classrooms depend on following instructors' preferences. One student answers, "No. because [sic] students should do as they are told," while another explains, "Stick to what is acceptable by [sic] professor." Such reasoning shows students both downplaying the importance of intellectual risk and disagreeing with composition pedagogy's fundamental evaluation principles.

This view may arise from students' general perceptions of college. One student explains, "Most college professors are very traditional in their ways so that breaking convention could leave a bad impression + a bad grade." It may prove hard to break the view that the academy rewards those who parrot their professors and grasp tightly to conventions. Encouraging intellectual risk-taking may thus require that we show its value early and often, possibly providing extra support for those who avoid risk-taking for fear of harming their grade.

Scaffolding risk-taking might also help students willingly work outside their comfort zones. A professional writing student supports this approach: "Yes, but only if they have chance [sic] to go over them with a professional writing advisor/teacher. I think it is always good to try new stuff, but not in a 'wrong' way, or ineffective way." Even some students who see the value of taking intellectual risks admit that they fear compromising their grades. "As students we should experiment since this is the time where the consequences are less severe," explains one student, though this student continues, "However I will not go out of my way to take such risks." Students, however, also counter this perspective: "School is about preparation for the real world, and breaking convention is risky there as well. Often the payoff is not worth the risk." Such metaphors that link risk-taking with monetary reward could indicate the prevalence of entrepreneurial conceptions of risk and underscore the value of presenting alternatives.

Teachers manifested a similar concern about payoff. When responding to the question on assigning intellectual risk-taking, an instructor comments, "I'd like to say yes, but I'm not sure what the conditions would be that might push students to want to take risks. What's the payoff for them, other than possible humiliation, demoralization, and a bad grade?" Another, who embraces teaching intellectual risk, nonetheless notes, "The students have to trust that I won't penalize them for not meeting 'expectations.'" The cost and benefit payoff approach to intellectual risk seems to temper the inventiveness students might otherwise display and perhaps limits what instructors might otherwise encourage.

Instructor responses also underscore an obligation to teach what course outcomes promise. For example, one teacher explains:

I sort of teach students about intellectual risk. I stress the idea of making an original contribution to an existing topic, which should make it clear to students that simply rehearsing common knowledge or familiar ideas is inappropriate for college writing. But I wouldn't say that I genuinely encourage students to take intellectual risks because I feel that such risks often make students' work more difficult than it would need to be in order to fulfill the course objectives.

Another argues, "From the first day on, I tell my students the old writing cliché 'you need to learn the rules before you can break them.' I think this applies to writing and thinking," and so delineates a need to teach conventional writing before encouraging risk-taking. Such comments suggest instructors do not oppose intellectual risk per se but rather see the concept in tension with their course goals. With students worried about good grades, and teachers focused on meeting objectives, evaluation creates multiple tensions. Intellectual risk-taking need not work against grades or objectives, but bringing intellectual risk into writing classes can require a serious perspective change in students and teachers, as well as deft assignment design.

Intellectual Risk versus Academic Integrity

A less-expected finding is how highly students associate intellectual risk with academic integrity, specifically plagiarism and intellectual property. These students seem to associate risk not with a possibility of success or reward, but rather with a chance of being caught for doing something improper. No instructor made this association.

Students who associated intellectual risk with academic integrity reveal another problematic tension with the concept's classroom enactment. One student defines intellectual risk as "The possibility of having ideas taken w/o consent" and explains that a safe way to write an academic paper means "to consult no sources other than the ones you document and cite." When asked to imagine ways that students can break the conventions of academic writing, the student explains, "I don't know how to challenge the conventions without plagiarizing or doing something else bad." This set of responses illustrates a notably common association of risk-taking with high-stakes rule-breaking.

Another student's definition draws out the connotation between *intellectual* and *property*. This student writes, "Intellectual risks are mistakes or misbehaviors people commit when producing works that either put their own intellectual products at risk such as plagiarism, being paraphrased in an offensive way and misuse or risk somebody else's work and therefore offend/violate their intellectual property right." This focus on intellectual property views risk-taking as a form of trespassing by taking a shortcut through improper use of someone else's work.

Given the discourse surrounding issues of plagiarism and academic integrity in student writing, students' association of risk-taking with (possibly inadvertently) trespassing on another's ideas or intellectual work may be understandable and even warranted. Sean Zwagerman points out university discourse around academic integrity often constructs a stark dichotomy between students who cheat or plagiarize and those who "[do their] own work" (682). Further, as Rebecca Moore Howard discusses, writing instructors themselves may have uncertain or conflicting definitions of what constitutes plagiarism. She argues students thus find themselves in the risky position of navigating a discursive environment in which some instructors may not have theoretical commitments to the possibility of fully acknowledging influences, or to creating authentically original work, while at the same time students are institutionally required to certify work as uniquely theirs. Howard, Tricia Serviss, and Tanya Rodrigue's findings also suggest that students often struggle to understand source material and to integrate it appropriately. Given students' documented challenges in positioning their ideas in relation to others', and the tense discursive environment surrounding academic integrity, it becomes clearer why those issues may immediately arise when students are asked about intellectual risk.

Students' associations of intellectual risk-taking with plagiarism or questions of academic integrity—and the disconnect between students' and instructors' views—are particularly interesting in light of our finding that assertions about objectivity and subjectivity arose in 12% of our students' responses; for example, students identify safe writing as writing that is "objective," and risky writing as including "personal input" or injecting one's own ideas. If, on the one hand, students experience themselves as at risk of inadvertently "stealing" others' ideas, and, on the other, find it risky to assert their own personal stance, perspective, or arguments (assuming objective writing is the coin of the realm), how comfortable can they feel articulating any ideas at all?

These findings suggest it may be important for instructors to consider how they frame concepts of originality and novelty in their classrooms, and that such discussions might be a necessary precursor to fostering intellectual risk-taking. At least by asking students to articulate what they see as risk-taking, teachers may better understand the unintended difficulties and pressures students face.

Intellectual Risk and Un/Conventional Ideas

The first two tensions demonstrate negative associations, but some students do cite positive associations. Their responses align with one existing line of research: that intellectual risk-taking is about engaging controversial ideas or unconventional topics. For example, some responses suggest that students value writing that is novel, unconventional, even daring—a stark contrast from those discussed above who wish only to tell professors what they want to hear. A student who associated intellectual risk-taking with the creation of strong arguments said, "I think that in order to make good arguments, students must challenge pre-concieved [sic], strong arguments with new, novel ones whenever possible." This student presents an alternative, though complementary, view of risk-taking as it relates to novelty. This is not so different from those who view risk-taking as an academic integrity issue in that the safe route is to support accepted arguments and the risk lies in venturing out on one's own to draw from new sources and new ideas.

When viewed as challenging conventional ideas, intellectual risk-taking can sometimes mean resisting authority. When asked how to write a safe academic paper, one student replied, "To me, a 'safe' academic paper is the approach a majority of students take, specifically this means that a safe paper would contain arguments that are widely accepted versus a view that is unconventional." When supporting widely accepted arguments, students may be learning the desired rhetorical moves, but they may be falling short of the kind of critical engagement that we may also strive to foster. As one student explains, "Intellectual risk is an act of defying norms and challenging theories and preconditions established by professionals with high prestige." Is this not the kind of civic and intellectual habit we would wish for our students and ourselves? Yet pushing against the norm requires much from students, especially when those who establish the norm are "professionals with high prestige" while our students are novices just learning the conventions. But for students to be independent thinkers and civic participants, some intellectual risk is required. At the same time, those who take such risks can open themselves up to scrutiny and put their grades in jeopardy.

Such responses indicate that invoking intellectual risk in a college classroom—or even holding it as an implicit evaluation ideal—could lead more to confusion than educational transformation. These findings suggest that fostering intellectual risk likely requires explicit scaffolding, definition, and assessment feedback.

Navigating the Tensions

We have shown intellectual risk's popularity in institutional discourse and charted the conflicting definitions associated with the concept. We assume colleges and universities will continue to view first-year composition classrooms as good places to foster academic values like intellectual risk, so it is a concept that deserves close attention.

Yet instructors surveyed appeared ambivalent about the value of intellectual risk. Fyc is frequently grounded in teaching shared conventions rather than novelty or risk-taking, since fy students are often "inventing" a discourse (Bartholomae). Students' responses also pointed to this as a concern. For example, our survey results show students may associate safe writing with the discourse conventions and rhetorical knowledge that some composition classrooms strive to teach. One student defined a safe paper as having "A strong thesis with corresponding topic sentences. Strong evidence, strong argument, and, most importantly, infallible and insightful logical deduction." If students associate safe writing with a well-structured, well-supported argument, then encouraging students to take intellectual risks—which could include discarding such conventions—may put our pedagogical goals at odds. How could our classes reconceive themselves if a new outcome is to foster intellectual risk-taking?

One approach to navigating these tensions is to steer away from intellectual risk—leave it to upper-level classes. However, we see the values of the rhetorical tradition as a resource for imagining a writing pedagogy that contextualizes intellectual risk within our field's existing practices and suggests a path toward its continued place in our classrooms.

A Rhetorical Approach to Intellectual Risk-Taking

Our findings reveal that students conceptualize intellectual risk in terms of the constraints of the university context itself; they worry about how to position their work in light of intellectual property concerns or how challenging convention may undermine their grades. While these concerns may be unsurprising, students' contextual realities are often downplayed in scholarship that embraces intellectual risk-taking. Our findings prompt us to suggest that we need a *rhetorical* approach to risk-taking, one that accounts for students' entire rhetorical situations, including the implications of their writing for readers and themselves. This approach aligns intellectual risk-taking with the rhetorical values of context, the copiousness possible through invention, and with rhetoric's traditional attention to deliberate choices made or stances taken with always-partial, tentative information. In viewing intellectual risk-taking as situated, emergent, and interactive, a rhetorical approach asks that we as instructors consider not only the process by which students decide to take intellectual risks, but how we can create conditions that build students' critical awareness of risk-taking as an aspect of their learning.

Fostering this rhetorical approach thus begins by de-centering the individual student learner as the only person impacted by risk-taking and considering instead the situational constraints of the contemporary university. Our study finds that students are unsure about taking risks for three primary reasons: (1) they perceive unclear expectations for what constitutes successful work; (2) they don't always know what counts as appropriate risk-taking when it comes to language and writing; and (3) they are dissuaded from taking intellectual risks because of grade penalties and other structural factors. These issues suggest that embracing intellectual risk-taking requires us to consider how we enable it throughout our pedagogy, from the writing process through assessment. This is not to advocate jettisoning current approaches; rather, we suggest that instructors can build from current practices. We can foster a rhetorical approach to risk-taking by engaging students in invention habits, offering reflection opportunities, making evaluation more dialogic, and taking into account students' perceptions of their own learning and risk-taking. Such practices, taken together, may help to address students' concerns. More concretely, we might do the following:

1. Scaffold classroom activities for students to test out safe and risky approaches to writing.

Inviting intellectual risk-taking during invention could involve students proposing several paper topics, explicitly inviting both risky topics and those deemed safe and asking students to provide rationales for such identifications. These invitations can be tied to contextualized discussions of what constitutes original or unconventional topics as well as how students can articulate the relation between their own and others' ideas.

Writing classrooms then become places where students consciously appraise risk-taking opportunities instead of instinctively shun or embrace them. This classroom approach pushes students to see how taking an intellectual risk is like a decision to pursue more research or switch from drafting to revising. Such an approach brings together previous composition scholarship that separately focused on risk-taking through revision, such as in Wendy Bishop's work, or through invention, as modeled by Rankin. Most importantly, it explicitly shows that composition classes value deliberate intellectual risk-taking.

2. Incorporate opportunities for students to reflect on intellectual risks taken.

Foregrounding the importance of risk-taking encourages students to evaluate their own decisions, such as in reflection memos that articulate the intellectual risks they took in relation to their rhetorical situations. Reflection memos could pose questions like the following: What risks do my work pose for my long-term beliefs, habits, and future learning? What risks am I asking a reader to take in reading this? Such an approach does not guarantee that students actually take intellectual risks, but it does signal risk-taking's value and offers opportunities for metacognition and reflection, which scholars such as Anne Beaufort and Rebecca Nowacek name as necessary precursors to transfer of learning. Raffaella Negretti similarly shows how such work fosters students' agency as writers. We see guided reflections being particularly useful in helping students identify places where they were concerned about plagiarism or stylistic choices, such as when to incorporate first-person voice and their own perspective—two issues that appeared prominently in survey responses. Further, articulating choices explicitly within reflections provides students a chance to grapple with potential rhetorical trade-offs involved in risky approaches to argument, convention, and language, and for instructors to access those struggles and potentially intervene if students seem to misunderstand key concepts or practices.

3. Create evaluation guidelines that clearly emphasize and reward intellectual risk-taking.

Approaching intellectual risk-taking rhetorically can also help navigate our introductory grading dilemma by reframing classroom evaluation as a dialogic, intersubjective process. We draw inspiration from composition scholars like Bishop who claim to encourage intellectual risk-taking by "deferring product grades to final portfolios … and by offering significant participation credit" (111). Ruth Mirtz and Rankin each stress students' justifications, assuming that evaluating intellectual risk requires both student and teacher to understand decisions made. Such approaches emphasize the rhetorical nature of risk-taking by attending to writers' deliberate choices and the reasoning behind them.

With intellectual risk-taking as a guiding value, we might reframe evaluation priorities. Following Kastely, we might assess writing by asking whether an assignment encourages students "to take more risks in the future" (240). Emphasizing risk-taking in assessment cannot eliminate the grading dilemma we outlined at the beginning, but it refocuses the issue. Furthermore, intellectual risk-taking does not replace rigor or expectations to meet certain disciplinary conventions, but it clarifies what is most important to evaluate.

In short, intellectual risk draws attention to the classroom as a space where the very real questions of students' subjectivity and their relationship to institutional discourse—that is, the question of what it means to take risks in education—are discussed, made central, and explored as an aspect of learning. Asking students to identify and evaluate what they experience as risky thus enables students to render tangible, specific, and personal the often amorphous institutional values that higher education discourse maps onto their educational experiences. In this way, writing classrooms can create space for students to articulate what these institutional values do and do not mean for the lives they shape.

While we see promise in this rhetorical approach, our preliminary study cannot conclude the conversation over intellectual risk-taking; rather, we see it prompting areas for future inquiry.

Institutional Context and Teacher Preparation

Our study focuses on a single institution: future studies might examine whether student responses vary depending on institutional context. We also note that institutional context may have shaped instructors' responses; particularly, our survey respondents were all graduate and adjunct instructors. Do variations in teacher preparation or institutional security shape how intellectual risk-taking is viewed by instructors? What challenges does embracing intellectual risk pose for teacher training and WPA work? Asking these questions, we argue, should occur in tandem with inquiry into how institutional context shapes intellectual risk's classroom enactment.

Student Identity and Educational Development

While our study aggregates responses from students across multiple courses, further research could tease out how risk-taking may be related to students' development levels. How might students approach risk-taking differently in first-year versus upper-level courses? In disciplinary or writing in the disciplines courses? Similarly, the literature and our study suggest that more research is needed into how intellectual risk-taking relates to students' socialization and sense of identity. James Byrnes, David Miller, and William D. Schafer's psychological research has found genders may be socialized in divergent ways that affect their behaviors around risk-taking. If we implicitly define risk-taking as a uniform practice, we could unintentionally reinforce extant disparities.

Intellectual risk's popularity in education discourse and connection to multiple pedagogies calls for research and intervention. What risks do we want students to take? And what can we as writing instructors do to actually help students take those risks? A rhetorical approach to intellectual risk-taking foregrounds these interconnected questions and directs our gaze to the values in tension. It provides space to take seriously Matthew Heard's curriculum design approach, which advocates "a habit of dwelling in tensions and complexities that connect studies of composition to larger ethical, ontological, and epistemological questions" (321). Rather than shunning intellectual risk, this approach encourages taking up these tensions. Doing so may create space for writing classrooms to help productively shape the continuing life of intellectual risk-taking in the academy.

Acknowledgments

We would like to thank the teachers and students that participated in our study as well as Laura Micciche, Christopher C. Burnham, and an anonymous peer reviewer for helpful suggestions.

Appendix: Survey Design

Like Carol P. Hartzog's study of writing program administration, we see surveys as the starting point of an iterative process (cited in Anderson et al. 62). Our goal for this survey was to begin eliciting how students and teachers define intellectual risk and to identify concepts and practices that both groups associate with it. We approached *intellectual risk-taking* similarly to a sensitizing concept as defined by Joop Hox (62) and sought to elaborate on its meanings within the particular context of academic writing classrooms. This ground-up method is similar to the "heuristic" approach Margaret Himley used to explore how students in Syracuse University's first-year writing program conceptualized diversity.

We explicitly asked survey respondents to define intellectual risk (Q1). To further elucidate how respondents define risk, we also asked all respondents for concepts or practices that they associate with the ostensible opposite of risk-taking; thus, Q3 uses familiar terms like *safe* and *conventional* to connote ideas commonly associated with non-risky practices within composition discourse.

In addition to exploring definitions, we sought to further illuminate students' and teachers' attitudes toward risk-taking in order to better understand its role and value within actual classrooms. Q5 asks whether respondents believe students should take intellectual risks in writing. We also asked instructors to describe any specific classroom practices used to teach intellectual risk and for general thoughts about its place in their classrooms (Q2).

Because responses were voluntary and uncompensated, we kept our survey brief. Since our study was exploratory and designed to generate hypotheses and potential directions for future inquiry, we limited our sample to one institution.

Survey Questions

All participants were asked the same questions except where noted.

Q1. How would you define intellectual risk?

Q2. Student Version. Have you taken any writing courses that were designed to prepare you for the kind of academic writing you will be expected to do in college? If so, please list them.

Q2. Instructor Version. Do you explicitly or implicitly teach students about intellectual risks in writing assignments? Why and how or why not?

Q3. What would you consider to be a "safe" way to write an academic paper? What do you see as the generally accepted "correct" or "conventional" characteristics of an academic paper?

Q4. In what ways can students challenge the conventions of academic writing? (What are some things that you would consider "risky" to do in an academic paper? What makes them "risky"?)

Q5. Do you think students should take these kinds of risks when they write academic papers? Please explain why or why not.

Works Cited

Anderson, Daniel, et al. "Integrating Multimodality into Composition Curricula: Survey Methodology and Results from a CCCC Research Grant." *Composition Studies*, vol. 34, no. 2, Fall 2006, pp. 59-84.

Bartholomae, David. "Inventing the University." *When a Writer Can't Write: Studies in Writer's Block*, edited by Mike Rose, Guilford P, 1985, pp. 134-66.

Beaufort, Anne. "'College Writing and Beyond': Five Years Later." *Composition Forum*, vol. 26, Fall 2012, www.compositionforum.com/issue/26/college-writing-beyond.php.

Beghetto, Ronald. "Correlates of Intellectual Risk Taking in Elementary School Science." *Journal of Research in Science Teaching*, vol. 46, no. 2, December 2008, pp. 210-23.

Berman, Jeffrey. *Risky Writing: Self-Disclosure and Self-Transformation in the Classroom*, UMass Amherst P, 2001.

Bharucha, Jamshed. "America Can Teach Asia a lot about Science, Technology, and Math." *The Chronicle of Higher Education*, vol. 54, no. 20, p. A33, 25 Jan. 2008.

Bishop, Wendy. "Contracts, Radical Revision, Writing Portfolios, and the Risks of Writing." *Power and Identity in the Creative Writing Classroom: The Authority Project*, edited by Anna Leahy, Multilingual Matters, Limited, 2005, pp.109-20.

Byrnes, James P., David Miller, and William D. Schafer. "Gender Differences in Risk Taking: A Meta-Analysis." *Psychological Bulletin*, vol. 125, no. 3, 1999, pp. 367-83. doi: 10.1037/0033-2909.125.3.367.

Carter, Joyce Locke. "Call for Program Proposals: Risk and Reward." National Council of Teachers of English, 2015. www.ncte.org/library/NCTEFiles/Groups/CCCC/Convention/2015/2015_4C_CFP.pdf.

Dutro, Elizabeth. "Writing Wounded: Trauma, Testimony, and Critical Witness in Literacy Classrooms." *English Education*, vol. 43, no. 2, Jan. 2011, pp. 193-211.

Florida SouthWestern State College. "Honors Scholar Program Mission and Values." www.fsw.edu/honors/mission.

Foster, Drew. "Private Journals versus Public Blogs: The Impact of Peer Readership on Low-stakes Reflective Writing." *Teaching Sociology*, vol. 43, no. 2, Apr. 2015, pp. 104-14.

Friel, Terri. "Art Schools Teach Too Much 'Gimmickry,' With Not Enough Real Education." [Letter to the editor]. *The Chronicle of Higher Education*, vol. 46, no. 38, 26 May 2000, p. B3.

Garrison, D. Randy, et al. "Revisiting Methodological Issues in Transcript Analysis: Negotiated Coding and Reliability." *Internet and Higher Education*, vol. 9, no. 1, 2006, pp. 1-8. doi: 10.1016/j.iheduc.2005.11.001.

Haas, Christina, Pamela Takayoshi, and Brandon Carr. "Analytic Strategies, Competent Inquiries, and Methodological Tensions in the Study of Writing." *Writing Studies Research in Practice: Methods and Methodologies,* edited by Lee Nickoson and Mary P. Sheridan, SIUP, 2012, pp. 51-62.

Haswell, Janis, Richard Haswell, and Glenn Blalock. "Hospitality in College Composition Courses." *CCC*, vol. 60, no. 4, June 2009, pp. 707-27.

Heard, Matthew. "Repositioning Curriculum Design: Broadening the Who and How of Curricular Invention." *College English*, vol. 76, no. 4, Mar. 2014, pp. 315-36.

Hebel, Sara. "An Analyst's Unusual Influence over Higher-Education Debates." *The Chronicle of Higher Education*, vol. 46, no. 27, 10 Mar. 2000, pp. A32-34.

Himley, Margaret. "Response to Phillip P. Marzluf, 'Diversity Writing: Natural and Authentic Voices.'" *CCC*, vol. 58, no. 3, Feb. 2007, pp. 449-63.

Howard, Rebecca Moore. "Sexuality, Textuality: The Cultural Work of Plagiarism." *College English*, vol. 62, no. 4, Mar. 2000, pp. 473-91.

Howard, Rebecca Moore, Tricia Serviss, and Tanya K. Rodrigue. "Writing from Sources, Writing from Sentences." *Writing & Pedagogy*, vol. 2, no. 2, 2010, pp. 177-92, doi: 10.1558/wap.v2i2.177.

Hox, Joop J. "From Theoretical Concept to Survey Question." *Survey Measurement and Process Quality,* edited by Lars E. Lyberg, et al., John Wiley & Sons, 1997, pp. 47-69, doi: 10.1002/9781118490013.ch2.

Hu, Alice. "A Letter to the Harvard Class of 2019." Harvard University, www.college.harvard.edu/admissions/hear-our-students/student-blog/letter-harvard-class-2019.

Kantor, Ken. "Evaluating Creative Writing: A Different Ball Game." *The English Journal*, vol. 64, no. 4, Apr. 1975, pp. 72-74.

Kastely, James L. "From Formalism to Inquiry: A Model of Argument in *Antigone*." *College English*, vol. 62, no. 2, Nov. 1999, pp. 222-41, doi: 10.2307/379019.

Kelty, Ryan, and Bridget A. Bunten. "Introduction." *Risk-Taking in Higher Education: The Importance of Negotiating Intellectual Challenge in the College Classroom*, edited by Ryan Kelty and Bridget A. Bunten, Rowman & Littlefield, 2017, pp. xv-xxviii.

Kimball, Bruce. *Orators and Philosophers: A History of the Idea of Liberal Education*, Teachers CP, 1986.

Mirtz, Ruth. "'You Want Us to Do What?' How to Get the Most Out of Unexpected Writing Assignments." *Elements of Alternate Style: Essays on Writing and Revision*, edited by Wendy Bishop, Boynton/Cook, 1997, pp. 105-15.

Monson, Connie, and Jacqueline Rhodes. "Risking Queer: Pedagogy, Performativity, and Desire in Writing Classrooms." *JAC*, vol. 24, no. 1, 2004, pp. 79-91.

"National Liberal Arts College Rankings." *U.S. News and World Report*, 2015.

"National University Rankings." *U.S. News and World Report*, 2015.

Negretti, Raffaella. "Metacognition in Student Academic Writing: A Longitudinal Study of Metacognitive Awareness and Its Relation to Task Perception, Self-Regulation, and Evaluation of Performance." *Written Communication*, vol. 29, no. 2, Apr. 2012, pp. 142-79. doi: 10.1177/0741088312438529.

Nowacek, Rebecca S. *Agents of Integration: Understanding Transfer as a Rhetorical Act.* SIUP, 2011.

Philadelphia University. "Hallmark Goals Descriptions." www.philau.edu/Hallmarks/ goalDescriptions.html.

Rankin, Elizabeth. "It's Not Just Mumbo Jumbo: Taking Risks with Academic Writing." *Elements of Alternate Style: Essays on Writing and Revision*, edited by Wendy Bishop, Boynton/Cook, 1997, pp. 67-74.

Roderick, Noah. "In Defense of Grade Grubbers." *The Chronicle of Higher Education*, vol. 57, no. 23, 06 Feb. 2011.

Scott, Tony. "Animated by the Entrepreneurial Spirit: Austerity, Dispossession, and Composition's Last Living Act." *Composition in the Age of Austerity*, edited by Nancy Welch and Tony Scott, UP Colorado, 2016, pp. 205-19.

University of Washington. "Undergraduate Research Program." www.washington.edu/ undergradresearch/about/.

Young, Mallory. "It's Not Just French 101. It's an Introduction to 'Tout Le Monde.'" *The Chronicle of Higher Education*, vol. 47, no. 35, 11 May 2001, p. B12.

Zwagerman, Sean. "The Scarlet P: Plagiarism, Panopticism, and the Rhetoric of Academic Integrity." *CCC*, vol. 59, no. 4, June 2008, pp. 676-710.

Course Designs

Advanced Exposition: Writing through Podcasts

Jacob Greene

Course Description

ENC 3310 Advanced Exposition is an upper-level writing course offered by the English department at the University of Florida. To enroll, students must be in good standing in their major and have taken at least two 1000- or 2000-level English courses. Although this course is open to all students, it mostly attracts junior and senior English majors. According to the undergraduate catalog, ENC 3310 is intended to introduce students to the "methods of exposition," including "definition, classification, comparison and contrast, analysis, illustration and identification." Due to the generalized nature of ENC 3310, the English department encourages instructors to organize their sections around a specific theme, genre, or modality. As such, ENC 3310 Writing through Podcasts, uses a semester-length podcasting project to teach expository writing. In this course, students demonstrate expository writing techniques through both print and sound-based media within the context of three major assignments: (1) a podcast analysis essay, (2) a podcast proposal assignment, and (3) a four-episode podcast mini-series. The section of ENC 3310 I discuss in this course design was taught over an accelerated six-week semester in summer 2017 that met Monday through Friday for 75-minute periods.

Institutional Context

The University of Florida English major has four composition courses at the 3000 level: ENC 3250: Professional Communication, ENC: 3310 Advanced Exposition, ENC 3312: Advanced Argumentative Writing, and ENC 3414: Hypermedia. Together, these courses offer advanced undergraduates further training in various genres and media of writing. Since the department began archiving all syllabi in 2013, only one out of five sections of ENC 3310 incorporated at least one multimodal writing assignment. Due to a variety of departmental factors, sections of ENC 3414: Hypermedia are being taught less frequently. As a result, junior and senior students in the English major are presented with fewer opportunities to engage in multimodal writing projects in their upper-level writing courses. Thus, Writing through Podcasts fills an important gap in the English major curricula with the aim of preparing students for future careers, internships, and graduate school programs where they are increasingly required to communicate through a variety of new media genres.

Of the archived sections of ENC 3310 that I was able to survey, a majority ascribe to an assignment sequence that moves students through the established genres of expository writing: definition, classification, analysis, and comparison/contrast. However, by isolating the modes of exposition into individual assignments, such sequencing tends to decontextualize the rhetorical function of expository writing. In other words, it is not enough that students simply know *how* to define a term or classify a concept, but that they learn to recognize the most opportune moments for doing so within the context of a broader rhetorical goal. Thus, rather than moving through this established assignment sequence, my section of ENC 3310 challenges students to apply the modes of exposition in their creation of a four-episode podcast mini-series.

Students who enroll in ENC 3310 are typically strong writers with little experience in sound editing or multimedia production. Because the University of Florida requires all undergraduate students to have "access to and on-going use of a computer," students are able to create podcasts and audio stories that are close to professional quality with their own laptops through the use of an inexpensive USB microphone and a free open-source audio editing software ("Student Computing Requirements"). Indeed, during in-class listening sessions, students would frequently remark that their peers' projects sounded like "real podcasts." Students' discovery that high-quality audio stories can be created with relatively inexpensive hardware and software made them much more invested in the overall quality of their podcasts.

Prior to Writing through Podcasts, most of the students were not regular podcast listeners. Informal surveys and class discussions revealed that students typically preferred listening to music over podcasts. Moreover, many admitted that they perceived podcasts as either boring (e.g., news and political analysis) or trivial (e.g., shows about quirky facts, interviews with celebrities, etc.). However, after listening to popular podcasts like *Serial, 99% Invisible, Radiolab*, and *This American Life*, students began to revise this perception and came to see that podcasting can be an engaging and immersive platform for telling stories and communicating information about important issues. Indeed, by the end of the semester, most students stated that they began to listen to episodes from these podcasts on their own time.

Theoretical Rationale

Since the establishment of the journal *Computers and Composition* in 1985, scholars such as Cynthia Selfe and Gail Hawisher have been leading the call for the inclusion of alternative modalities within the first-year writing classroom. A multimodal approach to the teaching of writing, they claim, allows students to develop rhetorical acuity within the emerging new media genres they are increasingly expected to produce (Hawisher and Selfe 642). However, as Jonathan Alexander and Jacqueline Rhodes point out, it is not enough for writing teachers to simply assign a generic "multimodal project" and call it a day. Rather, as they write in their recent book *On Multimodality: New Media in Composition Studies*, many writing teachers who assign multimodal projects "rarely address the specific invention, delivery, and rhetorical possibilities of other types of composition" (3). In many writing courses, multimodality is often tacked on as an afterthought at the end of the semester after students have already completed the standard sequence of print-based genres (analysis, synthesis, argument, etc.). Through this, students come to conceive of alternate modalities like podcasts as subordinate to alphabetic text, or, at best, a kind of additional rhetorical "flare" used to liven up a written argument by adapting it to a video-, image-, or audio-essay. Because of this separation between "writing assignments" and "multimodal assignments," we (and our students) miss out on the "distinct modes, logics, methods, processes, and capabilities" of specific media forms (Alexander and Rhodes 4).

Technically, a podcast is simply a pre-recorded audio file that has been uploaded to an online database or audio-streaming service (e.g., iTunes, Soundcloud, etc.). Although pre-recorded audio broadcasting has been around since the early days of radio, "podcasting," as the name implies, is uniquely tied to the growth of the Internet and the proliferation of portable digital music players. The emergence of mobile devices in the early 2000s offered audio storytellers— from professional journalists to amateur raconteurs—an entirely new delivery network for circulating audio files. Much like the term "blogging," "podcasting" refers to not only a medium or technology but to an emerging genre ecology encompassing a range of topics, styles, and formats.

Podcasts have grown in popularity year after year. According to a recent report from Edison research, the number of people who listen to podcasts on a regular basis now totals over 42 million ("The Infinite Dial"). Another surprising data point revealed in the report is that most people listen to podcasts from home rather than while driving or commuting. Although home media consumption is still dominated by cable television and video streaming platforms, professionally produced and highly bingeable podcast mini-series like *Serial* and *S-Town* have pushed podcasting into a mass-listening medium, simultaneously ushering in an entirely new genre of audio storytelling that combines elements of investigative journalism, narrative nonfiction, and literary symbolism.

Although sound-based composition pedagogy is not (and should not be) synonymous with podcasting, I chose to organize ENC 3310 around podcasting for three main reasons. For one, there is a seemingly endless variety of highly engaging and informative podcasts that students can access and use as models for their own podcasts. NPR podcasts like *Planet Money* frequently draw on expository modes like definition and comparison/contrast in their reporting, often in highly engaging and stylistically nuanced ways. Second, podcasts often exhibit the same stylistic qualities that we value in effective writing—concision, clarity, coherent organization, showing versus telling, etc. Because a listener cannot simply reread a sentence or flip back a few pages if they do not understand something, audio is often less forgiving than print. Students are then challenged to script their episodes with clear transitions and signposting so as to keep the listener engaged and informed. Lastly, in creating a podcast mini-series that they could upload to Soundcloud—a free audio hosting website—students left the course with a digital project that they could embed on a personal website or online portfolio.

As Adam Banks pointed out in his 2015 Chair's Address at the Conference on College Composition and Communication, our writing pedagogies must evolve as "composing becomes more and more enmeshed in digital environments" (274). Ultimately, my primary objective in designing and teaching Writing through Podcasts is to provide students with a solid rhetorical foundation for composing with audio media that they can apply to their future courses, careers, and post-graduation plans.

The objectives of an expository writing course align well with the rhetorical skills required to create an effective podcast. Exposition finds its roots in the four traditional modes of discourse: narration, description, exposition, and argumentation. Expository texts are the most didactic of the four modes; they seek to explain, describe, and inform. Expository writing pedagogies typically work through an established genre sequence, moving from simpler modes like definition and classification and gradually building into more complex ones like analysis and comparison/contrast. Professionally produced podcasts draw on the modes of exposition on a regular basis, often in creative and engaging ways. For instance, a *Planet Money* episode on the history of American banking employs a creative use of a comparison/contrast structure to introduce the two main characters ("The Bank War"). By using these podcasts as models for their own assignments, students learn how to employ the modes of exposition within the context of a larger project and, more importantly, come to see that expository writing is not simply a series of isolated exercises but rather a compositional technique used by writers in specific situations to create rhetorical effects for a target audience.

I am fortunate enough to teach in a department that supports and even encourages instructors to assign multimodal projects. ENC 3310 Writing through Podcasts is organized around a three-part, project-based learning assignment: (1) a podcast analysis essay, (2) a podcast proposal, and (3) a four-episode podcast mini-series. Project-based pedagogies ask students to propose a solution to an authentic problem that they see in the real world and then create a project that responds to this problem within the parameters set by the instructor. For example, a project-based learning assignment might ask students to create a website that educates community members about the local effects of climate change. Through this, students achieve the learning outcomes that the project was designed to teach, such as communicating to a public audience through digital media. Writing through Podcasts utilizes a project-based learning model to teach expository writing. At the beginning of the semester, students choose a topic for their podcast miniseries (e.g., immigration) and then survey the existing podcasts related to this topic, focusing specifically on any informational gaps in how this particular topic is represented. Then, students propose a four-episode podcast mini-series that addresses this informational gap.

The major assignments of Writing through Podcasts align with our three course units: analyzing podcasts, planning podcasts, and creating podcasts. The first unit, analyzing podcasts, introduces different podcasting genres and the rhetorical affordances of audio more generally. Students learn how to:

- Isolate the rhetorical affordances of print and audio texts
- Classify basic narrative structures and genres of podcasting
- Define key podcasting terms
- Analyze and explain specific podcasting techniques

The podcast analysis assignment asks students to subscribe to a podcast series and analyze how the podcaster uses sound (e.g., music, sound effects, voice narration, etc.) and expository writing techniques to create specific rhetorical effects. During this unit, students listen to a variety of podcast episodes inside and outside of class in order to isolate how podcasters draw on the specific "methods, processes, and capabilities" of sound to create informative and engaging episodes (Alexander and Rhodes 4). This section of the course also covered some of the basic modes of expository writing (definition, comparison, etc.). Students would analyze podcast episodes in class and identify how podcasters use these modes rhetorically to persuade their listeners or more clearly illustrate a difficult concept.

A particularly valuable resource during this first unit and throughout the course was the online podcasting resource Transom.org. The Transom website is supported by the National Endowment for the Arts, and it provides resources for aspiring audio storytellers, from technical tutorials on specific audio editing platforms to guides on crafting effective interview questions. Transom also hosts a podcast series called *Howsound* that proved an invaluable tool for the students of 3310. Each *Howsound* episode focuses on a specific audio storytelling technique (e.g., using silence, writing introductions, structuring an audio story, etc.) and uses examples from professional podcasts and radio broadcasts to illustrate each one. *Howsound* episodes are under 20 minutes, which made it very easy for students to listen to episodes together in class and discuss how they might apply the technique to their own podcasts. *Howsound* was also useful in providing students with examples of things to look for when analyzing a podcast.

For the second unit, planning podcasts, students used a compare and contrast structure to propose an original podcast miniseries. In their proposals, students were required to research any podcasts that were in the same general topic area as their podcast (e.g., environmental podcasts, music podcasts, etc.) and then articulate how their miniseries filled an important informational gap in how this particular topic has been represented. An important component of project-based learning pedagogies is creating assignments that have significance beyond the classroom. By researching existing podcasts, students were able to consider how their podcast fits within a broader media ecology comprised of public listeners who have a vested interest in the topic. In their proposals, students were also required to write an outline of their mini-series in which they delineated the focus and general format of each episode. In this way, the podcast proposal helped students achieve the primary objectives for unit two:

- Use a compare and contrast structure to propose an original podcast mini-series
- Write a detailed outline for an original podcast miniseries

The final unit, creating podcasts, took up the final four weeks of the course and was split into one-week subunits: narrative journalism, audio vérite, interviews, and freestyle. During each subunit, we listened to podcasts and read articles associated with that week's theme. In addition, each subunit corresponded to a specific podcasting format or technique that students were required to include in that week's episode. In the narrative journalism subunit, students introduced their topic using structures of audio storytelling popularized by radio journalists and professional podcasters. In the audio vérite subunit, students incorporated live audio from impromptu interviews conducted around campus, and in the interview subunit, students conducted more in-depth interviews with experts on their topic. For the final subunit, freestyle, students could incorporate any technique and/or format from the first three subunits. On the Friday of each week, students submitted their episode and we held an in-class listening party during which students provided feedback on their peers' episodes before submitting their final episode over the weekend. Together, these four episodes aligned with the overarching objectives for Writing through Podcasts:

- Script and produce different podcast episodes in a variety of formats
- Layer discursive and non-discursive audio (e.g., background music, sound effects, etc.) to create specific rhetorical effects
- Adapt the modes of exposition to audio
- Critique and revise podcast episodes

For episode one, students analyzed the structure of popular narrative podcasts and then used these structures to script their podcast episodes. For the most part, students used what Rob Rosenthal, the host of *Howsound*, describes as the "e" method for structuring an audio story, a popular expository technique used frequently by podcasts like *99% Invisible* ("Story Structure: The 'e'."). Rosenthal describes this technique as the "e" structure because it follows the same four-part directional logic of how most people write a lowercase "e": (1) The podcast starts out with a short anecdote related to the episode topic; (2) moves out into a discussion of the topic more generally; (3) circles back to the anecdote and contextualizes it within the information gathered from step 2; and (4) moves into a discussion of the underlying implications of this topic for the future. Students were able to build on and modify this "e" story structure in subsequent episodes as they incorporated more advanced podcasting techniques and sound design principles.

For their second episode, students were required to incorporate "vox pop." Vox pop is journalistic shorthand for "Vox Populi," or "voice of the people," and it refers to short, impromptu interviews conducted in a public space. Students incorporated vox pop into their podcasts in a variety of clever and creative ways. For instance, one student, Lissa, went around campus asking random students how to pronounce the word "Iran." She then used this audio as the introduction for one of her podcast episodes about American perceptions of Iranian culture[1]. Another student, Kevin, used vox pop in his podcast about immigration to ask people how their family ended up in the United States[2]. The disparate responses he received helped to illuminate why immigration can be such a divisive and highly personal topic.

For their third episode, students were required to include an interview. In preparation for this episode, students practiced interviewing techniques and workshopped potential questions. The episode "Interviewing with Your Skeptical Brain" from Transom's *Howsound* podcast was particularly instructive during this subunit. In this episode, reporter Sally Helm interviews a talkative (and somewhat recalcitrant) interview subject and discusses methods for interrupting interviewees with counter-arguments and asking questions that help move the story forward. For the most part, students' interview subjects fell into one of two groups: (1) an expert on their topic, and/or (2) a representative member of a community. For instance, one student took this latter approach and interviewed an avid videogame player for her podcast about the social and emotional benefits of video games. In this episode, the student uses specific audio editing techniques we had discussed in class—summarizing interviewee responses, cutting out her original audio, etc.—to make the interview flow more naturally within the narrative structure of her episode[3].

Due to the time constraints of creating a five-to-ten-minute podcast episode each week, students spent ample time in class workshopping their scripts and learning how to add background music, media clips, and other sound effects to their podcasts. As students scripted their episodes at the start of each week, we discussed how the modes of exposition they had learned earlier in the course might be incorporated into their episodes. For instance, some students chose to structure their episode around a set of key terms that were important for the listener to understand throughout the rest of the podcast series. One student, Johana, structured the first episode of her podcast about contemporary feminism around three concepts important to feminist theory: the concrete wall, the glass ceiling, and the labyrinth. By drawing on the mode of definition and then moving into a broader historical narrative about contemporary feminism, Johana was able to create an informative and engaging introductory episode for her podcast[4].

Students used a variety of expository modes throughout the podcasting assignment. For instance, Emily used a compare and contrast structure throughout her podcast mini-series, which explored how Attention Deficit Hyperactive Disorder (ADHD) is diagnosed differently in men and women. This structure made it easier for the listener to comprehend how ADHD often goes undiagnosed in adolescent girls[5]. Instead of forcing students to work within a prescribed sequence of expository modes, the podcasting assignment allowed them to select the modes that were most well-suited for their specific rhetorical aims for their podcast series. By incorporating these expository modes into a larger project, students came to see that "expository writing" is not synonymous with "objective writing." Rather, they see that expository modes are rhetorical structures that they can draw upon as writers to present information in such a way that will lead the reader (or listener) to a particular action or belief.

In addition to specific podcasting and audio editing techniques, each subunit explored the broader cultural and ethical issues associated with that week's theme. For example, during our subunit on Audio Vérite, I screened the documentary *Shut Up Little Man!*, which explores the murky ethical underpinnings of one of the first pieces of "viral media" in a pre-internet era. Audio vérite refers to raw, unedited audio that has been recorded surreptitiously. In the documentary, two young men secretly record their neighbors and then distribute cassette tapes of these recordings throughout the United States. Along with this documentary, I had students listen to an episode of *Howsound* titled "The Ethics of Audio Trespassing and Secret Recording." In this episode, Rob Rosenthal interviews Jack Rodolico, a radio reporter who used audio from a surreptitiously recorded interview in his reporting on abuse allegations at a New Hampshire mental health hospital. Afterwards, students discussed the ethics of audio vérite and whether it's permissible to use secretly recorded audio, either for entertainment (as in *Shut Up Little Man!*) or to promote a broader public good (as in the *Howsound* podcast).

An important outcome of the Creating Podcasts unit was for students to recognize that "Writing through Podcasts" is more than simply reading a script into a microphone. Rather, students needed to learn that in adapting their writing to a podcast they must utilize the unique rhetorical capacities that sound offers us as a medium—layering sounds, voice intonation and rhythm, etc. As Steph Ceraso points out in her article for *College English*, "(Re)Educating the Senses: Multimodal Listening, Bodily Learning, and the Composition of Sonic Experiences," multimodal writing courses rarely approach sound as "a distinct mode with distinct affordances" (113). Ceraso goes on to describe how sound is an embodied event, and that by attuning students to the non-discursive affordances of podcasting and audio storytelling we help them to see (and hear) "how sound works as an affective mode . . . [and] how their own sonic compositions might affect audiences" (115).

To help students grasp the more affective, non-discursive affordances of sound writing early in the semester, I had them create a 60-second audio story using only sound effects and instrumental music. The goal of this mini-project was to teach students that non-discursive sound can be used to convey information to the listener, such as creating a sense of location or establishing a particular mood. Assigning this mini-project earlier in the semester had the added advantage of teaching students basic audio production skills like downloading copyright-free sounds, layering tracks in Audacity, and mixing audio levels. Moreover, I was able to reference this mini-project throughout the class as a way of encouraging students to incorporate non-discursive audio into their podcasting assignment.

Of course, as Ceraso also points out, composition instructors should be careful not to conflate all sound-based assignments with podcasting. Rather, in encouraging students to consider the rhetorical possibilities of sound, Ceraso and Kati Fargo Ahern claim that we should challenge them "to pay attention to how sound shapes and is shaped by different contexts, material objects, and embodied, multisensory experiences" ("Composing with Sound"). To introduce students to the "multisensory" aspects of sound, my spring version of ENC 3310 included a location-based audio tour assignment. For this assignment, students used the website geotourist.com to link their audio files to specific GPS coordinates associated with their audio tour, such as a local city park or an historic building on campus. Thus, students were challenged to consider how the embodied experience of the listener within a particular location might affect their sound design. For instance, one student, Savannah, designed her audio tour as a guide for our campus sculpture garden. She used different sound effects and musical interludes to help translate the visual-material perception of the sculptures into a soundscape that played alongside her narration of each artwork[6].

By extending their audio compositions out into physical spaces, students were able to explore the intersection of sound writing and multimodal invention strategies. Because audio tours necessarily incorporate a range of rhetorical modes and senses, including physical movement, sight, touch, speech, and sound, students came to re-envision their role within the audio tour assignment less as the author of the tour and more as the facilitator of a dynamic, multimodal experience that they are co-authoring alongside the rhetorical contingencies of the location. Patricia Dunn and Kathleen Dunn De Mers point out that when students compose in multiple media, they begin to "reconceptualize" their approach to a given topic as they "re-think, reshape, and revise their work" for a different mode. In this way, they claim, we can think of multimodality as not merely the crafting of a final product but as "a broad set of invention activities" through which writers can explore multiple perspectives in relation to an idea, issue, or (in the case of the audio tour assignment) location.

Students' writing abilities are "enriched rather than diminished by [the] semiotic dimensionality" of multimodal writing (Selfe 618). As communication continues to splinter into new genres and modalities, the field of writing studies should continue to adapt its pedagogies to accommodate not only the unique rhetorics specific to media like sound and podcasting but also specific genres, formats, and techniques like interviews and vox pop. By incorporating the modes of exposition into a podcast, students come to see expository writing as more than just a series of isolated exercises. Rather, they begin to develop a sense of exposition as rhetorical and audience-specific as they draw upon different organizational structures in order to communicate to listeners beyond the classroom walls.

Critical Reflection

In having the opportunity to teach English 3310 twice, I was able to address some of the initial difficulties I experienced. In the first iteration of the course, students submitted their podcasting assignment all at once, and I used in-class workshops and one-on-one conferences to stay up to date with students' progress. Although this structure was useful in allowing students ample time to work on their projects as a whole, it did not allow enough time for students to improve on an episode-to-episode basis.

Thus, in the second iteration of the course, I made a few changes to the flow of the main podcasting assignment. Considering what I had learned in the spring semester (along with the fast-paced nature of a summer course), I decided to split the podcasting assignment into a serialized project so that students could complete an individual episode each week before moving on to the next one. This proved to be a determining factor in improving the overall quality of student work. By breaking up the podcasting assignment into a serialized project, students were able not only to improve their audio production skills from episode to episode but also to spend more time learning and incorporating specific podcasting formats (e.g., vox pop, interviews, etc.).

The final four weeks of the course corresponded to the four episodes that students need to create for the podcasting assignment. Each week in this final unit followed the same sequence: On Mondays and Tuesdays, I introduced students to that week's podcasting format through a combination of mini-lectures, group work, and in-class podcast listening. On Wednesdays, I worked with students in small groups to workshop their scripts. On Thursday, I conducted technology workshops with Audacity, and students were required to bring in their laptops and condenser microphones so that they could finalize that week's episode. On Fridays, students listened to their peer's episodes and provided constructive feedback within a shared Google document. A majority of students found this weekly sequence helpful in providing them with the skills and resources necessary to learn the technical and rhetorical aspects of podcasting (see fig. 1).

In receiving feedback from myself as well as their peers after each episode, my hope was that the quality of students' podcasts would gradually improve throughout the semester. Indeed, many students demonstrated a marked improvement in their podcasts from episode to episode. Specifically, most students grew more comfortable editing their podcast episodes in Audacity and incorporating background music, sound effects, and media clips to create rhetorical effects.

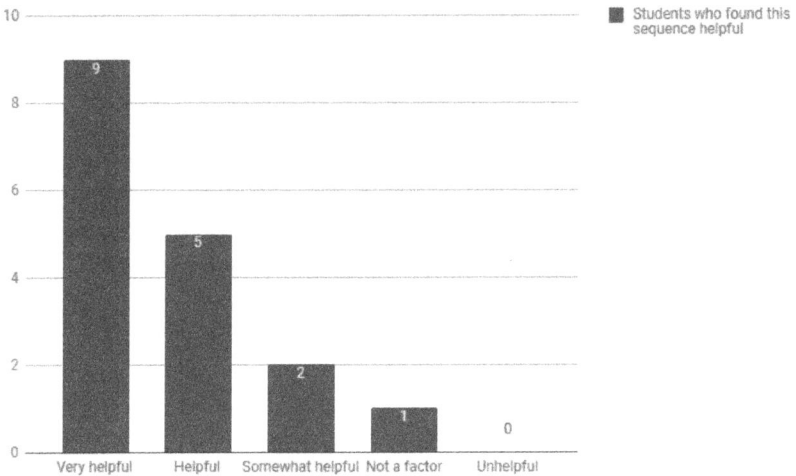

Fig. 1. Responses to the following question on an anonymous course evaluation survey: "On a scale of 1 to 5, how helpful have you found the weekly sequence of classes?"

However, some students struggled to make the transition from writing a print essay to writing a podcast script. In particular, students who were somewhat familiar with the narrative style and structure of podcasting prior to the course continued to create compelling episodes with dynamic and engaging audio narration. Meanwhile, students who were less familiar with podcasting continued to sound like they were simply reading a print essay. In subsequent iterations of this course, I would address this issue by dedicating more class time to workshopping the actual narration of students' podcasts, either through in-class peer review or in one-on-one conferences. Through this, students would come to see how writing for audio is more than just reading into a microphone. It requires careful attention sentence structure, pacing, and vocal inflection.

Another major change I made in the summer version of ENC 3310 was dedicating more time to listening to and analyzing podcasts in class. By diagramming and outlining different elements of a podcast episode—introductions, transitions, pacing, sound effects, etc.—students learned how to structure a podcast episode and employ the affordances of audio to create specific rhetorical effects. In a mid-semester evaluation survey, many students reported that this component of the course was the most helpful in scripting and producing their podcast episodes (see fig. 2).

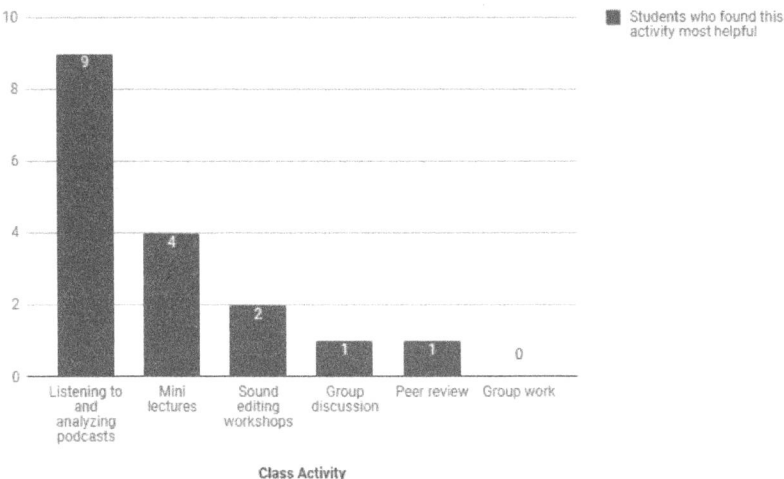

Fig. 2. Responses to the following question on an anonymous course evaluation survey: "What component of the course have you found most helpful?"

As the graph in figure two demonstrates, only a handful of students found the peer review component of the course helpful. At the end of the course, many students expressed frustration over our Friday listening sessions, noting that while they gave detailed feedback on other student's episodes they received only a couple of vague comments on their own episode. Logistically, I organized podcast peer review by compiling all of the students' podcast episodes into a shared Google document. Then, students would listen to at least three of their peer's episodes through headphones and provide feedback based on evaluative criteria I had displayed on a slide at the front of the class. Because students commented anonymously, many of them may have felt less accountable to their feedback. Peer review could have been improved if students had been able to listen to podcasts collectively rather than individually through headphones. In subsequent versions of this course, I would place students in listening groups where they would listen to one another's episodes one at a time and then provide feedback verbally. As Glynn Washington, the host of the critically acclaimed *Snap Judgment!* podcast points out, listening groups are common to audio editing practices because they help a podcaster understand how a listener might respond to their episode in real time, cluing them into those parts where people seem bored or confused (Abel 172).

Because the student learning outcomes of ENC 3310 are still primarily invested in the modes of exposition as they play out within print-genres, the podcasting assignment was somewhat limited in its emphasis on highly scripted audio storytelling. Although the main podcasting project aligned well with the learning outcomes of ENC 3310, these pedagogical goals sometimes prevented us from exploring more experimental and unscripted podcasting formats. For instance, many students expressed interest in creating a conversational style episode during the freestyle unit. In conversational podcasts, three or four speakers exchange ideas and opinions on a given topic in a loosely organized, organic format. Conversational podcasts are growing in popularity, and they can be rhetorically powerful texts for providing listeners with insight into the real-time thought processes and debates that come to inform people's opinions about nuanced, controversial topics. NPR's *Code Switch* podcast, for instance, employs a conversational style format while addressing a variety of cultural issues related to race, such as microaggressions, media stereotypes, and appropriation, among many others. Through this, *Code Switch* establishes a tone of exploration and discovery, thereby making the listener feel as if they are learning this information alongside the speakers.

However, conversation is not something that is usually taught in a writing course. Conversations are often unstructured, meandering, conflicted, and disorganized; they are antithetical to the clear and concise writing we emphasize in most writing courses. But polarizing issues are often difficult to work through in a clear and concise manner, and the genre of conversational podcasts offers writers a means for opening up alternative discursive frameworks for exploring controversial or nuanced topics. Thus, in future iterations of this course, I would consider adding a Composing for Conversations unit in which students learn effective rhetorical strategies for facilitating and leading productive and informative conversations, a skill that is becoming increasingly important in today's partisan political climate.

Conclusion

Ultimately, sound-based writing pedagogies should continue to pursue course designs that encourage students to compose within the unique genres and affordances of sound-media, from specific podcasting formats to non-discursive, embodied explorations of the rhetorics of sound. When we teach students how to compose in multiple media, we are teaching the same rhetorical and compositional skills we emphasize in courses with print-based assignments: audience, modes of exposition, rhetorical situation, etc. In fact, as I discovered in both semesters that I taught ENC 3310, allowing students to write in alternate modalities can sometimes work better than print assignments in encouraging revision and self-editing. As Jason Palmeri points out, audio essays challenge students "to carefully compose and rework their words over time (by writing, revising, and reperforming their alphabetic script)" (83). When students are required to perform their writing (even if into a microphone), they often take greater care with the structure and flow of their writing at the sentence and paragraph level. Indeed, in course feedback, many students reported increased awareness of stylistic concerns such as clarity and concision because they were challenged to read aloud and record their writing in a more permanent and public manner.

Composition teachers who are hesitant to assign multimodal work often operate under the false assumption that teaching students how to communicate through an alternate modality requires technical mastery by the instructor. However, such a belief betrays a fundamental misconception about the purpose of teaching multimodality in a writing course, which is not to turn writing students into multimedia production students but rather to introduce them to other "means of communicating effectively and productively" in a society in which information increasingly circulates through a variety of digital and non-digital platforms (Takayoshi and Selfe 9). Through this course design, I hope to inspire other writing teachers to pursue multimodal courses and assignments. In particular, I encourage those already incorporating multimodal work into their classes to consider taking a media-specific approach, if not through sound then through another medium like photography or video. A media-specific approach to multimodal composing is not only more feasible to execute logistically but also provides students with more time and resources to explore the rhetorical capabilities of a specific media form.

Acknowledgments

I am indebted to a number of rhetoric and composition scholars whose research and publicly available syllabi were influential to my decision to design a sound-based writing course, in particular, Byron Hawk, Casey Boyle, Steph Ceraso, and Eric Detweiler. I would also like to thank Shannon Butts and Madison Jones for their insightful feedback on my syllabus and course design drafts. Lastly, many thanks to the University of Florida English Department, in particular Sid Dobrin and Marsha Bryant, for giving me the opportunity to design a podcast-themed writing course for ENC 3310.

Notes

1. To listen to Lissa's minimal yet effective use of vox pop, listen to her podcast *WTF is Iran?* at https://soundcloud.com/lissa-a-639475725/wtf-is-iran-ep-2.

2. To listen to Kevin's use of vox pop in his podcast *American Borders*, visit https://soundcloud.com/kevin-artiga-941918905/american-borders-2.

3. To listen to this student's episode, visit https://soundcloud.com/kasey-veltman/dragon-age-and-story.

4. To listen to Johana's podcast *The Labyrinth,* visit https://soundcloud.com/thelabyrinthshow.

5. To listen to Emily's podcast *Dopa-Men...and Women*, visit https://soundcloud.com/user-242031722.

6. You can listen to this component of Savannah's location-based audio tour at https://soundcloud.com/user-577630566/alachuafrench-fries. Due to time constraints, I was not able to include a location-based audio tour assignment in my summer section of this course.

Works Cited

Abel, Jessica. *Out on the Wire: The Storytelling Secrets of the New Masters of Radio.* Broadway Books, 2015.

Alexander, Jonathan, and Jacqueline Rhodes. *On Multimodality: New Media in Composition Studies.* CCCC/NCTE, 2014.

Banks, Adam. "2015 CCCC Chair's Address: Ain't No Walls behind the Sky, Baby! Funk, Flight, Freedom." *CCC*, vol. 67, no. 2, 2015, pp. 267-79, ncte.org/library/NCTEFiles/Resources/Journals/CCC/0672-dec2015/CCC0672Address.pdf.

Ceraso, Steph. "(Re)Educating the Senses: Multimodal Listening, Bodily Learning, and the Composition of Sonic Experiences." *College English*, vol. 77, no. 2, 2014, pp. 102-23.

Ceraso, Steph, and Kati Fargo Ahern. "Composing with Sound." *Composition Studies*, vol. 43, no. 2, 2015, uc.edu/journals/composition-studies/issues/ceraso-and-ahern.html.

Dunn, Patricia, and Kathleen Dunn De Mers. "Reversing Notions of Disability and Accommodation: Embracing Universal Design in Writing Pedagogy and Web Space." *Kairos*, vol. 7, no. 1, spring 2002, technorhetoric.net/7.1/binder2.html?coverweb/dunn_demers/index.html.

Hawisher, Gail E., and Cynthia L. Selfe with Brittney Moraski and Melissa Pearson. "Becoming Literate in the Information Age: Cultural Ecologies and the Literacies of Technology." *CCC*, vol. 55, no. 4, Jun 2004, pp. 642-92.

"Interviewing with Your Skeptical Brain." *Howsound*, Transom, 12 Jan. 2016, transom.org/2016/interviewing-with-your-skeptical-brain/.

Palmeri, Jason. *Remixing Composition: A History of Multimodal Writing Pedagogy.* SIUP, 2012.

Selfe, Cynthia L. "The Movement of Air, the Breath of Meaning: Aurality and Multimodal Composing." *CCC*, vol. 60, no. 4, 2009, pp. 616-63.

Shut Up Little Man! Directed by Matthew Bate, Filmlab, 2011.

"Story Structure: The 'e'." *HowSound*, Transom, 11 Jan. 2016, transom.org/2016/story-structure-e/.

"Student Computing Requirements." *University of Florida-Information Technology*, 7 Aug. 2017, it.ufl.edu/policies/student-computing-requirements/.

Takayoshi, Pamela, and Cynthia L. Selfe. "Thinking about Multimodality." *Multimodal Composition: Resources for Teachers*, edited by Cynthia L. Selfe, Hampton, 2007.

"The Bank War." *Planet Money*, NPR, 24 Mar 2017, www.npr.org/sections/money/2017/03/24/521436839/episode-761-the-bank-war.

"The Ethics of Trespassing and Secret Recording." *Howsound*, Transom, 31 May 2016, transom.org/2016/ethics-trespassing-secret-recording/.

"The Infinite Dial." *Edison Research*, 2017. www.edisonresearch.com/infinite-dial-2017/.

Syllabus

ENC 3310: Writing through Podcasts

Course Overview

In general, expository writing simply refers to how writers use different organizational structures to present information in a clear, accessible manner. In fact, we draw on these various modes of exposition on a daily basis: we compare and contrast different ideas, we link causes to effects, and we describe problems and offer solutions. ENC 3310: Writing through Podcasts explores how the modes of exposition—definition, classification, etc.—are evolving alongside new modalities of writing. Specifically, this course will examine how the emergence of podcasting is transforming how writers explain, define, summarize, compare, and contrast different types of information through audio media. To this end, this course provides students with opportunities to demonstrate expository writing techniques through both print and sound-based media.

Course Objectives

- Identify expository writing techniques in print and audio media
- Classify basic narrative structures of podcasting
- Define key podcasting terms
- Analyze and explain specific audio storytelling techniques
- Compare and contrast different podcasting formats
- Script and produce a podcast mini-series
- Layer discursive and non-discursive audio (e.g., background music, sound effects, etc.) for rhetorical effect
- Adapt modes of expository writing to various podcasting formats
- Critique and revise audio texts

Major Assignments

Podcast Analysis, 200 points
Analyze how a podcaster(s) uses audio to tell a story, explore an idea, provide information, and/or to persuade an audience. Your analysis can be about a particular episode of the podcast or a technique you have observed throughout several different episodes. Prior to submitting your analysis, ensure that you have (1) clearly described the overall goals of the podcast and its intended audience, (2) focused on a specific audio technique used in the podcast (e.g., background music), (3) used specific examples in making claims about the podcast, and (4) built your analysis into a focused claim about the podcast's use of sound design (e.g., "*Radiolab* uses background

noises, music, and sound effects to induce subtle mood shifts in the listener.")

Podcast Proposal, 150 points
Write a proposal for a four-part podcast mini-series. Your proposal should include (1) a title, logo, and (optional) tagline for the podcast, (2) a survey of similar podcasts in your topic area and how your podcast is similar/different, and (3) a brief overview of your podcast miniseries including description of its format and ideas for specific episodes.

Podcasting, 400 points (100 per episode)
Create four episodes of a podcast related to a topic of your choosing. Each episode should be 5-10 minutes in length. Although you can make your podcast about any topic, each episode should follow a different format based on that week's theme. For the final episode, you can use any format or combination of formats.

- Ep. 1: Narrative
- Ep. 2: Vox pop
- Ep. 3: Interview
- Ep. 4: Freestyle

I will evaluate your podcast according to the following criteria:

- Does the podcast have a specific topic with clear, focused episodes?
- Does the podcast use background music and sound effects when appropriate?
- Is the narration written in a style appropriate to the podcast topic?
- Does the podcast introduce and organize ideas in a clear and effective manner?
- Do the podcast episodes have engaging introductions, clear transitions, and fully developed conclusions?
- Do the podcast episodes utilize appropriate narrative structures?

Discussion Posts, 150 points
At the beginning of each week, I will post links to several exemplary podcasts that will serve as models for that week's episode. Listen to at least one episode from each weekly list and write a discussion post about a specific technique used by the podcaster. For instance, you might describe how the podcaster uses music to create tone shifts, or you might describe the podcaster's unique style of interviewing.

Discussion Leader, 100 points
Sign up for one class period to lead discussion on that day's reading/

listening. Students signed up for that day should come prepared with at least 2-3 engaging questions about the day's texts. No more than four students can sign up to lead discussion for a given class period.

Course Materials

- Abel, Jessica. *Out on the Wire: The Storytelling Secrets of the New Masters of Radio*. Broadway Books, 2015.
- External USB condenser microphone. Do not rely on your built-in laptop/computer/smartphone microphone. Amazon has quite a few for sale under $50. Just read the reviews to make sure you're getting a good deal. Here are a few options:
  - Samson Go Mic ($36.30)
  - CAD U37 USB Studio Condenser Mic ($36.56)

Podcasting Resources

- TapeACall (https://www.tapeacall.com/)
- Getting Started with Audacity (http://multimedia.journalism.berkeley.edu/tutorials/audacity/)
- Found Sounds—Archiving Field Recordings (https://foundsounds.me/)
- Freesound.org (https://freesound.org/)
- YouTube Audio Library (https://www.youtube.com/audiolibrary/music)

Digital Texts (podcasts, online articles, etc.)

"8-bit Sounds." *Twenty Thousand Hertz* from Defacto Sound, n.d., https://www.20k.org/episodes/8-bit.

"3300 Greenmount." *Out of the Blocks* from WYPR, 25 May 2012, http://programs.wypr.org/podcast/out-blocks-%E2%80%93-3300-greenmount.

"After Party." *the memory palace* from Radiotopia, 14 Sep. 2012, http://thememorypalace.us/tag/donner-party/.

Allison, Jay. "The Basics." Transom, 4 Sep 2013, https://transom.org/2013/the-basics/.

"Chapter 1." *S-Town* from *Serial* and *This American Life*, 28 Mar. 2017 https://stownpodcast.org/chapter/1.

Clegg, River. "Honest Museum Audio Tour." *The New Yorker*, 5 Dec 2016, http://www.newyorker.com/magazine/2016/12/05/honest-museum-audio-tour.

"Could Solving This One Problem Solve All the Others?" *Freakonomics*,

5 Apr 2017, http://freakonomics.com/podcast/solving-one-problem-solve-others/.

"Cruel and Unusual." *More Perfect* from WNYC, 2 Jun 2016, http://www.wnyc.org/story/cruel-and-unusual/.

D'Angelo, Frank. "The Rhetoric of Ekphrasis." *Journal of Advanced Composition*, vol. 18, no. 3, 1998, pp. 439-47.

"Do Crickets Sing Hymns?" *Here Be Monsters* from KCRW, 16 Nov. 2013, http://www.hbmpodcast.com/podcast/hbm029-do-crickets-sing-hymns

"Doorstepping: The Uninvited Interview." *HowSound* from Transom, 20 Sep. 2016, https://transom.org/2016/doorstepping-uninvited-interview/.

"Finding Emilie." *Radiolab* from WNYC, n.d., http://www.radiolab.org/story/110206-finding-emilie/.

"Fracking." *Science Vs.* from Gimlet Media, 26 July 2016, https://gimletmedia.com/episode/fracking/.

Herships, Sally. "The Art Of the Pre-Interview." Transom, 25 Oct 2016, https://transom.org/2016/art-pre-interview/.

"How Not to Pitch a Billionaire." *StartUp* from Gimlet Media, 5 Sep. 2014, https://gimletmedia.com/episode/1-how-not-to-pitch-a-billionaire/.

"How Not to Write for Radio." *HowSound* from Transom, 23 Aug. 2016, https://transom.org/2016/not-write-radio/.

"Is Podcasting the Future or the Past?" *StartUp* from Gimlet Media, 5 Sep. 2014, https://gimletmedia.com/episode/2-is-podcasting-the-future-or-the-past/.

"Making the Hippo Dance." *Radiolab* from WNYC, 9 Sep. 2008, http://www.radiolab.org/story/91863-making-the-hippo-dance/.

McKibben, Bill. "The Pen is Easier Than the Mic." Transom, 2 Nov. 2006, https://transom.org/2006/the-pen-is-easier-than-the-mic/.

"Messy Nobel." *Planet Money* from NPR, 18 Nov 2016, http://www.npr.org/sections/money/2016/11/18/502475485/episode-736-messy-nobel.

"Mojave Phone Booth." *99% Invisible* from Radiotopia, 1 March 2016, http://99percentinvisible.org/episode/mojave-phone-booth/.

"On Your Mark. Get Set. Start Your Story." *HowSound* from Transom, 29 Nov. 2016, https://transom.org/2016/mark-get-set-start-story/.

"Open Office." *Planet Money* from NPR, 3 June 2016, http://www.npr.org/sections/money/2016/06/03/480625378/episode-704-open-office.

"Radio Rookies DIY Toolkit: How to Do Voxpop." WNYC, 16 Sep. 2013, https://www.youtube.com/watch?v=9ybkE3jEuzg.

"Radio Silence." *HowSound* from Transom, 12 Jul 2016, https://transom.org/2016/radio-silence/.

"Regrets, I've Had a Few." *This American Life* from WBEZ, 5 Dec 2014, https://www.thisamericanlife.org/radio-archives/episode/541/regrets-ive-had-a-few.

"Revealing Selfies. Not Like That." *Note to Self* from WNYC, 19 April 2017, http://www.wnyc.org/story/photo-metadata-translation/.

"Show, Don't Tell." *HowSound* from Transom, 4 April 2012, https://transom.org/2012/show-dont-tell/.

Shut Up Little Man! Directed by Matthew Bate, Filmlab, 2011.

"Sound Matters." *HowSound* from Transom, 9 Aug. 2016, https://transom.org/2016/sound-matters/.

"Sounds Natural." *99% Invisible* from Radiotopia, 18 April 2017, http://99percentinvisible.org/episode/sounds-natural/.

"Story Structure: The 'e'." *HowSound* from Transom, 11 Jan. 2016, https://transom.org/2016/story-structure-e/.

"The Alibi." *Serial* from This American Life, 3 Oct. 2014, https://serialpodcast.org/season-one/1/the-alibi.

"The Code Switch Guide to Handling Casual Racism." Code Switch from NPR, 28 Sep 2016, http://one.npr.org/?sharedMediaId=495473701:495719078.

"The Ethics of Trespassing and Secret Recording." *HowSound* from Transom, 31 May 2016, https://transom.org/2016/ethics-trespassing-secret-recording/.

"The Magnetic Fields." *Song Exploder* from Radiotopia, 12 Sep. 2015, http://songexploder.net/magnetic-fields

"The Sizzle." *99% Invisible* from Radiotopia, 13 Jan. 2015, http://99percentinvisible.org/episode/the-sizzle/.

"Tinkering with Sound Design." HowSound from Transom, 22 Mar 2016, https://transom.org/2016/tinkering-with-sound-design/.

Towne, Jeff. "Podcasting Basics, Part 2." *Transom*, 15 Mar. 2015, https://transom.org/2015/podcast-basics-part-2-software/.

"Underdog." *Reply All* from Gimlet Media, 8 Apr 2015, https://gimletmedia.com/episode/19-underdog/.

Weiner, Jonah. "What Makes Podcasts so Addictive and Pleasurable?" *Slate*, 14 Dec. 2014, http://www.slate.com/articles/arts/ten_years_in_your_ears/2014/12/what_makes_podcasts_so_addictive_and_pleasurable.html.

"What the Falcon's Up with Qatar?" *Planet Money* from NPR, 16 June 2017, http://www.npr.org/sections/money/2017/06/16/533272737/episode-778-what-the-falconS-up-with-qatar.

Course Schedule

Week 1: Analyzing Podcasts

- Science versus "Fracking"
- Planet Money, "Open Office"
- Serial, "The Alibi"

Monday
- Read:
  - Syllabus, major assignment descriptions
  - Bill McKibben, "The Pen is Easier Than the Mic"
- In-Class: 99% Invisible, The Sizzle

Tuesday
- Listen: Howsound, "Story Structure"
- In-Class: Analyzing Podcasts
  - Group 1: Here Be Monsters, "Do Crickets Sing Hymns?"
  - Group 2: Planet Money, "What the Falcon's Up with Qatar?"
  - Group 3: Startup, "Is Podcasting the Future or the Past"
  - Group 4: Note to Self, "Revealing Selfies. Not Like That."
  - Group 5: 99% Invisible, "Sounds Natural"

Wednesday
- Read: Jonah Weiner, "What makes podcasts so addictive and pleasurable?"
- Listen: S-Town, "Chapter 1"
- In-class: Podcast analysis examples

Thursday
- Read: Jeff Towne, "Podcasting Basics, Part 2"
- In-class: Audio workshop (Bring in condenser mic)
  - Downloading software
  - Setting up recording environment
  - Importing/exporting files
  - Basic audio editing

Friday
- Due: Podcast analysis (bring two copies printed and stapled to class)
- In-class: Introduce podcasting assignment

Week 2: Planning Podcasts
- Radiolab, "Making the Hippo Dance"
- 99% Invisible, "Mojave Phone Booth"
- Startup, "How Not to Pitch to a Billionaire"

Monday
- Read: "Out on the Wire" (p. 1-43)

Tuesday
- No Class (holiday)

Wednesday
- Read: "Out on the Wire" (p. 47-76)
- Listen: Howsound, "How not to write for Radio"
- In-class: Radiolab, "Finding Emilie"

Thursday
- Listen: Howsound, "Sound Matters"
- In-class: Audio Editing Workshop
    - Recording audio
    - Audio effects (compressor, noise reducer)
    - Create podcast intros
    - Friday
- Due: Podcast Proposal
- In-class: Peer-review proposals (bring in three copies, printed and stapled)

Week 3: Narrative
- The Memory Palace, "After Party"
- Here Be Monsters, "Do Crickets Sing Hymns?"
- Twenty-Thousand Hertz, "8-bit Sounds"

Monday
- Listen: HowSound, "On Your Mark. Get Set. Start Your Story"
- In-Class: Workshop introductions

Tuesday
- Read: Frank D'Angelo, "The Rhetoric of Ekphrasis"
- Listen: Howsound, "Show don't tell"
- In-class: Discussion, Ekphrasis activity

Wednesday
- In-class: Individual conferences, workshop scripts

Thursday
- In-class: Audio Workshop
    - Sound effects
    - Adding music
    - Editing podcast episodes
    - Soundcloud

Friday
- Due: Podcast episode one

Week 4: Audio Vérite
- More Perfect, "Cruel and Unusual"
- Out of the Blocks, "3300 Greenmount"

Monday
- Listen: HowSound, "Doorstepping"
- Read: "Out on the Wire" (p. 109-143)
- In-class: "How to do Vox pop" YouTube video, Voxpop workshop/planning

Tuesday
- In-class: *Shut up Little Man!* screening

Wednesday
- Read: "Out on the Wire" (p. 147-201)
- Listen: Howsound, "The Ethics of Trespassing and Secret Recording"
- In-class: Discuss ethics of audio verite

Thursday
- In-class: Audio editing workshop

Friday
- Due: Podcast episode two

Week 5: Interviews
- Song Exploder, "The Magnetic Fields"
- Freakonomics, "Could Solving This One Problem Solve All the Others?"
- Reply All, "Underdog"

Monday
- Read: Jay Allison, "The Basics"
- Listen: This American Life, "Regrets, I've Had a Few"
- In-class: Conducting Interviews mini-lesson

Tuesday
- Read: Sally Herships, "The Art of the Pre-Interview"
- In-class: Workshop interview questions

Wednesday
- Listen: Howsound, "Tinkering with Sound Design"
- In-class: sound design adaptation activity

Thursday
- In-class: workshop on editing raw audio from interview

Friday
- Due: Podcast episode three

Week 6: Freestyle
- Planet Money, "Messy Nobel"
- Code Switch, "The Code Switch Guide to Handling Casual Racism"

Monday
- Listen: Howsound, "Radio Silence"

Writing through Podcasts 161

Tuesday
- In-class: Class discussion on use of silence as rhetorical

- Listen: Janet Cardiff "The Missing Voice: Case Study B Part One"
- In-class: River Clegg, "Honest Museum Audio Tour

Wednesday
- In-class: Workshop scripts

Thursday
- In-class: Troubleshooting final episode

Friday
- Due: Podcast episode four
- In-class: Course wrap up discussion

Sociolinguistics for Language and Literacy Educators

Missy Watson

Research in sociolinguistics offers important understandings of the social dynamics impacting how language is acquired, used, perceived, and treated in the U.S. and beyond. It provides opportunities to critically examine societal structures and attitudes surrounding language (including our own beliefs) that create and uphold social and racial hierarchies—a worthwhile pursuit for any educator. As teachers of composition, we are implicated by these and other social, linguistic, raced, gendered, and political realities, which not only affect our students and us, but also reflect and maintain our pedagogies and the educational systems in which we participate.

In the graduate course I describe, Sociolinguistics for Language and Literacy Educators (SLLE), students examine research in sociolinguistics to better understand how language and society are entangled. Through this examination, they contemplate how and why teachers of language and literacy might better understand and address such interrelations. This course serves as one example for how graduate programs in composition and rhetoric might develop seminars that introduce to new teachers the relevant and too often overlooked scholarship coming out of sociolinguistics.

Institutional Context

This graduate seminar is part of the Master's Program in Language and Literacy at City College of New York (City College). City College is part of the City University of New York (CUNY) structure, a massive and strikingly diverse public university system connecting twenty-four higher education institutions in New York City ("Colleges and Schools"). Collectively, the quarter of a million students enrolled in CUNY colleges ("Total Enrollment") speak over 170 languages ("A Profile") and represent more than 125 countries ("Country of Birth"). City College, which enrolls approximately 16,000 students each year ("Total Enrollment"), was the first college established in the CUNY system as well as first in the nation to offer free higher education, beginning in 1874 ("Our History"). The institution, and the CUNY system more generally, has also been the site of public debate surrounding open enrollment in the 1970s (Lavin and Hyllegard), "remediation phase-out" controversies in 2000 (Gleason "Remediation"), as well as the site of important research in the fields of composition and basic writing, namely from scholars Mina Shaughnessy, Marilyn Sternglass, and Mary Soliday.

The English Department at City College has the largest faculty on campus and is home to a first-year composition program, four undergraduate programs (Literature, Secondary English Education, Creative Writing, and an English Minor), and three graduate programs (Language and Literacy, English Literature, and Creative Writing). The Language and Literacy MA program (hereafter L&L) was developed in 1975 by Mina Shaughnessy and was reconfigured and re-named by Marilyn Sternglass who envisioned the program as preparing English language and literacy teachers working in high school, college, and community settings (Gleason "Reasoning"). Barbara Gleason, who has directed the graduate program since 2003, shifted the program's theoretical and pedagogical focus to prepare teachers to primarily work with adult learners. Thus, the program is distinctive not only for its historical status and urban location, but also for its blending of linguistics and composition and its emphasis on teaching adult English language learners across institutional and community contexts.

Each year, the L&L program serves an average of twenty-eight matriculated students who are diverse in their interests, identities, and cultural and linguistic backgrounds. Most, however, are natives or long-time residents of New York City who work full-time, with some already working or volunteering as English teachers or tutors in community centers, language institutes, libraries, high schools, and colleges. The MA program requires students to complete four core courses, six electives, and a foreign language requirement. Core courses include Introduction to Language Studies, Second Language Acquisition, Theories and Models of Literacy, and Adult Learners of Language and Literacy. Sociolinguistics[1] is one of a handful of electives available in and beyond the L&L program that students may take to fulfill elective requirements. SLLE is my version of this course. Other recently offered electives include Digital Literacies, Contemporary Composition Pedagogies, Introduction to Teaching Composition and Literature, Basic Writing Theory and Practice, and Teaching Adult Writers in Diverse Contexts.

Over the fifteen-week semester, students of SLLE engage in cross-disciplinary readings, a range of reflective and research assignments, and weekly seminar discussions. The course invites students to examine how language attitudes impact the material realities of their current and future students and how standard language ideology shapes their own perceptions and practices as new or developing teachers of English language and composition. The course begins with a survey of sociolinguistics research to introduce fundamental findings on linguistic variance, cultural perceptions of language, the bonds between identity and language, and the sociopolitical dynamics of accents, dialects, and multilingualism. Building from this foundational knowledge in sociolinguistics, students then study (and interrogate) an array of linguistic myths, such as the myth of non-accents, the myth of standard language, and the myth of nonstandardized varieties being inadequate or substandard. Then, the bulk of the course's content is to attend carefully to what sociolinguistics teaches us about the ways language is used in the U.S. to identify, subordinate, and discriminate against groups of people, while the assignments and class discussions ask students to draw connections between research in sociolinguistics and in composition studies and to reflect on their own experiences with language and teaching.

Theoretical Rationale

This course emerged from my perspective that teachers of English language and literacy are long overdue in coming to terms with the ways our classrooms perpetuate standard language ideology, a belief system that has for decades been exposed as oppressive to marginalized groups of people. Based on the research of James Milroy and Rosina-Lippi Green, I have elsewhere defined standard language ideology as "the unquestioned belief system that assigns the written language variety of a privileged group as standard (and superior) and all others nonstandard (and inferior), a worldview uncritically assumed neutral and commonsensical but used as an instrument for social stratification and maintaining the interests of privileged groups" (Watson). Since standard language ideology works to uphold social and racial hierarchies, it seems essential that all instructors of writing, new and seasoned alike, examine the ways this harmful belief system permeates our field's teaching practices. However, while numerous scholars across fields have revealed for nearly fifty years the problems with privileging and standardizing American Academic English[2] (among other standardized varieties across the globe), we have consistently faltered in composition studies and in higher education at large to determine an effective and ethical path forward. In a field that prides itself on striving for social justice, the very essence of our identity—being experts of standardized English—is wrapped up in this problematic and harmful ideology. This must be acknowledged and tended to in a variety of ways, including through the training of new teachers. In the past, I have typically drawn on research from composition studies to examine monolingualist ideologies with undergraduate students, graduate students, and new writing teachers. However, and importantly, it wasn't until I began focusing on research in sociolinguists that I actually felt successful in effectively introducing and exploring with newcomers the sociopolitics of language and monolingualist ideologies.

Thus, I see a focus on sociolinguistics, especially research on standard language ideology, as instrumental in compelling new teachers to begin reassessing their own affinities for Standardized English (SE) and their roles in perpetuating standard language ideology. I concur with Melinda J. McBee Orzulak that "writing teacher education may benefit from a more explicit focus on language, specifically standard language ideology" primarily because, as she argues, "The traditional position of writing teachers as standard-bearers, or 'gatekeepers,' creates potential conflicting ideologies for pre-service teachers who are also taught about language variety and culturally relevant pedagogy during teacher education" (12). While McBee Orzulak's research is on pre-service teachers destined for K-12 institutional contexts, her findings are relevant for college composition. As she indicates, we send a contradictory message when we impress upon new teachers the need to treat students and their writing in more linguistically and culturally inclusive ways without also simultaneously deconstructing the age-old tradition of focusing on rhetorical and grammatical deviations of SE and honoring our profession's deeply entrenched (but linguistically false) assumptions about the superiority of SE. Examining research on sociolinguistics and standard language ideology helps with this sort of deconstruction process.

I'll be the first to say that a single course taught, even at multiple institutions across the nation, will not solve the problem of standard language ideology. Training new teachers about the ills of standard language ideology is far from all that needs done, but I believe it should be part of what we do. When we teach composition, we should examine with students standard language ideology, and when we train new teachers, we should examine with them standard language ideology (Watson and Shapiro). I should also emphasize that this argument for infusing sociolinguistics into the research and teaching of composition studies is far from new. In the 1970s we saw our interest in borrowing from sociolinguistics peak with the movement and research leading up to the "CCCC Resolution on Students Right to Their Own Language," a statement that primarily prevails on the research of sociolinguists. My course is one effort suggesting that we still have much to gain by returning to sociolinguistics.

That said, I adjusted the title of my course from Sociolinguistics to Sociolinguistics for Language and Literacy Educators to represent my objective to narrow the course's focus to the specific areas of inquiry in sociolinguistics that are particularly useful and applicable for the teaching of English and composition. Our field's distancing from linguistics and other language studies (Matsuda "Composition Studies") has led composition instructors and researchers to feel resistant to (or simply unaware of) arguments on the benefits of familiarizing ourselves with its literature and of discovering ways to borrow from its findings. A subfield of linguistics that centers on social, cultural, political, and rhetorical aspects of languaging, sociolinguistics is already closely aligned to our field's research and pedagogies. Thus, the course aims to introduce composition newcomers to the research in sociolinguistics that reveals how languaging works and how social and political dynamics impact language use and users.

Importantly, the three main texts I use are written for newcomers or outsiders, and so the texts offer accessible introductions without overuse of disciplinary-specific knowledge or language. The first text students read is John Edwards *Sociolinguistics: A Very Short Introduction*, which covers the research of the field in a short enough text to make a comprehensive survey manageable and beneficial. In the first half of the text, Edwards discusses the field's findings that demonstrate the undeniable connections between language and identity. This realization alone can be fundamental for composition teachers who may have not fully considered the ways that our assessments of students' language and writing, no matter our best intentions and mindful pedagogies, ultimately function as assessments of students' identities. The second text that students read is Laurie Bauer and Peter Trudgill's *Language Myths*, which can be likened to *Bad Ideas about Writing*, edited by Cheryl E. Ball and Drew M. Loewe. Both are edited collections written for public audiences, with each chapter written by a different expert in the field and focusing on deconstructing a specific myth about language or writing, respectively. As far as I'm concerned, Bauer and Trudgill's text is a must-read for anyone still steeped in harmful myths about the value of language variance, the validity of dialects, and the relationship between grammaticality, communicability, and rhetorical effectiveness.

Finally, the third and most central text in the course is Rosina Lippi-Green's *English with an Accent: Language, Ideology, and Discrimination in the United States*. The textbook reveals and challenges unfounded beliefs that fuel our uncritical acceptance of standard language ideology. In her first chapter, "Linguistic Facts of Life," Lippi-Green unpacks the following notions about language, which are common knowledge in linguistics and sociolinguistics:

- All spoken language changes.
- All spoken languages are equal in linguistic terms.
- Grammaticality does not equal communicative effectiveness.
- Written language and spoken language are historically, structurally, and functionally fundamentally different creatures.
- Variation is intrinsic to all spoken language at every level. (6-7)

These facts, based on empirical research in linguistics, help show how nonsensical it is to try to control and standardize language, to hierarchize languages and their users, to assume standardized grammar is necessary for communication, to conflate our expectations for writing and speaking, and to seek the homogenization of languages. What makes this text so compelling is Lippi-Green's relentlessness in providing case after case of how standard language ideology has guided the subordination of languages and language communities by way of educational practices and standards, the authorizing endeavors of pundits and teachers, representations of language difference in the media (including children's cartoons), housing and workplace policies, the judicial system, and so much more. This is an important outcome afforded by research in sociolinguistics and especially by this text.

In addition to being more mindful of including sociolinguistics research, SLLE serves as a response to calls for fostering in teachers translingual dispositions toward writing (Horner et al.) and for accessing the decades worth of scholarship beyond our field on language theories and pedagogies (Atkinson; Matsuda "Composition Studies"). However, when we in composition studies look to other disciplines (such as sociolinguistics but also education, TESOL, and second language writing) for insights on how language and language teaching works, we should be mindful of the explicitly political and praxis-driven approaches, or lack thereof, that accompany cross-disciplinary research and pedagogy.[3] Not all disciplines and researchers are as determined to actively intervene in the ways that standard language ideology serves to hierarchize languages and language users.

We in composition have long recognized that all pedagogies represent and perpetuate certain ideologies of the instructor, department, institution, discipline, and local and cultural contexts. As James Berlin put it in 1988, "a way of teaching is never innocent. Every pedagogy is imbricated in ideology, in a set of tacit assumptions about what is real, what is good, what is possible, and how power ought to be distributed" (492). In the context of our teaching and research, we must acknowledge our own individual subjectivities, how dominant discourses shape our subjectivities, and how that plays out in our work. As indicated above, the design of this course stems from my own political commitments to combat standard language ideology. I realize that in countering standard language ideology through what and how I teach SLLE, I am endorsing and promoting a new competing ideology, one based in critical language studies and critical pedagogies. As I discuss in the next section, among other topics, explicitly embracing and owning a political approach affords various benefits and challenges.

Critical Reflections

SLLE invites examinations of the oft invisible and unacknowledged language ideologies engrained within our institutions, our classrooms, and our very own perspectives and practices. Because such inquiries can be intellectually and emotionally staggering, I aimed to provide various outlets for dialogue and reflection. Alongside weekly seminar discussions, I designed and implemented various avenues for dialogue and reflection, which, from my perspective, were of the most beneficial pedagogical moves I made. Importantly,

I treated "the personal" and storytelling as part of our shared content and practice from the start. This propelled us into interpersonal engagement, and it set the stage for a semester-long commitment to our respective narratives, community building, and critical reflection. At the end of the semester, numerous students cited the practice of sharing narratives as among the most memorable and meaningful moments of the class.

But I found the reflective writing assignments students completed to be the most instrumental to shaping learning. Students wrote four short reflections at various points in the semester wherein they communicated to me thoughts they wanted to share on the course and its content, including but not limited to their interpretations of the texts, their ideas about projects, their questions about sticky concepts, their reactions (positive and negative) to the readings, and, often, personal anecdotes representing a full range of emotions. I wrote each student back, responding to their specific ideas and questions, posing additional questions to consider, providing my own narratives that resonated with theirs, and/or directing them to readings or other resources. At the end of the semester, all students indicated that they found this "pen-pal" assignment to be of the most significant throughout the semester in developing their thinking about the topic as well as enhancing teacher/student communications and fostering individualized mentorship. Then, for their final reflection essay, students revisited and closely analyzed their four reflections, extrapolating the most meaningful developments in their thinking.

As the instructor, I found writing back-and-forth with students to be instrumental in getting to know them and their interests, learning more about their ideas and needs, picking up on issues and questions overlooked or unattended to in class, and providing individualized feedback on a semi-regular basis. While not all students were convinced by the purposes and power of reflection, I concluded that this was an unavoidable and not necessarily unwanted outcome when engaging with such politicized content. I cherished the moments of groundbreaking realizations I witnessed, but I also found invaluable the responses focused more on summarizing readings or those that provided offhand rants over semi-related topics. The choice of topic and style was theirs to make, and I can't assume which approaches would or should prove more meaningful to students.

Challenges with Applying Theory to Practice

Although I'm pleased to report that students' responses to the course have been overwhelmingly positive, there remain various challenges and limitations to the design. A major concern that I continue to grapple with is how to best respond to those students who want to resist standard language ideology but also feel at a loss over how to do so. I realized after teaching a previous version of the course in 2014 that I offered too few opportunities to brainstorm teaching applications. In response, I designed in 2017 a different major assignment, the praxis project, which tasked students with selecting and exploring a topic we covered in class and then designing a lesson plan demonstrating their applications of theory into practice. The final product was to resemble more or less the very genre in which I'm writing now (although written prospectively rather than retrospectively). While I found the praxis project a worthwhile method for applying sociolinguistics theory to pedagogical design, the assignment needs some rethinking and needs to be supplemented by other opportunities for practical applications. Some students expressed disappointment over not being able to immerse themselves more within certain course topics that interested them, while some of the newer students expressed wanting to get better acquainted with the field and pedagogy more generally before designing and theoretically grounding teaching materials.

After much consideration, and as my appended syllabus shows, I offered students the option to engage in a more exploratory and research-driven project, the extended researched essay, instead of completing the praxis project. This option also provided those students who were unconvinced by or uninterested in arguments for contesting standard language ideology the choice to explore what they felt were more pragmatic topics. Of seventeen students, ten chose the extended researched essay over the praxis project. It's worth noting, however, that this option did not prove to be an "out" for students uncomfortable with the controversies examined in our course. Nine out of ten students who completed the researched essay chose to study more closely standard language ideology (based on Lippi-Green's text) or anti-racist assessment (based on Inoue's *Antiracist Writing Assessment Ecologies: Teaching and Assessing Writing for a Socially Just Future*), while just one student in the class selected a more general topic in sociolinguistics to investigate. Moving forward, I intend to continue providing both options, despite being worried that opportunities to apply sociolinguistics research to pedagogical design will then be more limited for those who choose the researched essay.

No matter their choice for the final assignment, students seemed to be aligned in their concern over the dominance of standard language ideology but baffled over what will truly help unravel it. And, as I assured them, they are far from alone and have good reason to feel so unsettled. It may feel daunting if not futile when tackling problems in the classroom that are ideologically engrained in the fabric of our society. Furthermore, composition studies has not fully come to terms with standard language ideology, nor have we settled on the best practices that should emerge from contesting the dominance of SE. Thus, I certainly cannot anticipate a seamless process from engagement in these controversial topics to practical application in my graduate classroom. In future classes, however, I may include scholarship contesting monolingualist ideologies from scholars working in translingualism, SRTOL, second language writing, basic writing, assessment, transnational literacies, and/or new literacy studies. At the very least, I intend to continue grappling with this dilemma, remaining patient with and forgiving of how incomplete, flawed, or unwieldy our ideas for pedagogical transformation will inevitably be.

Political Teaching and the Emotional Labor that Follows

It's safe to say that most teachers of English language and literacy seek and continue working in this profession with the best intentions to help students harness the language of power. This is certainly the case for graduate students in the L&L program who typically pursue the degree in hopes of attaining teaching positions in New York City programs and institutions that serve primarily people of color, adult English language learners, refugees, immigrants, and the children of immigrants. Serving these populations makes it difficult at times for teachers to come to grips with the effects of unquestioned privileging of SE. In short, it hurts some English instructors to discover that SE, the tool of their trade and source of their expertise, is not linguistically superior and that SE often works to sustain rather than level the socioeconomic gaps in the U.S.

Even knowing this, I was interested in how much time and debate we as a group needed to recognize the myth of SE's superiority and to debunk beliefs that it is more valid, versatile, appropriate, effective, and accessible than other language varieties. I happened to teach Lippi-Green's chapter on "The Standard Language Myth" to L&L students the same week I taught it in my undergraduate composition classrooms. I observed with interest (as did my graduate student teaching mentee who participated in both classroom discussions) how quickly my undergraduate students grasped and concurred with the ideas in this chapter, while my graduate students needed a bit more time to process it and flesh out all their (many) counter arguments.

Explicitly addressing the politics of standard language ideology in any classroom is likely to make the instructor and students feel uncomfortable at times, and not all parties are going to welcome the sort of emotional labor required to "stay" with and emerge out of such discomfort (Micciche). Even instructors and students who willingly devote the affective labors needed to grapple with ideological controversies will find themselves feeling troubled at times with content or conversations surrounding content. The range of stances students took, coupled with the fact that many of our topics were political and controversial, placed additional (but arguably important and fruitful) demands on students as well as me as the instructor. Research that invites teachers of

English to consider the importance of contesting standard language ideology is likely to invite challenges and require more time and different strategies from instructors.

I endeavored to steer classroom dialogue diplomatically without, at the same time, avoiding the productive discomfort that may arise from conflicting stances on the politics of standard language ideology, including my own. There were some students who digested the course with great interest and without any reservations, but most expressed (at some point or another) feeling uneasy, shocked, angry, overwhelmed, even exhausted by the content. In students' written reflections, I heard repeatedly that the content was emotionally draining on them—that, especially when tackling the latter half of Lippi-Green's book, it was just too discouraging for them to keep reading week after week cases where language was used as a tool for discrimination in the U.S. Further, a handful of students shared in their reflections emotional accounts detailing how they had been judged or mistreated due to language differences or, alternatively, how they themselves had judged or mistreated others for the same reason. The new interpretations of past events that were gained when processing course content proved upsetting to some. And since these anecdotes, as mentioned above, often transferred over to classroom discussion, other students were pulled into the emotional labor upon hearing about their classmates' experiences. To be clear, no students indicated experiencing any sort of serious distress requiring special attention or treatment in or beyond the classroom, but it is also safe to assume that the content of the course and the reflection-based assignments invited more affective processing as compared to other courses students had taken in our program.

While I consider the negotiations of emotional labor to be one of the ongoing challenges of this course, I also consider it an essential and necessary feature and, ultimately, a benefit. And I should add that the emotions experienced weren't always grim—far from it. Students frequently expressed feelings of intense curiosity, intrigue, hope, and relief that these topics were being addressed, and determination about coming to terms with standard language ideology in the teaching of English language and literacy. And, of course, not all students delved so emotionally deep into the topics we covered; indeed, two students indicated to me in their final reflection essays that they wished the course focused instead on a more neutral examination of sociolinguistics as a field.

At the end of the semester, one of these students also offered me valuable criticism of the course. The student expressed disapproval of how political the classroom had become and how much agreement there was over the importance of contesting standard language ideology through our approaches to teaching English language and literacy. Although the student appreciated that our discussions of sociolinguistic theory and pedagogical practice were centered on social justice, a focus the student likewise appreciated, the student worried that emphasizing the reshaping of pedagogies to suit the linguistic needs and strengths of oppressed groups would eventually work to reverse (rather than level) social, racial, and linguistic hierarchies. I explained that the student was not alone in this concern and that similar criticisms had been made recently against translingual approaches to writing (see Jordan; Matsuda "The Lure"; Shipka). We spent time together discussing how revealing injustice and working to dismantle oppressive ideologies and practices does not and should not equate to, as Jody Shipka puts it in her discussion of translingualism and transmodality, "inverting existing hierarchies, substituting one set of sign systems, meaning-making strategies, and communicative technologies for another while working to denigrate what has come before" (255-56). I emphasized this point by referring to the work of feminists and racial justice workers, who aim to end inequality, not attain superiority for women and people of color. Our dialogue was collegial and seemed fruitful. I find this student's perspective important and I'll be sure to raise it more explicitly when I teach the course again.

I intend to continue being explicit about my political position on advocating for new pedagogical approaches in light of what sociolinguists have uncovered about the oppressive nature of SE. I will continue to invite and respect perspectives that conflict with my and others' stances, and I will emphasize that while the choice for what to do with this information is theirs to make, we can no longer ignore or deny the oppressive realities of SE and our role as teachers in maintaining its privileged status. Finally, I am interested in seeing the content of this course be transferred to one of the L&L MA program's required courses, Introduction to Language, making the sociopolitics of language and standard language ideology more central to our students' introductory inquiries. My greater hope, however, is that other instructors across institutions will likewise work to see examinations of sociolinguistics and standard language ideology become a regularly offered course topic in composition graduate programs.

Acknowledgments

I'd like to thank Barbara Gleason and Laura Micciche for their careful reading of this manuscript and the invaluable feedback they offered.

Notes

1. The official title and description for this course at City College is as follows: English B6100, "Sociolinguistics: Variation in language from a social, linguistic and cultural orientation."

2. See the works of Suresh Canagarajah, Keith Gilyard, Nancy H. Hornberger, Bruce Horner, Braj B. Kachru, Ryuko Kubota, Rosina Lippi-Green, Min-Zhan Lu,

James Milroy, Leslie Milroy, Alastair Pennycook, Robert Phillipson, James Sledd, Geneva Smitherman, John Trimbur, Victor Villanueva, Terrence G. Wiley, Walt Wolfram, and Vershawn Ashanti Young, among many others.

3. In particular, I found myself struggling some with teaching John Edward's book, *A Short Introduction to Sociolinguistics* given his disavowing of more critical approaches to studying and revitalizing languages. Of course, it was useful to have students engage this perspective because it is part of a much larger trend whereby scholars *observe what is* rather than *take a stance and intervene in what's problematic*. Because of the inevitable but important epistemological and political differences across fields of study, interdisciplinary readings can require more time unpacking the histories and ideologies that inform the scholarship and scholars we read.

Works Cited

Atkinson, Dwight; Crusan, Deborah; Matsuda, Paul Kei; Ortmeier-Hooper, Christina; et al. "Clarifying the Relationship between L2 Writing and Translingual Writing: An Open Letter to Writing Studies Editors and Organization Leaders." *College English*, vol. 77, no. 4, 2015, pp. 383-86.

Ball, Cheryl E., and Drew M. Loewe, editors. *Bad Ideas About Writing*. West Virginia University Libraries Digital Publishing Institute, 2017.

Bauer, Laurie, and Peter Trudgill, editors. *Language Myths*. Vol. 20, Penguin UK, 1998.

Berlin, James A. "Rhetoric and Ideology in the Writing Class." *College English*, vol. 50, no. 5, 1988, pp. 477-94.

"Colleges and Schools." *City University of New York*, www2.cuny.edu/about/colleges-schools/.

Conference on College Composition and Communication, *CCCC Resolution on Students' Right to Their Own Language*. CCCC, 1974.

Edwards, John. *Sociolinguistics: A Very Short Introduction*. Vol. 365, Oxford UP, 2013.

Gleason, Barbara. "Reasoning the Need: Graduate Education and Basic Writing." *Journal of Basic Writing*, vol. 25, no. 2, 2006, pp. 49-75.

—. "Remediation Phase-out at CUNY: The 'Equity versus Excellence' Controversy." *CCC*, vol. 51, no. 3, 2000, pp. 488-91.

Horner, Bruce, Min-Zhan Lu, Jacqueline Jones Royster, and John Trimbur. "Language Difference in Writing: Toward a Translingual Approach." *College English*, vol. 73, no. 3, 2011, pp. 303-21.

Inoue, Asao. *Antiracist Writing Assessment Ecologies: Teaching and Assessing Writing for a Socially Just Future*. Parlor Press, 2015.

Jordan, Jay. "Material Translingual Ecologies." *College English*, vol. 77, no. 4, 2015, pp. 364-82.

Lavin, David E., and David Hyllegard. *Changing the Odds. Open Admissions and the Life Chances of the Disadvantaged*. Yale UP, 1996.

Lippi-Green, Rosina. *English With an Accent: Language, Ideology, and Discrimination in the United States*. 2nd ed., Routledge, 2012.

Matsuda, Paul Kei. "Composition Studies and ESL Writing: A Disciplinary Division of Labor." *CCC*, vol. 50, no. 4, 1999, pp. 699-721.

—. "The Lure of Translingual Writing." *PMLA*, vol. 129, no. 3, 2014, pp. 478-83.

McBee Orzulak, Melinda J. "Gatekeepers and Guides: Preparing Future Writing Teachers to Negotiate Standard Language Ideology." *Teaching/Writing: The Journal of Writing Teacher Education*, vol. 2, no. 1, 2013, pp. 12-21.

Micciche, Laura. "Staying with Emotion." *Composition Forum*, vol. 34, 2016.

"Our History." *The City College of New York*, www.ccny.cuny.edu/about/history.

"A Profile of Undergraduates at CUNY Senior and Community Colleges: Fall 2016." *Current Student Data Book by Subject*. Office of Institutional Research, City University Of New York, www2.cuny.edu/wp-content/uploads/sites/4/page-assets/about/administration/offices/oira/institutional/data/current-student-data-book-by-subject/ug_student_profile_f16.pdf.

Shipka, Jody. "Transmodality in/and Processes of Making: Changing Dispositions and Practice." *College English*, vol. 78, no. 3, 2016, pp. 250-57.

"Total Enrollment by Undergraduate and Graduate Level, Full-time/Part-time Attendance, and College, Fall 2016." *Current Student Data Book by Subject*. Office of Institutional Research, City University Of New York, www.cuny.edu/irdatabook/rpts2_AY_current/ENRL_0001_UGGR_FTPT.rpt.pdf.

Watson, Missy. "Contesting Standardized English." *Academe*, May-June 2018.

Watson, Missy, and Rachael Shapiro. "Clarifying the Multiple Dimensions of Monolingualism: Keeping Our Sights on Language Politics." *Composition Forum*, vol. 38, spring 2018.

Syllabus: Sociolinguistics for the Language & Literacy Educator

Description and Trajectory

In this course, we will study some of the ways language and society are entangled, and we will explore how and why teachers of language and literacy might better understand and address such interrelations. Sociolinguistics provides an important backdrop for understanding the social dynamics behind how language is used, perceived, and treated in the U.S. and beyond. It provides opportunities to critically examine societal structures and attitudes surrounding language (including our own beliefs) that create and uphold social hierarchies—a worthwhile pursuit for any educator. As teachers of language and literacy, we are implicated by these and other social, linguistic, raced, gendered, and political realities, which not only affect our students and us but also reflect and maintain our pedagogies and the educational systems in which we participate.

We'll begin with a survey of the field's collective knowledge on cultural perceptions of language; the bonds between identity and language; linguistic histories, variance, and change; as well as the social and political dynamics of accents, dialects, and multilingualism. Building from this knowledge, we will study (and interrogate) an array of linguistic myths, such as the myth of non-accents, the myth of standard language, and the myth of nonstandardized varieties being inadequate, and we'll consider what sociolinguists say about how language is used in the U.S. to identify, subordinate, and discriminate against groups of people. Later, we'll examine the implications of sociolinguistics and standard language ideology as they apply to assessment practices in rhetoric and composition. Throughout, you will complete a variety of reading response and reflection assignments as well as a research project wherein you apply some of your new knowledge to synthesize themes and design teaching materials.

Course Outcomes

In this class, you will

- acquire broad knowledge of the scope of sociolinguistic research and theory
- acquire deep knowledge of contemporary sociolinguistic theories, including critical language studies and language ideology
- conduct independent research on topics in sociolinguistics and write essays to explore disciplinary knowledge and gain deeper understandings of pedagogical theory and practice

- recognize how experiential learning about language / literacy inform your work as teachers and your students' lives as learners

Course Texts and Materials

Bauer, Laurie, and Peter Trudgill. *Language Myths*. Penguin UK, 1998. ISBN: 978-0140260236

Edwards, John. *Sociolinguistics: A Very Short Introduction*. Oxford UP, 2013. ISBN: 978-0199858613

Greenfield, Laura. "The 'Standard English' Fairy Tale: A Rhetorical Analysis of Racist Pedagogies and Commonplace Assumptions about Language Diversity." *Writing Centers and the New Racism: A call for Sustainable Dialogue and Change*, edited by Laura Greenfield and Karen Rowan, Utah State UP, 2011, pp. 33-60.

Inoue, Asao. *Antiracist Writing Assessment Ecologies: Teaching and Assessing Writing for a Socially Just Future*. Parlor Press, 2015. ISBN: 978-1602357730. Download free PDF version here: wac.colostate.edu/books/inoue/ecologies.pdf.

Lippi-Green, Rosina. *English With an Accent: Language, Ideology, and Discrimination in the United States*, 2nd edition. Routledge, 2012. ISBN: 978-0415559119

Villanueva, Victor. "Blind: Talking about the New Racism." *Writing Center Journal*, vol. 26, no. 1, 2006, 3-19.

Journals Relative to Our Course

Useful journals in sociolinguistics: *Journal of Sociolinguistics, Language in Society, Journal of Linguistic Anthropology, Narrative Inquiry, American Speech, Multilingua: Journal of Cross-Cultural and Interlanguage Communication, Intercultural Pragmatics.*

Useful journals in the fields of TESOL and Second Language Writing: *Journal of Second Language Writing, Journal of Second Language Teaching and Research, TESOL Journal, TESOL Quarterly.*

Useful journals in the field of Composition and Rhetoric: *Composition Studies, Composition Forum, College English, College Composition and Communication, Writing on the Edge, Journal of Basic Writing, The Journal of Writing Assessment.*

Other useful journals available online: *Critical Race Theory in Education, The Freire Project: International Journal of Critical Pedagogy, Pedagogy.*

Descriptions of Major Assignments

Reading Notes (10%). The goal for this task is for us to work together to keep a record of our readings and discussions—information that we can build on and refer to as needed. You will be the "Note Taker" for one of our class periods, and your task is twofold: <u>First</u>, you will compile in a single document a 400-500-word summary of the portion of that week's readings you're responsible for (there will be 2 note takers per class), a list of key words with definitions, 2-5 important quotations, and a complete citation. Use headings to help organize and present information and post these notes to our Blackboard Discussion Board Forum >24 hours before our class meets. <u>Second</u>, you will collaborate with the other note taker to compile notes for that class discussion (noting that day's events, the main topics of discussion, any important questions posed, any announcements, etc.). Please word-process these notes, paste your Personal Responses (see below) as the introduction, include your names and the date, and post the document as a thread under the week's Forum within 48 hours of our class meeting. For both of your BB posts, please copy/paste your summary and attach it as a .doc or .rtf text file.

Personal Responses (10%). You will be assigned as a "Responder" the same day you are a "Note Taker." As a responder, you are tasked with composing a short (*<260-word*) response that you will read aloud the day it's due. Responses can take any form and be as (in)formal or (non)standard as you like. The only requirement is that your response is *inspired* by that week's readings, and that you can read it aloud in two minutes or less. But I do encourage you all to make it personal; it is *your response* after all. Poetry, ranting, sampling, and storytelling are most welcome! Know that we likely will not explicitly address responses in class after they're shared; instead, the goal is for your voices and perspectives to set the tone of each class and to get us thinking.

Reflections (15%). This semester you will write four short reflections (each should be ≥250 words). These must be printed and submitted in class the day they are due. The four due dates on the calendar correspond to the group you're assigned (and so I will determine groups the first day of class). In the reflection, your task is simply to communicate to me (and me alone) some of the ideas you're drawn to (or wrestling with) in this course and to ask any questions you may have. The goal is for you and me to be in regular communication about your learning, and so I will be responding to each of your reflections. I'm not particular about exact word counts here, but I am asking that you shoot for 250+ words, that you word process your reflection, and that you fit it on one side of one sheet of paper. Feel free to adjust font, margins, and spacing as needed. I'll use the blank side of the page to respond to you.

Final Reflection Essay (15%). This assignment is an extended analysis of and discussion on your semester's reflections. Your goal is to take stock of your most meaningful thinking and learning this semester in hopes that you might better articulate, concretize, and preserve your new knowledge and perspectives. There are two requirements: 1) *Articulate explicitly* the ways in which your perceptions of sociolinguistics, language ideology, and the teaching of language and literacy have evolved; and 2) *Provide evidence* (quoting your previous reflections or narrating specific learning moments) to show how you have developed as a thinker and teacher. In the case that you feel you have not evolved in your thinking and learning, identify and explain (with evidence) the ways in which you have not progressed (either because you didn't spend enough time with the materials or you feel that you had a strong start in those areas). The reflection essay should be 1250-1500 *words*.

Praxis Project or Extended Research Essay (50%). See the assignment prompts below for more details.

Assignment Prompt: Praxis Project

Part of being a knowledgeable and effective literacy and language teacher is working to ensure your teaching practices are informed by pedagogical research and theory. This Praxis Project challenges you to do just that. For this project, you will inquire more deeply into one of the topics covered in (or closely related to) our course for the purposes of (1) writing a short *Researched Essay*; and (2) using your new knowledge to design a *lesson plan* for a specific language or literacy teaching situation.

Your goal for the *Researched Essay* (2000-2500 words) is to *represent* and *respond* to a narrow topic of inquiry circulating in research on the teaching of language and literacy, a topic that connects to or is implicated by sociolinguistic research. You'll *represent* the topic by summarizing and synthesizing some of the theories and findings from our readings and from your own research. You will also *respond* to your source use by introducing ideas, contextualizing sources, drawing connections across texts, and providing *your own* interpretations, experiences, analyses, claims, and conclusions. The essay should

- engage in complicated and contemporary ways of thinking about the social and political aspects of teaching language and literacy;

- include close work with the texts, in which you summarize specific ideas from the texts and select key passages to closely examine or to use as evidence for your ideas;
- include synthesis of sources, in which you make clear the relationship across sources (does one idea from one source *illustrate*, *extend*, *contest*, or *complicate* an idea from another source?);
- make explicit your interpretations and stance on the topic in relation to the key passages from the sources on which you're drawing (If I had to quantify how much of the essay should be devoted to *your* ideas, *your* interpretations, *your* thinking, I'd say about 40%.);
- be organized so that readers are effectively oriented to the specific topic of inquiry, guided through your synthesis of themes/sources, and presented with conclusions that illustrate the implications of your research, review, and analysis; and
- be edited for clarity and formatted to meet MLA or APA style guidelines.

Your goal for the *Lesson Plan* (another 500-750 words + lesson materials) is to apply the new pedagogical knowledge you've gained from the scholarship synthesized in your Researched Essay to design and describe a lesson plan for any imagined or real language or literacy teaching situation. If you are already teaching language or literacy, you are encouraged to design context-specific materials that you actually intend to use. You are also welcome to adapt a lesson plan that you've discovered or that you've used in the past. Your Lesson Plan should

- demonstrate your ability to apply theory in your teaching practice;
- include explicit mention of class objectives, connections to course goals, and the various procedures and time allotments set for introducing, executing, and concluding the lesson;
- present information so that unfamiliar teachers could effectively adopt/adapt your lesson;
- include any relevant supporting materials (i.e., readings, handouts, images, clips, prompts);
- be preceded by a 500-750 foreword that accomplishes the following: introduce the type of lesson and materials you will provide, their intended outcomes, and the value they aim to offer; describe in detail the teaching context in which the materials are intended; narrate your intentions for how the lesson should be carried out; and reflect on the pedagogical benefits and potential limitations of

the materials, explicitly referring back to the literature you reviewed in your Researched Essay.

Selecting your topic. Your first task is to decide on a topic of inquiry. You have 3 options:

1. Language ideology in the language/writing classroom (drawing on Lippi-Green).
2. Anti-racist assessment in the language/writing classroom (drawing on Inoue).
3. Another theoretical topic of your choice that deals with inclusion and/or diversity initiatives in the language or writing classroom (e.g., universal design; critical pedagogy and problem-posing education; etc.). Run idea(s) by me.

Researching your topic. You are required to draw on Lippi-Green or Inoue (either one chapter or smaller excerpts from across the chapters) and then to locate an additional four journal articles or book chapters connected to the topic you choose. Meticulously select sources so that you not only have *enough* sources but also have the *best* sources to nuance your discussion. See the syllabus for a list of useful journals.

Drafting a Proposal. For your first written product due for this assignment, you'll draft a proposal (worth 5% of your final grade and due on BB). Your proposal should accomplish the following in 2-3 pages: *Introduce* and contextualize the topic you're taking up. Briefly explain the significance of this topic of investigation (to you, this class, the field, or larger social issues). *Summarize* your plans for drawing on research articles to describe some of the major issues your topic addresses and your ideas for designing a lesson plan. *Provide* a bibliography of eight potential journal articles or book chapters you may use for this project. Use complete MLA or APA citation style. Note: It is not necessary to read all of your sources before writing this proposal. For now, skim over each to make sure it is reputable and relevant.

Drafting an Annotated Bibliography. In your AB (*worth 5%* of your final grade and due on BB), begin with an updated summary of your project's goals (see #s 1 and 2 above) and then provide the following for each of the five sources you intend to use: a correct MLA or APA Citation; a concise summary of the source's main argument, purpose, and evidence; a brief reflection on how the source fits into your research (how does this source help *illustrate, extend, contest*, or *complicate* the issue you're investigating?); a quotable quote or two (with page numbers). Each entry should be ~250 words.

Drafting, workshopping, and finalizing your Praxis Project. Based on this prompt, you may rightly assume I'm a big fan of scaffolding writing assignments. And I believe it's especially important to take full advantage of any opportunity for peer review. We'll dedicate class time to workshopping a *full* draft (>1750 words + lesson plan) of your Praxis Project (*worth 10%* of your final grade and due on BB). Your final draft is due two weeks later (*worth 30%* of your final grade and due on BB). It should be carefully revised, edited, and formatted, and should include a separate works cited or bibliography page.

Assignment Prompt: Extended Researched Essay

Rather than completing the Praxis Project, you have the option of engaging instead in a more traditional research project, the Extended Researched Essay. For the Extended Researched Essay, you are tasked with inquiring more deeply into *any topic* of your choice covered in either John Edwards's book, *Sociolinguistics: A Very Short Introduction*, or Rosina Lippi-Green's *English with an Accent: Language, Ideology, and Discrimination in the United States.*

Your goal for the *Extended Researched Essay* (2500-3000 words) is to *represent* and *respond* to a narrow topic of inquiry circulating in sociolinguistic research. See the Praxis Project prompt's section on the "Researched Essay" for a list of criteria required for completing the essay.

Selecting your topic. First, select a specific, contemporary sociolinguistics topic or theory from Edwards or Lippi-Green that you'd like to further investigate. What's most important (and useful) is to choose an issue that you are genuinely interested in or curious about. Please run your ideas by me.

Researching your topic. You are required to draw on Edwards or Lippi-Green (either one chapter or smaller excerpts from across the chapters) and then to locate an additional five journal articles or book chapters related to your topic. Your sources should be meticulously selected to ensure you not only have *enough* sources but also have the *best* sources to nuance your inquiry. See the Praxis Project prompt for a list of useful journals in sociolinguistics.

Drafting a Proposal, Annotated Bibliography, and Extended Researched Essay. See the Praxis Project prompt for details.

Course Calendar

WEEK/DATE	READING DUE	WRITING DUE
Week 1	Introductions to the course and to each other Review syllabus. Buy textbooks.	
Week 2 *Survey 1 of Sociolinguistics*	Edwards, *Sociolinguistics*, pp. 1-60 Ch 1 Coming to Terms Ch 2 Variation and Change Ch 3 Perceptions of Language Ch 4 Protecting Language	Take notes on 'takeaways'
Week 3 *Survey 2 of Sociolinguistics*	Edwards, *Sociolinguistics*, pp. 61-118 Ch 5 Languages Great and Small Ch 6 Loyalty, Maintenance, Shift, Loss, and Revival Ch 7 Multilingualism Ch 8 Name, Sex, and Religion	Take notes on 'takeaways' G1 Reflection 1
Week 4 *Linguistic Facts of Life*	Lippi-Green, *English with an Accent*, pp. xix-xxii; 1-26 Preface + Introduction: Language Ideology or Science Fiction? Ch 1 The Linguistic Facts of Life Bauer & Trudgill, *Language Myths*, pp. 1-8; 50-57; 77-84 Myth 1 Meanings of Words Should Not be Allowed to Vary… Myth 7 Some Languages Are Harder than Others Myth 8 Children Can't Speak or Write Properly Any More Myth 10 Some Languages Have No Grammar	G2 Reflection 1
Week 5 *Myths about Accents and Standards*	Lippi-Green, *English with an Accent*, pp. 27-65 Ch 2 Language in Motion Ch 3 The Myth of Non-Accent Ch 4 The Standard Language Myth Bauer & Trudgill, *Language Myths*, pp. 9-14; 169-182 Myth 2 Some Languages are Just Not Good Enough Myth 20 Everyone Has an Accent Except Me Myth 21 America is Ruining the English Language	G1 Reflection 2
Week 6 *Language Ideology in Action 1*	Lippi-Green, *English with an Accent*, pp. 66-129 Ch 5 Language Subordination Ch 6 The Educational System: Fixing the Message in Stone Ch 7 Teaching Children How to Discriminate	G2 Reflection 2

WEEK/DATE	READING DUE	WRITING DUE
Week 7 *More Language Myths*	Bauer & Trudgill, *Language Myths*, pp. 15-22; 32-49; 85-131; 139-149 Myth 3 The Media Are Ruining English Myth 5 English Spelling is Kattastroffik Myth 6 Women Talk too Much Myth 11 Italian is Beautiful, German is Ugly Myth 12 Bad Grammar is Slovenly Myth 13 Black Children are Verbally Deprived Myth 14 Double Negatives Are Illogical Myth 15 TV Makes People Sound the Same Myth 17 They Speak Really Bad English Down South & in NYC	Participate on Blackboard Discussion Board
Week 8 *Language, Race, and Writing*	Villanueva, "The Rhetorics of the New Racism..." pp. 1-21 Greenfield, "The 'Standard English' Fairy Tale..." pp. 33-60 Inoue, *Antiracist Writing Assessment Ecologies*, pp. 3-24 Introduction: Writing Assessment Ecologies as Antiracist Projects	G1 Reflection 3
Week 9 *Race and Writing Assessment*	Inoue, *Antiracist Writing Assessment Ecologies*, pp. 25-118 Ch 1 The Function of Race in Writing Assessment Ch 2 Antiracist Writing Assessment Ecologies All read 77-85; then choose one of the next three sections: "As more than" (86-93), "As Interconnected" (93-104), or "As Marxian Ecology" (104-115); and then all read 115-118.	G2 Reflection 3
Week 10 *Language Ideology in Action 2*	Lippi-Green, *English with an Accent*, pp. 130-181; 322-331 Ch 8 The Information Industry Ch 9 Real People with a Real Language... Ch 17 Case Study 2: Profiling and Housing	Proposal Due*
Week 11	Read your selected sources and prepare annotated bib	Annotated Bibliography
Week 12 *U.S. Language Differences 1*	Lippi-Green, *English with an Accent*, pp. 182-234; 303-321 Ch 10 The Real Trouble with Black Language Ch 11 Hillbillies, Hicks, and Southern Belles: The Language Rebels Ch 16 Case Study 1: Moral Panic in Oakland	G1 Reflection 4

WEEK/DATE	READING DUE	WRITING DUE
Week 13 *U.S. Language Differences 2*	Lippi-Green, *English with an Accent*, pp. 235-302 Ch 12 Defying Paradise: Hawai'i Ch 13 The Other in the Mirror Ch 14 İYa Basta! Ch 15 The Unassimilable Races: What it Means to be Asian	G2 Reflection 4
Week 14 *Drafting*	Lippi-Green, *English with an Accent*, pp. 332-335 Conclusion: Civil (Dis)Obedience and the Shadow of Language	Full Draft of Final Project Print 3 copies
Week 15 *Conclusions*	Course Evaluations, In-Class Reflections, Celebrations	Final Reflection Essay
Finals Week	No class	Final Draft of Final Project

Where We Are: #MeToo and Academia

"Where We Are" highlights where we are as a field on matters current and compelling. This section brings together a small group of scholars at the forefront of a particular issue or practice to issue a progress report in 800-1200 words. –Editor's Note

Beyond a Hashtag: Considering Campus Policies in the Age of #MeToo

Laura Rosche

On October 15, 2017, actress Alyssa Milano tweeted a call for women who have been victims of sexual assault and harassment to speak out about their experiences, making #MeToo viral. However, Tarana Burke, who founded the movement over a decade ago, reminds us that #MeToo "is beyond a hashtag. It's the start of a larger conversation and a movement for radical community healing" (emphasis added). Burke's call for a "larger conversation" about sexual violence challenges us—participants, observers, and critics—to treat sexual violence as a social issue, one that can only be resolved through prolonged, meaningful discourse that leads to action. Though the objectives of the movement are many, what I find most significant for the field of composition is not Milano's call for disclosure, but Burke's insistence upon the need for discussion. The #MeToo movement implores us to treat sexual violence as a public problem, but what does that mean for the field of composition? For our classrooms? How do we make sure that #MeToo goes "beyond a hashtag" at our institutions so that we continue the "larger conversation" about sexual violence in our learning environments?

With 230 universities currently under investigation for possible mishandling of Title IX cases, the problem of sexual violence on college campuses demands attention ("Title IX: Tracking Sexual Assault Investigations"). The topic, however, is not often discussed in our composition classrooms. While our syllabi may include information about Title IX and offer the contact information of campus resources that help victims of sexual assault and harassment, a larger discussion about its relevance in our students' lives is generally lacking. It is not as if we are unprepared to address complex and unsettling social issues in our classrooms, though. Since the 1980s, cultural studies has influenced composition pedagogies, challenging instructors to ask "students to move their investigations [of language] out of the classroom" to discuss complicated issues such as race relations, gender biases, and ableism (George, et al. 105). This pedagogical approach asks students to analyze the ways in which language influences and is influenced by culture; it challenges students to think about the ideologies implicit in their everyday discourse; and it forces them to grapple with uncomfortable realities about the oppression they witness, experience, and may even be a part of. So why do we so often leave out texts and discussions about sexual violence when we can ask students to engage with that topic in similar ways? Is it that we think students are less willing to participate in conversations about sexual violence than in discussions about other cultural issues, or is it a reflection of university attitudes and policies? Unfortunately, I'm compelled to think the latter.

In December 2017, Glen Retief, an Associate Professor of English and Creative Writing at Susquehanna University, published an article in *Inside Higher Ed* that addresses the ways in which Title IX's mandatory-reporting requirements are negatively affecting university writing classrooms. This policy requires faculty members who have been designated as "Responsible Employees" to contact their Title IX office if a student discloses a sexual assault to them. This policy demands faculty report on behalf of their student even if the assault happened years ago, even if the student has worked through it in counseling, even if they ask us not to report. Retief writes that though this mandatory-reporting policy has had a "stifling effect" on his students when it comes to working with texts that address sexual assault or harassment, it appears to also impact instructors' willingness to approach such topics in their classrooms in the first place. Many instructors—myself included—feel uncomfortable with the requirement to report a student's experience of sexual violence. There are, of course, exceptions; if a student is in immediate danger, I want to offer all the help I can to keep them safe. However, if my class is discussing the rhetorical differences of identifying as a "sexual assault survivor" rather than a "sexual assault victim" and a student shares her own experience with sexual violence as a child—violence that happened years before she ever arrived on campus—I do not feel comfortable reporting the incident to my university's Title IX officer. The very possibility that I might have to do so has kept me from talking more candidly with my students about the rhetoric of sexual violence in my own composition classroom. Though the mandatory-reporting requirement does not, on the surface, make talking about sexual violence in our classrooms more difficult, it does have an impact on our willingness to do so if we value sexual assault survivors' right to self-determined disclosure. But, if we do not analyze sexual violence in our classrooms as we would racial injustices or ableist rhetorics, how can we expect its prevalence in our society to lessen? If we do not treat sexual violence as a topic we can learn and ask questions about, as a problem we can address through discourse, how will #MeToo ever move, as Burke urges, "beyond a hashtag"?

Despite the university policies in place that may make us hesitant to discuss sexual violence in our classrooms, I do think there is a way for composition instructors and students to participate in the "larger conversation" that #MeToo encourages; however, just as we ask our students to do in their assignments, we must work within the constraints of our rhetorical situation. For example, when we include information about Title IX on our syllabi, we can also outline what it means for faculty to be designated as mandatory-reporters, and we can discuss how we imagine that impacting our classroom dynamics. We can welcome discussion about and disclosure of sexual violence, while making sure that students understand the agency they have when participating in both. When we provide the contact information of resources for victims of sexual violence, we can include on- and off-campus options so as to encourage the treatment of sexual violence as a public issue. We can invite students into the conversation about sexual violence by asking them to treat university policies as objects of rhetorical analysis. We can, beyond the classroom, advocate for university policies that make easier our ability to talk about sexual violence with our students. We have options. We can talk about this, and—as the #MeToo movement suggests—we must.

Works Cited

Burke, Tarana (@TaranaBurke). "It's beyond a hashtag. It's the start of a larger conversation and a movement for radical community healing. Join us. #metoo." 15 Oct. 2017, 8:22 p.m. Tweet.

George, Diana, et al. "Cultural Studies and Composition." *A Guide to Composition Studies*, edited by Gary Tate, Amy Rupiper, Kurt Schick, and H. Brooke Hessler, Oxford UP, 2014, pp. 94-110.

Milano, Alyssa (@Alyssa_Milano). "If you've been sexually harassed or assaulted write 'me too' as a reply to this tweet." 15 Oct. 2017, 5:21 p.m. Tweet.

Retief, Glen. "Balancing Enforcement with Education." *Inside Higher Ed*, 19 Dec. 2017, https://www.insidehighered.com/views/2017/12/19/writing-and-other-classes-should-receive-exceptions-title-ix-mandatory-reporting. Accessed 1 Aug. 2018.

"Title IX: Tracking Sexual Assault Investigations." *The Chronicle of Higher Education*, 2018, https://projects.chronicle.com/titleix/. Accessed 3 Aug. 2018.

Literacy Narrative: Ways to Write #MeToo

Tessa Brown

Like many women who are raped in college, I was attacked during the first month of my freshman year. Studies dub this period the "red zone." Extremely drunk, I was led away from my friends, across the dance floor, and to an upstairs bathroom. This is how I became a survivor.

Soon, a version of my attack appeared in my creative writing class. After three weeks of dutifully imaginative submissions in which I invented a religion, satirized a school recreational schedule, and penned a dialogue between a man and a lion who wanted to eat him, I showed up one day with a sexually graphic story about a woman and a string of lovers—one of whom finds her on a dance floor, then pulls her into an upstairs room. Unlike me, this woman had chosen her encounter. Trauma theory says survivors repeat their trauma in order to control it. There it was on the page: 12-point font, one-inch margins, double-spaced. Controlled.

I still remember my instructor's comment written across the top of the paper, all caps: "AUDACIOUS." I think I was stunned.

Later, when I was an MFA student, my classmate walked me home after pushing drinks on me all night and then followed me into my apartment building after I'd left him outside, turning up minutes later with a bang on my door. I had already put my pajamas on. I remember his muddy boots on my carpet, him unzipping my sweatshirt while I sobbed. The thought of my bedroom behind me willed me to push him out.

The next morning, when I called him to tell him he crossed a line, he told me, "I'm tired of people telling me they don't want to do things they want to do," so I emailed our faculty. In a meeting with two professors, I resisted naming my classmate—to protect him?—and ended up speaking to the chair of the English department. We decided the chair would tell my classmate not to contact me again and that if he did I would call the police. I also filed a report with campus reporting services, who said they'd follow up but never did.

But then . . . I had to sit with my assailant in workshop every week. He did not show up to workshop my writing, but he emailed me comments that I didn't read. When his turn arrived, I emailed our workshop leader, the professor I'd originally reported my classmate to, to tell him that I wouldn't be attending workshop nor writing comments for my assailant-cum-classmate. My professor said that wasn't "the professional thing to do." I didn't care, and I said so.

A few years later, during my first day of TA training as an incoming doctoral student in composition and rhetoric, a man from campus psychological services came to talk to us, an auditorium full of new and returning grad students who would be teaching undergrads for the first time. He asked, in call-and-response fashion, "What do you think is the most common crime on this campus?"

Responses flew forward from the audience. "Robbery! Disorderly Conduct! Driving Under the Influence!"

"Rape!" I called, from the back of the room, ignored. But I knew I was right. Research had been part of my recovery from PTSD.

"Sexual assault," the man said, smirking because we hadn't known. Gotcha! Then he changed the subject, talking for ten minutes about what we as instructors should do if we suspected our students were homicidal—something he repeatedly insisted was vanishingly rare, yet we had to be prepared. He never returned to the subject of rape.

The following May, I took an intensive two-week creative nonfiction course determined to write about my attack. Like Laura Gray-Rosendale, I discovered that this project was an archival one. I didn't know exactly when my rape occurred, only that it was sometime during my freshman fall; but there, deep in hard drive backups of my old computers, was that short story from freshman year, dated to early September, with its uncanny repetition of that night. A realization dawned: I was raped during my first weeks of college. In the journal entries I wrote that year, the word "rape" appears once, in a narration of me telling my friend it certainly wasn't. Because after I was raped, it took five years for me to accept what had happened. Took going back to school for my MFA, a new campus triggering something in me, a me ready to face what I couldn't, hadn't, as a teen.

I am now teaching freshman composition at my third institution; this will be my ninth fall term at the front of the class. Last winter, in my "Hashtag Activism" freshman composition course, about one third of student papers were about #MeToo or the Brock Turner rape case, which resulted in hashtags like #thingslongerthanBrockTurnersrapesentence and the viral and successful #RecallPersky campaign. While I am forward with my students about many aspects of my identity, I am not out as a rape survivor. Yet I tell my students who I am so that they may feel emboldened to do the same. A few of them came out in their writing as survivors—should I say, "Me too"?

What would happen if our field said "Me, too"? Five years later, I am still thinking about that man at my TA training and how he talked for ten minutes about a crime that rarely happens and zero about a crime that happens every weekend. What *am* I supposed to do if I think my student has committed an assault? Or has survived one? Shouldn't we, as writing teachers, have answers to these questions—we, who engage more deeply with the contents of our students' thoughts than perhaps any other instructor at the college, who get to know the majority of freshmen on our campuses?

My syllabi now end with the following statement—a start, but not enough—which I invite you to use or adapt:

> **Sexual violence**. Many students arrive on campus as survivors of sexual violence; for female students, the risk of sexual assault is especially high during the fall of freshman year. If you are the victim of a sexual assault (defined as unwanted or nonconsensual touching, kissing, sexual contact or sexual intercourse, including while incapacitated), visit [this list of resources].

Questions linger: Is this unprofessional? Am I reenacting my trauma? What about my whole career, repeating freshman fall year after year? And: what else can I do?

Trauma drives survivors to write. I started with stories, diaries, a counseling intake form. I graduated to letters, essays, and blog posts. In this journal, we've gathered to write narratives, critiques, suggestions. Tarana Burke, who originated the phrase "me too," has said that uttering this phrase opens a necessary dialogue but must be followed by work for lasting change to occur. So let's keep writing: classroom studies, teacher-training syllabi, and administrative protocols, IRB forms, interview questions, and institutional histories. We must reckon with the reality of sexual violence on our campuses, in our classrooms, and in our own and our students' lives. Now that would be audacious.

Works Cited

Gray-Rosendale, Laura. *College Girl.* SUNY Press, 2013.

Herman, Judith. *Trauma and Recovery.* Basic Books, 1997.

Kimble, Matthew, Andrada D. Neacsiu, William F. Flack, and Jessica Horner. "Risk of Unwanted Sex for College Women: Evidence for a Red Zone." *Journal of American College* Health, vol. 57, no. 3, 2008, 331-38.

Natividad, Angela. "#MeToo Founder Tarana Burke Explains How the Simple Phrase Gave Voice to So Many." *Adweek*. 22 June 2018. Web. https://www.adweek.com/brand-marketing/metoo-founder-tarana-burke-explains-how-the-simple-phrase-gave-voice-to-so-many/. Accessed 10 August 2018.

Ohlheiser, Abby. "The woman behind 'Me Too' knew the power of the phrase when she created it — 10 years ago." *The Washington Post*. 19 October 2017. Web. https://www.washingtonpost.com/news/the-intersect/wp/2017/10/19/the-woman-behind-me-too-knew-the-power-of-the-phrase-when-she-created-it-10-years-ago/?utm_term=.6d8963234d93. Accessed 10 August 2018.

Richardson, Elaine. *PHD to Ph.D.: How Education Saved My Life.* New City Community P, 2013.

Misogyny in the Classroom: Two Women Lecturer's Experiences

Patricia Fancher and Ellen O'Connell Whittet

#MeToo began as calling out sexual harassment and has expanded to include a broader definition of misogynistic behavior, including abuse, intimidation, and physical threat. Public discourse and institutional policies focus, in particular, on the abuse of power by those in positions of authority. In the stories that follow, we seek to complicate this focus by addressing multidirectional power dynamics. When faculty experience misogyny in the classroom, they are met with a system that cannot support nor protect them until threats escalate.

Ellen's Story

One afternoon during office hours, a student told me another student, Joe,[1] claimed to a group I'd made sexual advances towards him.

Stunned, I defended myself. I explained it wasn't true, and wondered what signals had gotten crossed. "We all knew it wasn't true," she told me quietly. "but I thought you'd want to know."

I was disturbed to be discussed by students as a sexual object. Instead of simply doing my job, I was facing sexualization and second guessing my interactions.

A week or so later, Joe himself came into my office to "discuss something serious" with me. I felt self-conscious knowing what he'd claimed I'd done, and I asked him to leave the door open. He began talking loudly, telling me my courses were designed to alienate and threaten him. As he yelled, I began to calculate whether I could use a chair as a weapon or duck around him to run out the open door. He continued shouting, backing me into a corner with his body.

Another colleague heard the shouting and came to my open office door. He was taller than Joe, and using a louder voice told Joe to get out of here and leave me alone. I recognized that his masculinity had saved me, and I knew it was a weapon I'd never be able to brandish.

I went straight to the front office and told someone what had happened. She told me to call Distressed Student Services, who performed a wellness check. I received a phone call later that day to say Joe was not posing a threat to himself or anyone else. "What about the threat he already posed to me?" I wanted to ask. But no one seemed to know who to call about that.

Our front office staff told me I could call the police, but without any physical contact or harassment there was probably not much else to be done.

It was one of the times in my career I've felt the most vulnerable, and the least protected. The top-down hierarchy of a university meant I had to be harmed or repeatedly harassed for my complaint to go anywhere. Instead, the encounter was dropped, and the student signed up for another class with me the next quarter. When I told my department administrators I felt unsafe around him, they told me I should try to convince him to take another class with another professor.

Trish's Story:

After first-year composition student Dan submitted incomplete assignments, refused to answer questions in class, and regularly appeared distracted on his phone during class, I invited him to my office hours.

I asked Dan about his goals as a writer. He replied that he didn't care. I asked about his major and career goals. With enthusiasm, Dan talked about computer science and how he was going to be a programmer. I tried to connect his enthusiasm for his career goals to the learning goals in the class. When I turned to discuss what strategies tend to help him learn, Dan explained he liked online classes and would have preferred that my class be an online class because "if I'm in class and bored, I get annoyed at my teacher; I just want to punch her in the face."

Looking back, I'm proud I had the composure to remain calm and appear unfazed. I told Dan that the comment was inappropriate. It was a joke, he assured me. I reiterated that it wasn't an appropriate joke. He merely shrugged.

But, of course, I was fazed. I was alarmed. Dan's comment was a very thinly veiled threat of physical violence. With his comment, I became hyper aware of my body in the classroom. I carefully consider how to establish my ethos and authority as a professor, as I think most women do. In each new class, I feel like I have to earn my authority. However, I never thought I had to earn my physical safety. After Dan's comment, I felt unsafe, small, fearful. And while I was left feeling a loss of both safety and authority, he left the meeting having expressed his entitlement to physically threaten and disrespect a woman professor.

I was unsure of what to do. He hadn't hit me. And his expressed desire to punch a professor was hypothetical and not a threat. When I asked a mentor, she recommended that I write down the experience. And, if he threatened me again, then I should report the student. I continued to teach the class, always aware that one bored student in the back could one day act on his violent thoughts.

Reflection

These stories complicate the typical #MeToo narrative. For the most part, when we talk about Title IX and #MeToo, we focus on men in positions of power who use that power to solicit sex, intimidate or otherwise belittle women. Our stories remind us that even when men are not in positions of power, they can still have power. The hierarchy of the classroom suggests that the teachers have power and authority. But it's not that simple. Power dynamics move in multiple directions and, although we hold positions of academic authority, men in our classrooms can use misogyny in the classroom to undermine and intimidate us as professionals, people, and educators.

We realize the stories offered here are just two experiences. At the same time, these experiences reflect a broader problem for women faculty: misogyny in the classroom. This misogyny can make us feel unsafe and feel the need to work harder to earn the respect of students. This misogyny is often displayed in subtle, unconscious ways. And this misogyny is regularly visible in student evaluations, which time and time again, have been shown to reflect gender bias against women faculty (Arbuckle and Williams 2003; Boring 2017; MacNell, Driscoll and Hunt 2015).

We are contingent faculty and our job security is largely dependent on students' course evaluations. The physical threats undermined our confidence, safety, and ability to teach. While students have a voice in their course evaluations, faculty and staff have no chance to officially record experiences dismissed as "not that bad." When we faced misogyny from our students, the university and our departments couldn't or wouldn't protect us.

Note

1. All student names are pseudonyms.

Works Cited

Arbuckle, Julianne, and Benne D. Williams. "Students' Perceptions of Expressiveness: Age and Gender Effects on Teacher Evaluations." *Sex Roles*, vol. 49, no. 9-10, 2003, pp. 507-16.

Boring, Anne. "Gender Biases in Student Evaluations of Teaching." *Journal of Public Economics*, vol. 145, 2017, pp. 27-41.

MacNell, Lillian, Adam Driscoll, and Andrea N. Hunt. "What's in a Name: Exposing Gender Bias in Student Ratings of Teaching." *Innovative Higher Education*, vol. 40, no. 4, 2015, pp. 291-303.

A Vindication of the Rights of Faculty

Michelle Graber

"Isn't that just like a woman," I heard Joe Student mutter to his peer.

"That's five points for gender-disparaging language," I interrupted my lecture to reply.

"Naw, Ms. Graber—I made that comment toward Tom," Joe said. Then, he turned to Tom and said, "Typical woman. Thinks it's about her."

This time, the language *was* directed at me. The slam against Tom contained a dualistic gender slight stereotyping my femaleness and attacking Tom's maleness. I decided to make this a learning experience. We discussed labels like "loser" and "weird." We talked about bad women drivers and men's obsession with football. While these seemed harmless to the students at face value, I took the conversation into the uncomfortable waters of race and sexuality labels.

"What about words like chink? Or faggot? How do these words feel?" I asked. Students agreed; these words had more impact. I explained that I am offended when people disregard my words and actions just because I am a woman. Joe said he understood, and the incident ended on a positive note. But the next one didn't.

In a different class, a verbal scuffle between two students—whom I will call Lane and Ty—escalated into a full-on shoving match during a collaborative writing activity, turning a corner of my sardine-packed classroom into a boxing ring. I slid between the cramped chairs and computer laden tables to squeeze between the fighters, trying to end the round while protecting other students from possible blows.

"Get out of my class!" I shouted at them as I stepped between flying fists. "You need to leave. This is not acceptable classroom or workplace behavior. Go to the Dean of Students' office. I will be contacting the Dean and your program advisor about your behavior."

Lane shoved his materials into his bag and banged into each table and chair in his path on the way out; Ty meekly packed his bag and left the room, shoulders hunched.

After class, I found Lane and Ty pacing in front of my office door. Ty apologized, explaining why he thought his behavior was inappropriate. Lane piped up, "Yeah, I'm sorry too. We just didn't think." I admit to a bit of gender stereotyping, thinking *boys will be boys.* After all, my brothers were prone to physical confrontation when settling disputes. Still, the behavior put other students at risk for potential harm. The incident was reported, and the students returned to class with little consequence. I thought this would be the end of any issues. A week later, Lane refused to stop talking while I gave instructions about a group project. After three verbal warnings about being disruptive, I asked Lane to leave the classroom.

"Fuck you," Lane replied, deadpan and without heat. Although I was standing across the room from him, I felt gut punched. Heat flooded my face, and my hands began to shake with frustration and anger.

"You need to leave now," I told Lane firmly, but not shouting.

"Fuck you. You can't fuckin' tell me what to do. Nothing will fuckin' happen. I'm gonna fuckin' finish what the fuck I'm doing with my group, and I will fuckin' leave when I am ready. You can't fuckin' make me go. What the fuck are you going to do? Ha."

Lane had a point: I had no power. I stood in front of thirty students with no immediate recourse to Lane's verbal assault. During Lane's tirade, I typed a quick instant message to the Dean asking him to come to my classroom and pull Lane out of class for being disruptive and disrespectful. The Dean showed up and pulled Lane out of class.

Next class period, Lane was back.

I tried to swallow a new, unsettling anxiety. What should I do next? Lane received no adverse consequences for his behavior and made no apologies this time. I had lost face with my entire class. At graduation, Lane walked past me into the auditorium in his cap and gown and sneered, "See? You couldn't do anything about me. I still graduated. You have no power."

These student incidents had different outcomes—one positive, one negative. Although administration expressed concern and compassion about the situation, the response reinforced a different message to Lane: gender discrimination and harassment will be tolerated. Why did Joe and Ty acquiesce when confronted with the ethical implications of their behavior but Lane balk, rejecting my accusation of unethical behavior? How can faculty be vindicated for correcting unethical and harassing actions made by students when student behavior goes unpunished?

Faculty members are expected to be superheroes beyond reproach and manage seemingly impossible situations, even to the point of taking a bullet in an active shooter situation. Teachers who suffer the recriminations of student abuse in silence end up trapped between a harassing student and administrators underprepared to deal with the situations or a lack of policies to reinforce classroom harassment. Teachers walk a tightrope between the student and administration. Teachers tolerate poor student behavior or unethical conduct perhaps in fear of losing credibility or worse—termination for the inability to manage a classroom. Imagine the public response should a teacher dare to malign a student's wayward behavior to administrators in the public sphere, even if such a criticism were accurate. Unlike Bill Clinton and other pedestalized offenders (Zacharek et al.), faculty are ostracized for their inability to manage such situations in lieu of administrative policies, which ends up exculpating student offenders instead of vindicating faculty mistreatment.

A student called one of my colleagues a "c-you-next-tuesday" (cunt) during class. The student returned to class the next class period, and the teacher found herself undermined by a female administrator who told the student he could return to class. Female administrators, too, can be complicit in the acceptance of harassment. Permissiveness around gender-based harassment is not exclusive to men or women nor is it exclusive to heterosexuals, as the recent case against Avital Ronell demonstrates (see Greenberg).

A lot of scholarship addresses students who are harassed by other students or students who are harassed by faculty or even harassment between faculty members and administration, but scant scholarship addresses teachers harassed by students. Instances of teachers being harassed by students offer little opportunity for redress when discussions are not happening. The #MeToo movement has created a heightened awareness, yet the lack of a clear policy or set of consequences when students enact harassing behaviors against faculty are cause for action. Faculty must speak up when students harass them and work with administrators to find ways to establish policies which address these issues when policies and consequences fall short of the mark.

Works Cited

Greenberg, Zoe. "What Happens to #MeToo When a Feminist Is the Accused?" *The New York Times*. The New York Times, August 13, 2018.

Zacharek, Stephanie, Eliana Dockterman, and Haley Sweetland Edwards. "TIME Person of the Year 2017: The Silence Breakers." *Time*. Time, December 18, 2017.

Academic Spaces and Grad Student Harassment

Katelyn Lusher

Sexual harassment and assault are not confined to academic workplaces—they spread to other spaces academics occupy as well, like conferences and workshops where anonymity is possible. At large conferences in particular, it's likely that you will be in the company of thousands. Include alcohol, and there is a heightened chance for unwanted attention and/or assault. Such was the case when I attended my first ever 4Cs this year in Kansas City. I openly admit that talking about this is deeply uncomfortable for me because part of me feels like it's my fault, even though years of therapy tell me that it absolutely is not.

After attending pre-conference workshops, a friend and I went out for a few drinks. As the night wound down, we decided to make one last stop at a jazz bar. While we were there, we saw a group of three men sitting in a booth with their conference badges still hanging around their necks. Once we realized we were all there for 4Cs, my friend and I joined them at their table.

Everyone was obviously intoxicated. Since it was late and we were in a jazz bar, the place was dimly lit and nearly empty. The large glass pitcher of absinthe in the center of the table was nearly empty too, but the men claimed that there was no way they could finish it by themselves. I sat on the edge of the booth next to a tall man in his early fifties and recognized the name on his badge. The booth seats were cramped and brought everyone close together, but this man apparently wanted to be closer. When I refilled my cup from the pitcher, he put his arm around my shoulder. Surprised, I pretended to ignore it and sip from my glass. "Wow," he said. "You can drink a lot. What's your name?" When I answered, he pulled me closer and slid his hand down to my waist, inching lower. He leaned close and his lips tickled my ear as he said, "You're pretty cute, you know that?" I felt my insides squirm—his touch was far too intimate for someone I'd just met. I wasn't sure how to respond and kept sipping from my drink. Across the table, my friend seemed uneasy but unsure about what to do. I was the only woman in the group. I felt isolated. The man's hand stayed on my waist until my friend and I left a few minutes later. As we walked away from the bar, I laughed nervously at the strangeness of the situation. I didn't know what else to do. I was a PhD student, and this man was a fairly prominent professor in the field.

The next day, my friend and I went to dinner with some of his friends from other universities. At some point, I told them what happened the night before and laughed about it. They did not. "That's really not cool. Actually, that's pretty fucked up," one of them said. I laughed nervously and said that I really wasn't mad about it. Another colleague, a woman, looked at me knowingly and said, "You might not be mad about it now, but you probably will be later once you realize what happened." I was a bit taken aback by her bluntness and even felt a little annoyed. Over time, however, I've come to realize that this incident says much about power dynamics and the critical need for progress within the academy.

When I began grad school, I had a somewhat utopian belief that most professors were so "woke" they couldn't possibly subscribe to the misogyny I had felt in so many workplaces. What I quickly learned is that barely disguised sexism and harassment are as much a part of academia as conferences, publishing, and happy hours that go far into the night. Harassment is an insidious thread that hides under the guise of collegiality and professionalism, and it's a clear misuse of power. This behavior is easily abused by tenured male professors so assured in their positions that they don't think they could possibly suffer consequences. Such beliefs are not unlike the powerful men in Hollywood who have recently fallen from grace as a result of the #MeToo movement. They, too, had power, and consistently and systematically abused it. Although many in academia stress the importance of feminism and social justice, many are still illiterate about consent; it is easy to shrug off behaviors that are never appropriately addressed. In the jazz bar, the two other professors sitting in the booth could have addressed their friend's behavior, but neither did. Unfortunately—and rather disturbingly—I suspect that something like this had happened before and so did not faze them much.

Conferences are supposed to be mentoring environments for PhD students like myself. How are we supposed to be effectively mentored when our mentors can't treat us like equals who deserve respect? What does this teach us about the environment we can expect for our future? In a field where success on the job market is heavily dependent on faculty recommendation letters, academic connections, and an overall "clean" reputation, it is incredibly dangerous to speak out against someone who can easily threaten your future career. Silence is a cycle that reproduces abuse.

As time went on, I realized that my blunt colleague was right. I did feel angry later. When I see his name cited in an article or casually referenced, I am deeply unsettled, reminded of him touching me and getting close to me when I didn't ask for it. Even though we were in a bar, that shouldn't matter. I felt completely powerless and vulnerable. His behavior *was* messed up. It was *not* okay. And I am mad about it. I have every right to be angry. So many times I've tried to tell myself that I am overreacting and it really *wasn't* a big deal—but it was. And I know I'm not alone.

Centering the Conversation: Patriarchy, Academic Culture, and #MeToo

Anna Sicari

As an academic who is committed to the writing center, a space guided by one-on-one mentorship and collaboration with others, I am not a stranger to stories of abuse and assault committed by colleagues and coworkers. In this space, perhaps similar to that of a therapist's office or even a confessional, writers often disclose the traumatic experiences they suffer in academia: the L2 learner who just "can't write"; the doctoral candidate with an abusive and controlling advisor; or a young woman who experienced sexual assault on campus and has no one to confide in. While these acts of assault differ, they are all forms of systemic abuse within a patriarchal institution, and they are all experiences occurring daily that largely go ignored.

The #MeToo movement, with its rapid pace and platform for all voices, has the potential to have lasting and positive impact on the academy; for similar reasons, it has the potential to fade away. The trouble with the #MeToo movement is that it does not seem "to get that deep," as bell hooks has recently argued. She and other feminist thinkers have been troubled by the movement's relative silence on patriarchy. Even in academic conversations about the #MeToo movement, the focus has been on overt experiences of sexual assault, and white women have dominated the conversation, as seen in the WPA-listserv (WPA-L) conversation, "We have a Weinstein problem." If we want academic culture to change, and build on what #MeToo has started, then it is time we deepen this conversation: how we theorize it, whom we ask to participate, and what experiences we want to highlight. The writing center can serve as a starting point, as the center is a space for stories and dialogue, very often serving those who are struggling in the academy.

#MeToo is only step one in a long list of steps toward transformation: It simply exposes a problem in order to pose a problem. The majority white women who participated in the WPA-L Weinstein conversation described tales of male advisors sexually pursuing them, of colleagues making inappropriate jokes or comments, and other firsthand accounts of sexual harassment. Gradually, other marginalized bodies chimed in with their experiences of assault. A number of white men discussed their concerns of complacency and complicity in perpetuating sexual harassment. However, there were a number of cisgender white males who objected that #MeToo too quickly can become a "witch hunt," with several of these men expressing a fear of not being wanted in this conversation and feeling silenced. Melissa Nicolas responded to this thread and posed to readers, "But what about the endemic patriarchy IN OUR

FEMINIZED FIELD that creates the conditions for these criminal acts to occur? These technically not-criminal acts are probably happening as I AM TYPING THIS MESSAGE."

No one responded to this important question. We quickly turned to other issues in our field. I was left thinking that we need to reflect on our everyday practices, on how we treat our colleagues and students, and ways in which we perpetuate patriarchal ideologies regularly, without much thought. As a writing center director, I have witnessed and heard too many stories of harassment and abuse that one may not immediately see as connected to the #MeToo movement, as they are not necessarily about sexual harassment or assault but are experiences that nonetheless stem from patriarchy and power dynamics. *Out in the Center*, a collection of stories written by those who work in writing centers, explores how practitioners benefit from engaging in dialogue about issues of identity, power, and intersectionality to better navigate the academy. I believe #MeToo has brought attention to just how necessary it is to have these conversations in the academy, particularly in writing spaces. Through one-with-one writing sessions, writers and tutors have the opportunity to have a meaningful dialogue, openly discussing the feelings and emotions associated with writing and surviving the academy. Yet terms such as "safe space" and "trigger warnings" are frequently mocked or criticized as coddling students or not preparing students for difficult conversations, for "the real world." Writing centers often aim to be "safe spaces" on campuses (and I am aware that there is pushback in the writing center community regarding this term) and I believe both the space and term are feminized and seen as inferior, weak, or less than because of accepted patriarchal practices of marginalization and exclusion which fostered an environment of sexual harassment in academia.

Sara Ahmed writes of sexual harassment specifically in academia and claims that it "works—as does bullying more generally—by increasing the costs of fighting against something, making it easier to accept something than to struggle against something, even if that acceptance is itself the site of your own diminishment" (141). The academy is built on this type of acceptance, the "I got here, why can't you" attitude that all of us have experienced and even adopted. The #MeToo movement is important because it has brought narratives of assault and harassment out in the open. However, it will only bring long-lasting change to academia if we take these conversations a step further. If we're not deliberately looking for all marginalized voices to be included in this conversation, and if white feminists (like myself) are not seeing how they themselves are complicit in everyday experiences of assault and harassment stemming from patriarchy, and we're not discussing feelings with students and colleagues, then the #MeToo movement will end as quickly as it began.

I believe that campus writing spaces are primed to start this dialogue and build a sustainable community around advocacy work. And it is the work of the writing center, a space still often seen as marginalized in academia and as a site of support for those who are marginalized, that can serve as a model for academic scholars to dialogue about identity, intersectionalty, and collegiality.

Works Cited

Ahmed, Sara. *Living a Feminist Life*. Duke UP, 2017.

Denny, Harry, Robert Mundy, Lila Naydan, Richard Severe and Anna Sicari, editors. *Out in the Center*. Utah State UP, 2019.

Hitchenson, Melissa. "We have a Weinstein problem." *Writing Program Administration Listserv,* 19 Oct 2017, https://lists.asu.edu/cgi-bin/wa?A0=wpa-l.

hooks, bell. "bell hooks on the Roots of Male Violence Against Women." *The New Yorker Radio Hour*, interview by David Remnick, 17 Nov. 2017.

Nicolas, Melissa. "We have a Weinstein problem." *Writing Program Administration Listserv*, 19 Oct 2017, https://lists.asu.edu/cgi-bin/wa?A0=wpa-l.

Book Reviews

Here We Go Again: More Ways of "Making It," Circa 2018

Women's Professional Lives in Rhetoric and Composition: Choice, Chance, and Serendipity, edited by Elizabeth A. Flynn and Tiffany Bourelle. Ohio State UP, 2018. 286 pp.

Surviving Sexism in Academia: Strategies for Feminist Leadership, edited by Kirsti Cole and Holly Hassel. Routledge, 2017. 316 pp.

Reviewed by Michelle Ballif, University of Georgia; Diane Davis, University of Texas at Austin; Roxanne Mountford, University of Oklahoma

It is the ten-year anniversary of *Women's Ways of Making It in Rhetoric and Composition*; published early in 2008, the book emerged just months before the economic downturn that threw higher education into a crisis. By 2011, the American Association of University Professors was reporting a sharp rise in non-tenure track job openings and a similar drop in tenure-line openings, and those of us at doctoral-granting research institutions watched as our PhD students increasingly took fixed- or limited-term contract jobs or were turned away from the academic job market altogether. In such a market, Kristin Bivens, et al., flat-out asked, what use is there for a book like ours, focused as it is on traditional tenure-track career paths in rhetoric and composition? Our response, then and now, is that the current state of the market makes our book more necessary than ever for those who do aspire to that traditional path, where the available positions are few and extraordinarily competitive. While we would revise our book substantially for today's job market, it continues to be studied by graduate students and young professionals, from whom we still hear frequently, and who hope to learn from the successful women we profiled.

At the same time, graduate students and junior faculty in the field obviously need to learn and practice strategies for other sorts of successes as well, and they need to be open to other types of rewarding positions, inside and outside of the academy. So, over the past decade, we've read with interest a continuously growing list of publications focused on women's diversifying career paths and success strategies in higher education. Especially noteworthy among them is this journal's special issue in spring 2011, which focused on responding to and expanding the scope of our project. What we've learned is that women in the field today face many of the very same challenges they have always faced, in addition to some new ones wrought by the economic downturn and the recent, soul-crushing emboldenment of sexist, racist, and homophobic habits and practices that threaten our civil liberties. On the upside, though, the #MeToo and Time's Up movements may be indicative of an intensified collective will to aggressively address systemic sexist roadblocks.

It just so happens, to our utter delight, that the whimsical ABBA musical *Mamma Mia!*, a film that celebrates intimate relations among women—as mothers, daughters, friends—is also (my, my) celebrating the ten-year anniversary of its premier. So it's in honor of all these relations and of the field itself that we embraced the subtitle of the just-released sequel to *Mamma Mia!—Here We Go Again*—and agreed to read and respond to two recent edited volumes on women's challenges and strategies of success in academia—*Women's Professional Lives in Rhetoric and Composition* and *Surviving Sexism in Academia: Strategies for Feminist Leadership*—while revisiting our own.

Women's Professional Lives in Rhetoric and Composition extends our curiosity into how women "make it" in the profession by offering the stories of women who consider their careers through metaphors other than a "pathway." Intended to challenge what counts as a "normal" career, the volume's chapters are autobiographical reflections on how unexpected life events—death, depression, commuter marriage, a working-class upbringing—can be leveraged into a career. The introduction emphasizes "serendipity," but these stories illustrate shrewd and cunning use of opportunity when it arrives and perseverance when it does not. As Lynn Bloom states, "Making good choices positions you to take advantage of serendipity" (58). Readers will be familiar with many of the names in the volume: Linda Adler-Kassler, Lynn Z. Bloom, Lisa Ede, Elizabeth Flynn, Anne Ruggles Gere, Malea Powell, Jacqueline Rhodes, and Shirley Rose, all of whom have "made it" by conventional definitions. But the book also includes a woman who left academia to develop a business and several who serve or have served in non-tenure track positions. In this way, the book nicely straddles our book and Amy Goodburn, Donna LeCourt, and Carrie Leverenz's edited volume, *Rewriting Success in Rhetoric and Composition Careers*, which, in response to our book's focus, explores success in the field off the tenure track. Unlike our profiles, which were based on interviews, the authors in *Women's Professional Lives* freely explore the obstacles they encountered trying to succeed at their goals and the unconventional sources of wisdom that sustained them. By emphasizing serendipity and resilience and pathways to positions in our field that are far from linear, the chapters collected here offer hope to women who do not see their lives reflected in the existing literature.

The essays in *Surviving Sexism in Academia* depart both from our book and *Women's Professional Lives in Rhetoric and Composition* in important ways. Edited by Kirsti Cole, a rhetoric and composition scholar, and Holly Hassel, who works in both women's and gender studies and rhetoric and composition, this book addresses obstacles for women leaders in higher education across the academic spectrum and strategies for addressing these problems. Of particular interest are seven chapters that address discipline-specific contexts, such as philosophy—long a boy's club—and STEM disciplines. The book also explores ways to use shared governance, mentoring, coalition building (e.g., among mothers—the focus of four chapters), resistance, and interruption to overcome oppression. There are two chapters on how to respond to bullying—including one on dealing with the queen bee, a sad theme in our own book—and to intersectional oppressions (particularly of gender and race). The stories of men behaving badly in philosophy and geography will resonate with feminists in the humanities and social sciences—particularly the gaslighting that seems a universal strategy of bullies. The story of one geography department stuck with us because of a particularly innovative feature of the volume: comic-book and other forms of visual essays interspersed throughout the book. There is something deeply satisfying about seeing problematic faculty members rendered as monkeys in the comic-strip version of an interview study (thank you, Heather Rosenfeld). Practical and nuanced, this book will be welcomed by women leaders (the target audience) writ large: department chairs, deans, faculty senators, committee chairs, and reformers in the ranks. At the same time, graduate students might find the book helpful for gaining strategies not so much to *make it* but to *break it* when the system reveals racist, sexist, ableist, and cis-gendered bias on such issues as dressing professionally (cf. Katie Manthey).

Though the editors of *Women's Professional Lives* attempt to draw a semi-clear distinction between the "ways of making it" depicted in *Women's Ways* and those they spotlight, we noted considerable overlap among all three volumes. One of the key themes that runs through each is collaboration: in the lived experience of our multiplicitous connections, in scholarly productivity, and in any political effort to combat sexist challenges. Throughout *Women's Ways*, we noted the role of collaboration especially in women's professional and scholarly successes. Many of the contributors in *Women's Professional Lives* addressed the significant ways in which their collaborative relations with colleagues helped them personally, as well as how they collaborated professionally. Several chapters in *Surviving Sexism* point to a collaborative *political* approach (a sisters-are-doing-it-for-themselves approach), noting that *women* need to work to change sexism in higher education, and that advancing any "strategy for success" or way of "making it" will need to refigure a system that has always banked on the service of women—both in the university and in the home (care of partners, parents, children).

Unsurprisingly, not much seems to have changed since we addressed the question of how to balance the personal and the professional in *Women's Ways*.

Chapter thirteen of *Surviving Sexism in Academia*, by Kyrstia Nora, Rochelle Gregory, Ann-Marie Lopez, and Nicole A. Williams, devotes itself specifically to issues facing mothers in the field of rhetoric and composition, and the stories gathered from their survey echo many that we gathered in ours. There is no getting around it: teaching a writing course is a labor intensive endeavor; teaching multiple writing courses requires, as one of our own survey respondents wrote, "most of the energy I possess" (*Women's Ways* 9). (1). Writing teachers who also have children at home, the authors note, "can be overwhelmed by the second shift—the work of the home and caregiving" (Nora, Gregory, Lopez, and Williams 138). They discuss the "motherhood penalty" faced by many mothers in the field who say, again echoing our own survey respondents, that they have faced discrimination and belittling by colleagues who resent them for not being able to stay late when a meeting runs over or attend every departmental event because they have children at home.

Of course, this second shift involves more than raising children. Many of our survey respondents told us they had

> partners, children, aging parents, and/or ill siblings under their care; many women reported difficulty in maintaining two-career partnerships, especially when they had to live separately, in different parts of the country, or when they had to ask a husband or partner to relocate to accommodate a career move, or when they had to work in the same department and negotiate the challenges that arrangement invites. (*Women's Ways* 11)

To address these issues of care, Nora, Gregory, Lopez, and Williams propose that the enactment of "two sorts of universal policies" are necessary: first, programs designed to "increase awareness and sensitivity to parental and caregiver issues"; and second, policies that "provide multilayered structural support for mothers" (142). While we noted some of these strategies in *Women's Ways*, the chapters on motherhood and academic careers in *Surviving Sexism* are much more focused on advocacy, which make them a valuable addition to the conversation.

Obviously, and for stated reasons, *Women's Ways* focused on success in research intensive tenure-track positions in a more direct and linear way than most of the chapters in *Women's Professional Lives*. Still, the theme of serendipity, which is a major focus of the latter, runs through four of the nine profile chapters in *Women's Ways*, each of which is devoted to the strategies for success outlined by a successful woman in the field. *Women's Professional Lives* takes up serendipity at its point of convergence with choice and chance, kairos and resilience. As Elizabeth A. Flynn and Tiffany Bourelle write in their introduction:

> All of our contributors made choices within the constraints necessarily imposed by chance and serendipity involving changes in direction that seemed risky at first but that usually resulted in productive work involving teaching, administration, and research within rhetoric and composition. While our themes revolve around choice, chance, and serendipity within the contexts of kairos and resilience, these terms call to mind other concepts such as agency, control (or lack thereof) over one's path, and a general openness to various experiences. The intention of these narratives is not only to illustrate how scholarship and outside influences have impacted careers and lives but also to provide guidance form women and men who find themselves in similar situations. (3-4)

In her *Women's Ways* profile, Sharon Crowley notes that women tend to talk about their own success in terms of serendipity, as if they had no agency in it. Reflecting on her decision to follow her husband to the University of Northern Colorado at Greeley rather than going to the University of Iowa where she had also been accepted (but he had not), Crowley said: "It never occurred to me not to go with him. . . . For women, up to the second wave, we sort of went with the flow," she told us. "We did what we were told, and it did seem like serendipity if things happened for us. Or we were taught to rationalize it as serendipity. If we made it happen, we told ourselves it was luck" (218). There certainly is a great deal of chance in life, but women's tendency to consider their own hard-won paths to success as "luck" appears to be a problem that persists beyond the second wave.

By explicitly focusing on the "intersection of agency and accidental sagacity," *Women's Professional Lives* insists that serendipity is not "solely coincidence or luck but the willingness to act on hunches or trust one's own intuition—to learn from one's experience" (5). Their point is to challenge the debilitating sexist narrative that women *luck* into success and to urge women in the field to prepare themselves to recognize and seize upon serendipitous gifts, even when they sometimes take the form of sizeable challenges. Shirley Wilson Logan and Cindy Selfe described their professional success to us as serendipitous, being in the right place at the right time; yet it was clear that both had actively participated in the steering of chance situations into avenues for success. They both kind of "stumbled into a job," as Selfe put it, and then into administrative positions that aligned with their research interests (and vice versa) mainly by saying yes to challenges that presented themselves. These "lucky breaks" were obviously also a product of explicit choices they made and their general willingness to size up and accept a challenge. That is to say, they co-created much of the "luck" for which they then expressed gratitude.

Lynn Worsham deliberately created opportunities for a productive chance encounter in her research practices. She told us she spent every Friday afternoon browsing the current periodicals section of the library, discovering journals she didn't know about and reading articles she might otherwise not have found. "I learned a tremendous amount about my chosen field and various debates in other fields," she told us. And she added that "to use the internet databases, you have to have some idea of what you are looking for. What I learned on my Friday afternoons was the result of pure serendipity, and it made all the difference in my intellectual formation and development" (*Women's Ways* 309).

An especially shameful arena in which not much has changed for women in the academy over the last decade is what we called "queen bee" politics: dealing with senior women colleagues who make it in the profession precisely by making it impossible for other women to do the same. Although collaboration and sisterhood are the main messages in both the recent books under consideration here, bullying is not a male-only sport. At the time we were writing *Women's Ways*, one of us had experienced a queen bee along her career path and considered it an aberration, but we were shocked by the number of respondents to our survey who reported encountering a queen bee at a particularly vulnerable moment in her career. It led us to ask the women we interviewed for our profiles about the issue. One of the more entertaining responses we received was from Selfe, who opined that her husband Dickie raised bees, and she "never did much like the queen," who was far too "privileged" for her taste. Hanging out with the worker bees, she argued, was far better. "There's always one queen bee in the hive, but you *don't* have to *like* her, nor do you have to *be like* her. Do your own good work, help others, and feel good about yourself" (*Women's Ways* 145). Nevertheless, women bullies can be particularly pernicious, which is why we weave advice about them throughout our book—including in the chapter about life beyond tenure, in which we admonish women to be obnoxious if necessary, but *never* be the Queen Bee.

Unfortunately, the queen bee is still with us. In a chapter dedicated to this subject in *Surviving Sexism in Academia*, Fran Sepler offers a welcome review of more recent studies, including a 2011 survey that found that a whopping 95% of women respondents had been a recipient of what Sepler calls "quiet bullying" (e.g., gaslighting, shunning, gossip) by a woman colleague (298). Sepler has pioneered techniques for conducting workplace investigation and in her chapter offers advice both to the queen bee's target and to institutions. She goes much further than we did, pointing out that post-traumatic stress will emerge if the target of bullying does not receive help, and they should be prepared to leave for their own mental and physical health "when an institution has made protecting the bully a priority" (303). Sepler's chapter offers a taste of the practical wisdom in this edited volume.

If we were to put out a second edition of *Women's Ways* in 2018, we would make significant revisions in a few areas. First, while issues of racial injustice emerge through the profiles in *Women's Ways* (see, for example, particularly powerful statements by Royster) it is crystal clear to all three of us today, in hindsight, that we should have attended to race, sexual orientation, ableism, and intersectionality more explicitly and more carefully in *Women's Ways*. The book especially needs to be queered: it's a cis-gender story right from the opening scenes of closet-snooping and earring advice. We so appreciate E-K Daufin's chapter in *Surviving Sexism*, "The Problem with the Phrase 'Women and Minorities,'" which illustrates how important addressing these issues continues to be.

Second, we would address ways the profession has changed because of current market conditions and other sociocultural and economic shifts. Though neither *Women's Professional Lives* nor *Surviving Sexism in Academia* deals specifically with graduate student issues, that's a part of our book we think is in need of an update a decade later. Most preliminary job interviews in rhetoric and writing studies are now conducted via Skype rather than at the MLA convention, for example. In fact, Paula Krebs, the current executive director of the Modern Language Association of America, is now actively discouraging interviewing at the convention. Among other things, holding MLA interviews forces graduate student candidates to spend money they very likely do not have, Krebs argues. She admonishes her readers to go to the convention for the right reasons—to hear the latest research in your area, to catch up and/or drink with old friends from graduate school, to network, to learn new approaches to teaching or mentoring or hiring, etc. "But for the love of all that's good and holy," she pleads, "please stop going to the MLA convention to conduct first-round job interviews." In a new edition of *Women's Ways,* we'd therefore want to offer advice about preparing for video interviews, which come with their own singular challenges.

At most public universities, time to degree has shrunk substantially, too, so students have to get through their program more quickly or risk losing funding. We'd want to address the challenges this time constraint presents to graduate students, especially to their research program, and to offer some strategies for negotiating this squeeze while producing a quality dissertation without sacrificing academic integrity or professional marketability. And of course, given the sharp decline in tenure-track positions, we'd need to offer a variety of other models for professional success and ways students might prepare themselves at every level for the possibility of all sorts of fulfilling academic and alt-ac careers. Inside and outside the academy, today's market requires some familiarity with digital literacies, so we'd suggest a number of ways graduate students might incorporate emerging technologies in teaching and research, and we'd offer some advice about how to claim appropriate digital skills on their curriculum vitae or work them into the conversation during an interview.

Third, because the culture of abuse within universities is finally being aggressively exposed by the #MeToo movement and an invigorated enforcement of the Title IX law, it seems crucial to include sober and concrete discussions, especially for graduate students, about what constitutes actionable behavior and by whom, where to go if there don't appear to be safe reporting structures within the department, and what to expect from each stage of the Title IX process. For faculty, we'd want to discuss not only what to do when a student comes to you to report a potential Title IX infraction but also ways to advocate for and develop safe reporting structures at every level of the academy. It also seems necessary, on the flipside, to discuss ways (especially feminist and queer) faculty might protect themselves against potential allegations.

The themes shared across *Women's Ways, Women's Professional Lives in Rhetoric and Composition,* and *Surviving Sexism in Academia* suggest that "here we go again" isn't always a positive thing for women pursuing a career in our field. It would be wonderful, obviously, if the rising economy would spark renewed support for higher education and an accompanying increase in tenure-track positions, both in our field and in higher education more broadly. Since we see no evidence that such a shift is on the horizon, we highly recommend the important volumes edited by Flynn and Bourelle and Cole and Hassel. Their attention to ways one might have a life within the field (*Women's Professional Lives*) and ways one might survive and fight back against the injustices within our institutions (*Surviving Sexism in Academia*) are a welcome addition to and expansion of feminist interventions in higher education like ours.

Athens, GA; Austin, TX; Norman, OK

Notes

1. See also "From Feminized to Feminist Labor," Jennifer Heinert and Cassandra Philips's chapter in *Surviving Sexism*, where they argue that the academy's increasingly reliance on contingent laborers, "the majority of whom are women," has had a particularly crippling effect on writing teachers, who are also exceptionally vulnerable in this climate:

> Because the teaching of writing is process driven and labor intensive in both instruction and assessment, those who do it are disproportionately affected by universal cost-saving measures and often have neither the time nor the political or academic capital to effect change. As a result, teachers of writing have become even more vulnerable in political and budget climates that target feminized labor as expendable and non-essential. (127)

They contend that there has been very little change in this "problematic labor dynamic" since the 1990s; in fact, it could perhaps be argued that "conditions have worsened, largely because solutions to inequity often focus on things that women should or should not do to become visible or valued in the current system rather than challenging the system itself." They advocate the creation of "feminist working conditions," which "means engaging in the complex patriarchal system while simultaneously working to change the system itself" (127-28).

Works Cited

Bivens, Kristin, Martha McKay Canter, Kirsti Cole, Violet Dutcher, Morgan Gresham, Luisa Rodriguez-Connal, and Eileen Schell. "Sisyphus Rolls On: Reframing Women's Ways of 'Making It' in Rhetoric and Composition." *Harlot*, vol.10, 2013.

Composition Studies. Special Issue on "Wo/men's Ways of Making It in Writing Studies." Vol.39, no.1, Spring 2011.

Goodburn, Amy, Donna LeCourt, and Carrie Leverenz, editors. *Rewriting Success in Rhetoric and Composition Careers*. Parlor Press, 2012.

Krebs, Paula M. "Stop Asking Candidates to Pay for Job Interviews." *Inside Higher Education*. April 19, 2018. https://www.insidehighered.com/advice/2018/04/19/head-modern-language-assocation-explains-why-she-prefers-skype-over-convention.

Centering Research, Practice, and Perspectives: Writing Center Studies and the Continued Commitment to Inclusivity and Accessibility

The Oxford Guide for Writing Tutors: Practice and Research, by Lauren Fitzgerald and Melissa Ianetta. Oxford University Press, 2015. 597 pp.

Writing Centers and Disability, by Rebecca Day Babcock and Sharifa Daniels. Fountainhead Press, 2017. 356 pp.

Reviewed by Mike Haen, University of Wisconsin-Madison

The birth of writing center studies as an academic field can be traced back to the late 1970s and early 1980s, when *WLN: A Journal for Writing Center Scholarship* (formerly *The Writing Lab Newsletter*) and *Writing Center Journal (WCJ)* produced their first issues in 1976 and 1980, respectively. Influential figures in composition studies like Kenneth Bruffee, John Trimbur, and Andrea Lunsford helped establish the field, which focused on various pedagogical issues early on and into the 21st century—perhaps the most well-known being the directive/non-directive instructional continuum. As the field developed, scholars like Irene Clark, Evelyn Ashton-Jones, and Jeff Brooks addressed the development and effectiveness of directive and non-directive, or non-interventionist, approaches to writing center tutoring. More recently, research informed by rhetorical analysis (Corbett), discourse analysis (Mackiewicz and Thompson), and activity theory (Hall) has helped the field paint a more complicated picture of the directive/non-directive instructional continuum, especially its complex relationship to tutor and writer knowledge and identity. And although this concern remains an important touchstone in writing centers and in the field, contemporary scholars have turned their attention to new topics, which are taken up by the books reviewed in this essay.

Both texts are grounded in the history of the field and will help new and veteran tutors alike build their understanding of writing centers and their history. Both texts also provide a wealth of insight for individuals new to and familiar with writing center research and instruction. Most importantly for writing center studies, these texts reflect the field's ongoing commitment to inclusivity and accessibility in scholarship and in the day-to-day work of writing center practice.

The Oxford Guide for Writing Tutors: Practice and Research, edited by Lauren Fitzgerald and Melissa Ianetta, is a comprehensive yet flexible resource intended for a broad audience including new and veteran writing center tutors at the undergraduate and graduate-levels, writing fellows or course-specific writing tutors, and writing center administrators. Its central focus is on the preparation of new one-to-one teachers of writing, most commonly in tutor training courses or practicums. Importantly, the authors see tutors as active participants in the scholarly conversations happening in writing center studies. Fitzgerald and Ianetta advocate for this stance, in part, because they claim that tutors are experts on their own academic experiences and, as they draw on those experiences, tutors often recognize unexplored assumptions in writing center pedagogy and in the field more broadly. Therefore, to help tutors become active participants in the field, Fitzgerald and Ianetta argue that writing center professionals should expose tutors-in-training to research methods applied by scholars, encourage and guide tutors' research projects about writing and tutoring, and showcase tutors' research and findings in scholarly publications.

As Fitzgerald and Ianetta write in the book's preface, "this approach to tutor training…allows tutors to test their theories of *what* might work in a writing center session and helps them to move our professional conversation toward *why* such things happen" (xiv-xv). *The Oxford Guide* enacts this tutor-centered ethos by featuring a total of fifteen articles written by undergraduate and/or graduate student tutors. These articles were previously published in venues like *WCJ* and *Young Scholars in Writing* and appear in the final "Readings from the Research" section. That section complements the earlier three sections of the text, which address the history of writing centers; tutoring strategies, writing processes, and tutoring online and across different disciplines; and lastly, the kinds of research valued and conducted in the field.

The editors' choice to incorporate work written by undergraduate and graduate tutors demonstrates the field's continued commitment to promoting tutors' voices and knowledge. Fitzgerald and Ianetta's book is another marker of the field's inclusive ethos, which has been long-reflected in *WLN's* tutor-authored column appearing in issues since 1984. That is, the field makes space for arguments and insights from emerging scholars who are not professors or writing center directors, or even graduate students in many cases. They are often undergraduates new to the field who are eager to question and critique the methods they are trained in.

To help tutors contribute to the conversation, *The Oxford Guide* offers an in-depth overview of possible research methods for writing center researchers and of possible questions that can be asked and pursued using certain methods. Following section two, "A Tutor's Handbook," and its practical focus on topics like tutoring practices and online tutoring, the authors of *The Oxford Guide* provide an accessible synthesis of the distinction between lore and method in writing center studies and delineate key concepts like reliability and validity in chapter eight. Also in chapter eight, the authors describe four kinds of research in the field, including lore, theory-based research, historical research, and empirical research, and they provide resources for readers who want to design their own research projects.

Those resources might easily be incorporated into any tutor training course that requires a research project. Fitzgerald and Ianetta offer a "Research Method Heuristic" table (194) that models a research question (e.g., "Why do so few engineering students use our writing center?") and displays examples of general and specific questions that lore, theory-based research, historical research, and empirical research can answer. Based on that sample research question about engineering, the authors also include an example of how to brainstorm and plan one's research. In the planning and brainstorming example, Fitzgerald and Ianetta include pointed questions (e.g., "What are the expectations of the venue in which I'll share my research?" "Does my research plan seem valid?") and sample answers to those questions, which demonstrate how to plan a research project (198).

To encourage readers of the book to begin planning their own projects, the authors include a "Research Method Brainstorm" template that combines the "Research Method Heuristic" and poses the same questions posed in the sample planning example about engineering. Readers are encouraged to answer those questions themselves as they begin thinking critically about potential research topics in the field. Also in section three, Ianetta and Fitzgerald explain approaches to theoretically based inquiry, historical research, and empirical research in more depth. That is, they familiarize readers with the processes of doing archival history and oral histories, along with guides of how to proceed through each research process. Chapter eleven, which focuses on empirical research, provides an accessible outline of common approaches to quantitative research and qualitative research in writing center studies, with more emphasis on the qualitative. Ianetta and Fitzgerald cover how to craft surveys that correspond well to research questions, describe the use of critical discourse analysis for analyzing tutorial talk, and define the benefits and processes of the case study method. The book also addresses research ethics. Writing center directors are sure to find the overview of ethics and the Institutional Review Board (IRB), as well as the sample informed consent forms, helpful for getting students started with their research projects.

Beyond the practical research guidance that Fitzgerald and Ianetta provide, their text also includes a section with almost 300 pages of previously published scholarship, titled, "Readings from the Research," which includes landmark work like Kenneth Bruffee's "Peer Tutoring and the 'Conversation of Mankind'" and Neal Lerner's "Searching for Robert Moore," alongside work by undergraduate and graduate tutors. This final section is an eclectic collection of articles that focus on ESL tutoring, tutoring basic writing, motivating writers, navigating gender dynamics, and attending to what graduate student authors Mandy Suhr-Systsma and Shan-Estelle Brown describe as the "everyday language of oppression in the writing center" (508). These topics reflect a clear commitment to articulating strategies for building inclusive communities in local centers and throughout the field.

Writing Centers and Disability, edited by Rebecca Day Babcock and Sharifa Daniels, parallels *The Oxford Guide's* valuing of scholarly inclusivity by featuring work from authors beyond the boundaries of composition studies and writing center studies. Authors from around the globe (e.g., United Kingdom and South Africa) as well as from fields like educational psychology and library sciences, are represented in this collection. The book arrives a little over a decade after the Conference on College Composition and Communication's (CCCC) adoption of "A Policy on Disability in CCCC," and the International Writing Centers Association's (IWCA) adoption of a "Position Statement on Disability and Writing Centers" in 2006. Since those policy shifts, the interest in disability within composition studies and writing center studies has continued to grow and flourish with work by scholars like Margaret Price, Jay Dolmage, and Stephanie Kerschbaum. Altogether, *Writing Centers and Disability* is a timely text that contributes to ongoing scholarly conversations about intersections between disability and writing centers. And, like *The Oxford Guide*, it reflects an ongoing commitment to inclusivity and accessibility in the field and in day-to-day practice.

Interestingly, the IWCA's drafting of the position statement on disability motivated the book, as the drafting committee included the co-editors, Rebecca Day (now Babcock) and Sharifa Daniels. In their introduction (chapter one), Babcock and Daniels write that "in formulating this [IWCA] position statement, the committee realized that the topic was too important and relevant to leave at a simple statement, so the committee decided to pursue a book-length, thoughtful, and critical exploration of disability and writing centers" (2). Babcock and Daniels' primary aim is to fill the sizeable gap in writing center research on disability. *Writing Centers and Disability* is organized into three separate sections: Narratives: Descriptions of Experiences, Advice, and Suggestions; Research on the Intersections of Disability and Tutoring Writing; and Policies, Practices, and Programs for Students with Disabilities in the Writing Center. Babcock and Daniels see their collection as valuing *lore* (e.g., anecdote; narrative) in the history of writing center scholarship, while prioritizing RAD (replicable, aggregable, and data-driven) research as essential for the field to build understandings of how disability figures into and proves consequential for writing center work.

A central argument across the collection is that personal narratives of disability matter and should be paired with more formal research on students with disabilities to "enhance practice and better serve students" (332). And while Babcock and Daniels do not provide as comprehensive an introductory overview of writing center history and research methodology as Fitzgerald and Ianetta do in *The Oxford Guide*, each contributor to *Writing Centers and Disability* carefully outlines their theoretical and methodological approaches. This collection of empirical research by established scholars like Margaret Price provides a strong model for bourgeoning graduate student and undergraduate researchers who are interested in studying the experiences of students and writing center staff with disabilities and in creating conditions within writing centers that promote accessibility.

In the first section of *Writing Centers and Disability*, narrative essays by people with disabilities who work in writing centers focus on a range of health conditions in relation to tutorial work, including cerebral palsy, brain injury, and mental health disabilities (e.g., anxiety disorders). Citing arguments by disability scholars Cynthia Lewiecki-Wilson and Brenda Jo Bruggemann, Babcock and Daniels claim that these narratives have a place in their collection because listening and learning "about disability from the perspective of the disabled" is an important way for teachers to recognize and understand a need for pedagogical and institutional change and to begin thinking about how to work towards that change (8).

Chapters two to five make up section one. Chapter three by Carol Ellis, for instance, is a former writing center director's personal narrative account of sustaining a brain injury that altered her life and led to her difficulty with learning and adapting to changing technologies important to her employment (39). Her narrative, which is one of the more intense and vulnerable depictions of mental disabilities in the collection, draws connections between how disabled individuals are marginalized in academia and how writing centers have a marginalized status in the university. In addition to narratives like Ellis' that challenge normative assumptions and expectations about faculty ability within academia, the book includes stories about working with mentally disabled students. For example, in chapter four, Julie Garbus tells her story of working as a faculty member while experiencing postpartum depression, alongside stories of her experiences tutoring students affected by mental health disabilities including panic disorders and manic episodes. After telling anecdotes that play out in her center, she provides practical suggestions for helping students facing similar situations. Garbus recommends that writers set up ongoing appointments with the same tutor to build trust (64) and advises that tutors reconsider their typical reliance on nondirective approaches, which might confuse and overwhelm anxious students who need more direction and guidance (66). The essays in this first section offer valuable stories and suggestions for rethinking and refining pedagogical practices in writing center work.

In the collection's second section, there is a turn to original empirical research. As Babcock notes in the book's concluding chapter, "Research Review and Call to Research," before this edited collection, her past articles on deaf students were "the only formal published research studies based on observation of tutoring sessions with disabled students in the writing center" (329). Daniels and Babcock include four original research studies that draw on different methodologies. In one, Margaret Price reports results from her case study of Bella—a student with a seizure disorder and emotional disabilities (e.g., panic and anxiety disorders). Using semi-structured interviews and analysis of Bella's written texts, Price examines Bella's view of her identity as an English major by describing emerging themes like independence/dependence, singled out/blending in, response to authorities, and expertise in literary studies (140).

Price concludes that Bella's experiences reinforce the need for writing center practitioners to ask how each individual student learns best, and what tutors can do to best facilitate that learning. Another chapter by Babcock discusses her study using grounded theory to analyze transcripts of several tutoring sessions between deaf students, hearing tutors, and interpreters, and to examine follow-up interviews (192). She finds that deaf students focused more on grammar errors in their sessions than hearing students and suggests that when tutors are nondirective, deaf students might become more confused and frustrated (209). Babcock importantly points out how directness or what she calls "straight-talk" is one cultural value of the deaf community, which can conflict with the writing center pedagogical emphasis on non-directive feedback (210). Also in this second section, writing instructor Marshall M. Kitchens and his student Sandra Duhkie study the use of voice recognition software Dragon NaturallySpeaking 7 (DNS) for helping students with cognitive disabilities. They highlight the tutoring relationship between Micah, an adult with a cognitive impairment, and Sandra, a student enrolled in a college composition class. The piece chronicles what Micah and Sandra learn about the technology, its affordances, and its shortcomings, as they collaborated with one another and helped Micah complete tasks like sending emails and building multimedia presentations. Although it is certainly not generalizable to all contexts, this article might help tutors-in-training better understand and think critically about the affordances of voice recognition software and applications within tutorial contexts. Ultimately, the strength of this section is its modeling of approaches to empirical research projects on disability in the writing center context.

The final section of *Writing Centers and Disability* shifts its focus to policy in the writing center and academy. Four chapters discuss policies, practices, and innovative programs for students with disabilities in the writing center. For example, in chapter ten, UK scholars Sue Jackson and Margo Blythman recount their programmatic advances in working with mentally disabled students through their student support program at University of the Arts London. They look closely at strategies employed by their program to support four different students with a range of conditions such as obsessive-compulsive disorder and depression. The positive benefits they saw support their argument in favor of collaboration between academic departments and student health units in the academy. Later, in chapter thirteen, Sharifa Daniels and Doria Daniels discuss disability in South African higher education and examine inclusive practices of the writing center at a South African university. Whether these reports situated in local sites can be generalized to other settings is an open question and a notable but reasonable limitation with this kind of work. Nonetheless, this work forms a nice foundation for administrators when developing policies in the writing center and university.

Finally, another way that *Writing Centers and Disability* and *The Oxford Guide* each reflect an ongoing commitment to inclusivity is how they engage and challenge readers. In other words, readers are invited into the scholarly conversation initiated by each author in these collections. In Babcock and Daniels' book, the end of each chapter provides readers with a few critical questions that are meant to help generate further reflection and discussion about writing centers and disability. For example, at the end of her case study, Price asks readers to reflect on the themes that organize her analysis: "How might these themes create tensions for disabled students working with writing center tutors? How might they provide a source of enriched communication and collaboration between tutors and learners?" (161). Such questions make the collection relevant for both advanced scholars and undergraduate tutors-in-training who are concerned about practice and research. Fitzgerald and Ianetta also structure the reader's experience with "For Discussion" questions at the start of each chapter that aim to help reading comprehension and facilitate class discussion. "For Writing" questions dispersed throughout each chapter are more formal and may be used as starting points for journal entries or blog postings in which readers make connections between concepts. "For Inquiry" questions push readers to think generatively and critically about their plans for original research as well as how that research would fit into their current understanding of writing center work and the field.

About four decades since the emergence of writing center studies as a discipline, its ongoing commitment to issues of inclusivity and accessibility is clearly represented in both of these recent publications. The field, and the people who work in it, see the value of including many voices from varied scholarly backgrounds and experiences as well as from across the globe. By centering research, practice, and a multitude of perspectives, these texts offer exciting new directions for established and emerging scholars.

Madison, Wisconsin

Legible Sovereignties: Rhetoric, Representations, and Native American Museums, by Lisa King. Oregon State University Press, 2017. 163 pp.

Reviewed by Katie Bramlett, University of Maryland

As public memory and Indigenous scholarship are fast growing areas of study in composition and rhetoric (see Brown; Monberg; Morris; Ramos), work that explores the intersections therein is particularly timely. Lisa King's *Legible Sovereignties: Rhetoric, Representations, and Native American Museums* works at this intersection. King investigates the rhetorical impact of three tribal museums: the Chippewa Ziibiwing Center, Haskell Cultural Center and Museum, and the National Museum of the American Indian. Building on Scott Lyons's rhetorical sovereignty, or "the inherent right of [Indigenous] *peoples* to determine their own communicative needs and desires in this pursuit, to decide for themselves the goals, modes, styles, and languages of public discourse" (449-50), King examines how museums legibly claim rhetorical sovereignty. That is, she is interested in how museums make their history, culture, and ways of knowing accessible or understandable to visitors. Through three chapters, an introduction, and a conclusion, King argues for the importance of sites of public memory to enact sovereignty in a legible format.

The introduction of *Legible Sovereignties* lays the groundwork for the scholarship that King employs—Indigenous studies, public memory studies, and rhetoric—to examine how the three museums assert rhetorical sovereignty and, more importantly, make that sovereignty legible to an audience in a clear and sustained format. For King, the term sovereignty is flexible and meant "to encompass multiple routes and means to self-determination, and the intrinsic right of Native and Indigenous peoples, communities, and nations to self-represent in whatever means, modes, and public stages they choose as appropriate" (8). King believes that because museums have historically been colonized institutions, balancing sovereignty with audience reception is key to working within traditional understandings of museums and honoring Indigenous culture and history. Therefore, King dedicates her book to analyzing rhetorically the museums' displays in order to extrapolate the legibility of their discursive practices. This method includes a consideration of the effect on the audience and the tensions between the tribes' intentions and the museums' representations.

After establishing an analytical framework, chapter one analyzes the legibility of the Saginaw Chippewa Indian Tribe of Michigan's Ziibiwing Center of Anishinabe Culture and Lifeways near Mount Pleasant. King begins by describing the displays, mission statement and narrative of the Ziibiwing Center. She focuses on the choices the museum made to assert Saginaw Chippewa voices and to help make their sovereignty accessible to a diverse audience. She details the museum's aesthetic, architectural, and linguistic elements, analyzing each in relation to how they represent and express Anishinabe culture and history to visitors. King also considers the ways museums and cultural centers rhetorically shape and influence the world around them by analyzing the cultural events at the museum and their connections to the surrounding community. For the Ziibiwing Center, public outreach includes cultural celebrations and collaborations with the local university, even if the surrounding community has not always historically welcomed or honored the tribe. Overall, King finds that Ziibiwing has a rich cultural heritage that not only independently voices their own history and modern day contributions to the community but also challenges former adversaries to learn about the tribe.

In chapter two, King analyzes an intertribal college museum, the Haskell Cultural Center and Museum (HCCM) at Haskell Indian Nations University in Lawrence, Kansas. Her reading of HCCM is more complex than the Ziibiwing Center, as HCCM not only represents multiple tribes but also has an admittedly complicated past and present relationship with the government. According to King, Haskell University's origins are deeply embedded in colonial practices since its beginning as a boarding school for young Native children. In 2002, the campus community and surrounding neighborhood paid considerable attention to HCCM's grand opening. King highlights this attention by examining students' active participation in creating displays and hosting opening ceremonies. Further, she underscores several distinct challenges to HCCM's articulation of sovereignty after the initial fanfare of its opening. After a few years, student and community involvement declined and HCCM struggled to maintain adequate funding. King maps out ways HCCM continued to struggle to make their sovereignty rhetorically legible despite a lack of fiscal support. HCCM also updated their mission statement and added a new display in order to meet the communicative needs of the community. These changes struggled to integrate coherently the new and old displays within the existing space and failed to attract more visitors, raising questions their rhetorical success. While other museums may face similar struggles, King believes that a lack of funding instigated HCCM's problems. She expands legible sovereignties to include adequate fiscal support as a foundation for successful rhetorical display.

King's third chapter examines the National Museum of the American Indian (NMAI) in Washington, DC. According to King, upon its inaugural opening, the NMAI challenged traditional Western museum and display conventions in more overt ways than do HCCM and the Ziibiwing Center. NMAI seeks to challenge viewers' concept of Native Americans as antiques of the past by using a nonchronological organization and by celebrating differences of tribes across North and South America. King points out that the nonlinear, noncontrolling narrative that the museum employed upon opening was met with mixed reviews and left the majority of the visitors confused and unsure what to think. As a result, King argues that the initial opening of the NMAI failed to make intertribal rhetorical sovereignty legible to visitors. This tension between the communicative goal of the museum and audience interpretation is the primary purpose behind rhetorically legible sovereignty. For King, a balance between rhetorical intent and audience reception is essential for achieving successful self-representation. Several years after its opening, the NMAI responded to these critiques and provided a friendlier atmosphere for children and individuals who know little about Native Americans. King argues that this shift does not mean that the museum abandoned Native meaning making practices, but instead highlights the way the museum acknowledged the complicated relationship between rhetorical effectiveness, museums, and visitors.

The conclusion puts the struggles and accomplishments of the three museums in conversation with one another. King helps the reader to recognize patterns of decision making, visitor response, and community involvement of established by the three institutions. King's analysis identifies strategies tribal museums use to make their sovereignty legible in relation to diverse audiences. To communicate indigenous self-determination, King highlights the ways each museum uniquely struggled to create a legible message that would reach both tribal and nontribal visitors through cultural displays. As the Ziibiwing Center, HCCM, and NMAI employed unique methods in creating legible displays, she argues that because sovereignty is highly localized, different museums will make their sovereignties legible using distinct methods. King underscores that this process is ongoing and that tensions will always exist. Museums will continually need to consider audiences and combat colonizing histories endemic to such institutions. Attention to the museum's legibility opens opportunities to understand the representation of "the involved Native community the way it wishes to be understood" (King 162).

Overall, *Legible Sovereignties: Rhetoric, Representations, and Native American Museums* demonstrates the ongoing struggle for rhetorical sovereignty and the role museums play in articulating and educating the public. King weaves together three fields of study to reveal the need to understand how tribal museums are constructed, the message they hope to and do convey, and the ways a community can be changed and influenced by their presence. She attunes the audience to the intricate and complex meaning making processes a museum must consider, underscoring their potential as sites that challenge Western ideological practices. I recommend *Legible Sovereignties* primarily to scholars interested in public memory and Indigenous studies and secondarily to museum connoisseurs who seek insight into tribal museums and the cultural work they perform. In this regard, chapter three on the NMAI is most compelling in its focus on audience response as key to making effective changes. King considers the audiences' varied responses and shows how NMAI directly responded to these critiques by recomposing the displays for diverse audiences.

This response is important for composition and rhetoric as it models ways an academic analysis connects to cultural institutions. King provides insightful analyses of the museums, and it becomes clear that the "legibility" of a museum necessitates an audience that understands the museum's rhetorical message. She includes information from newspapers as well as interviews with curators and authors to show the museum's intent and general reception; however, the concrete ways museums can and do collect audience feedback to inspire effective change would further the supposition that understanding rhetorical legibility of a museum increases the overall message of sovereignty. Nonetheless, King lays the foundation for future work in understanding the relationship between sites of public memory, history, and continued community involvement, especially in relation to Native American history, culture, and rhetorical practices.

College Park, Maryland

Works Cited

Lyons, Scott Richard. "Rhetorical Sovereignty: What do American Indians Want from Writing?" *CCC,* vol. 51, no. 3, 2000, pp. 447-68.

Florida, edited by Jeff Rice. Parlor Press, 2015. 304 pp.

Reviewed by Jacob W. Craig, College of Charleston

Extending the lineage of composition studies research examining space (e.g., Nedra Reynolds' foundational *Writing Geographies*), *Florida* further develops the methodological approach first introduced by Jeff Rice in his monograph, *Digital Detroit: Rhetoric and Space in the Age of the Network*. Like *Digital Detroit*, *Florida* develops stories through details and fragments that are networked in choric or multiple, relational patterns of meaning. In his introduction to the edited collection, Rice encourages readers to approach *Florida* as neither a history nor a cultural critique but as a method for writing about space "that allows personal and non-personal meanings" to interact, making "a variety of identifications" of patterns possible (13). But while *Florida* and *Digital Detroit* share a similar intellectual frame and methodology for studying space, as an edited collection, *Florida* is a different project from *Digital Detroit*. Rather than developing a networked representation of *Florida* through his own memories and experiences, Rice provides for a wider range of meanings and patterns to emerge by inviting contributors to offer their own memories, experiences, observations, reflections, appreciations, and scholarship to develop a networked representation of Florida. Thus, *Florida* functions like "an internal Facebook page" that links Rice and his memories to other writers, other objects, other memories, and other sites of meaning beyond the Miami home that Rice describes in the introduction and in his contribution to the collection (8). As members of Rice's internal Facebook page, the other contributors draw on their experiences growing up in, studying in, or living in Florida, making a range of patterns available to trace, some of which include migration and mobility; dwelling and urban design; racial and religious discrimination; desire and psychosis. Ultimately, however, the patterns established in the book are left to the reader to identify and trace across the networked fragments that are curated in each chapter. In an effort to help readers identify patterns, the book is organized in five sections, each focused around a different approach to developing Florida's story as a networked space.

The first section, "Florida Patterns," is most informed by the concept of chora that frames the collection. Sean Morey's chapter, "A Network of Bones," is a strong beginning to this section and the book. Through his exploration of Key West as a choric space, Morey brings together his personal memories of fishing, Key West's topography, the legacies of Jimmy Buffett and Hemingway, and Key West's history as a pirate enclave that culminates in "the atmosphere of loss" that haunts Morey's Key West. Jeff Rice's contribution follows, wherein he develops a Certeau-like spatial story of Kendall, a suburb of Miami. Weaving together his childhood memories, his scholarship (particularly, *The Rhetoric of Cool*), James Brown, boxing, gangsters, JFK, UFOs, and Hurricane David, Rice's spatial story represents the feeling that Miami is a site for secrecy, conspiracy, and mystery. Charlie Hailey's chapter, "Florida Trouse," focuses on the intransient mobile homes that have been a consistent feature of Florida's landscape since the 1930s. Hailey traces the significance of mobile homes to Florida's history and culture, examining them as sites of domesticity, escape, shelter, and DIY improvisation that helped transform Florida into "not just a place to dwell but the place to dream" (69).

The second section, "Florida Stories," features four personal narratives interwoven with history and scholarship. The section begins with Todd Taylor's memories of living in Tampa, tracing how Tampa has referenced other places (for instance, New Orleans and Miami) and people (for instance, Midwesterners and Cubans) for its identity, ultimately creating a place without a distinguishing signature. Next, Cassandra Branham and Megan McIntyre describe their childhood in New Port Richie through an assemblage of photographs and fragmented stories, ultimately revealing that the assemblage of people, economics, environments, and communities that comprise New Port Richie is a reflection of Florida: also an assemblage of varied and often-competing fragments. Lillie Anne Brown offers her memories growing up in Florida's capital city, Tallahassee, in the 1960s during the struggle for civil rights in the Jim Crow South, ultimately demonstrating how segregation shaped local geographies and economics while reaffirming Florida's status as a Southern state despite the histories of migration from the north and Midwest that shaped central and southern Florida. Steve Neuman's chapter, the final one in this section, extends Brown's examination of the impact of race and class on the geography of cities by turning again to Kendall's Jewish community.

The third section takes a different approach than the previous two by using Florida's environment as a heuristic for theorizing networks, spectacle, non-places, and reading. The approach of this section, organized under the rubric of Florida Studies, strongly resembles ecocomposition as Sid Dobrin and Christian Weisser have previously theorized. Each contributor to this section ultimately considers "what effects discourse has in mapping, constructing, shaping, defining, and understanding" Florida and what effects Florida's ecology and environment have on discourse (Dobrin and Weisser 573). Through his case study aimed at representing networks with greater complexity, Dilger examines West Palm's canal system, tracing how cultural, political, and legal networks shape and are influenced by the network of waterways in and around West Palm. James Beasley follows, theorizing gaze and spectacle through his case study of Ponte Verde Beach, the site for the most watched tournament in golf, The Players. David Grant's chapter examines the non-placeness of Town 'n' Country, a census-designated suburb whose name, geography, and culture all contribute to a space vacant of history and master narratives, which can be productive sites for fabricating hopeful realities. Through his study of Florida's history of racial discrimination on beaches, Sidney Dobrin forwards the practice of "reading beaches" as paying attention to transitional spaces that affect, regulate, and discipline the bodies that occupy them (214).

In the final section, "Florida Theory," contributors bring together both personal and non-personal fragments of meaning in service of theory-making. Craig Saper with Adam Trowbridge and Jessica Westbrook's production and research group, Channel Two, examine Epcot's original designs and eventual realities to theorize Epcot as a site of psychosis and foreclosure: intentionally kept separate from reality and unable to fabricate successfully its utopic vision. Lauren Mitchell also focuses on the Orlando area, attending to "the city's boxes," particularly its various sites of retail, hospitality, domesticity, storage, and construction to consider how human desire influences Orlando's design, rendering the city's landscape incoherent and architects unable to design in ways that can improve the lives of inhabitants (250). Gregory Ulmer's concluding chapter returns to the book's framing concept of chora by creating a choragraphy different from Sean Morey's in the opening chapter. Focusing on a Superfund site of ground and air pollution outside of Gainesville, Florida, Ulmer samples an interactive exhibit that he terms a konsult: a genre that theorizes a region in order to amend a crisis in the "Well-Being" of the region (277). Ultimately, Ulmer's chapter both enacts choragraphy and forwards a design for choragraphy meant to educate and improve people's lives.

As indicated by Rice in the introduction, this book is an experiment in representing and analyzing space. Reading *Florida* feels somewhat like viewing a chaotic Prezi, jumping without warning from rhetorical and critical theory to creative nonfiction to descriptions of streets and cities to the historicization of places, objects, and people. Thus, reading this book feels much more like reading fragments than a coherent work, and that is very much the purpose. Knowing that one node links to another without a clear connection invites close consideration of what each fragment and memory means and how it relates to the rest of the network. Having spent time in Tallahassee for graduate school, I identified with the picture of Florida developed here: particularly, the sense that Florida's "boxes," specifically its strip malls, suggest that Florida is like anywhere while its history and landscape suggest that it is distinct from everywhere else. Living with these competing realities and patterns *is* Florida, and *Florida*'s approach makes that recognition possible. Thus, as an approach to studying and analyzing space, *Florida* is a provocative model of spatial scholarship, particularly for studying spaces like institutions and disciplinary formations that are also comprised of fragments rich in contradiction.

Charleston, SC

Works Cited

Dobrin, Sidney I., and Christian R. Weisser. "Breaking Ground in Ecocomposition: Exploring Relationships between Discourse and Environment." *College English*, vol. 64, no. 5, 2002, pp. 566-89.

Inside the Subject: A Theory of Identity for the Study of Writing, by Raúl Sánchez. NCTE, 2017. 127 pp.

Reviewed by Thomas Girshin, Ithaca College

Raúl Sánchez's *Inside the Subject: A Theory of Identity for the Study of Writing* is a refreshingly practical book about heavy theoretical terrain, addressing some of the most obdurate binaries of writing studies—individual/social, empiricism/postmodernism—with an unembellished acuteness that makes his view seem as if it had always been there, just waiting to be discovered.

Ultimately, Sánchez's purpose is to outline a thoroughly rhetorical definition of identity, one that adequately describes the function of identity in acts of writing. His project, therefore, nudges us to revise our thinking about identity in writing, which Sánchez argues relies on a series of foregone conclusions. According to Sánchez, identity has been repeatedly and rigorously critiqued but remains stubbornly at the center of the way the field seems to imagine writing nevertheless. Sánchez argues, however, that this persistence isn't a bad thing, that in fact the intractability of identity suggests that identity is a recurring function of writing, and therefore something observable in acts of writing.

Sánchez begins with the premise that when we think, talk, or write about writing, we do so from the assumption that there is something outside or beyond language that we're representing, some referent we're aiming at, or grasping for, even when, as good postmodernists, we know better (8).

To illustrate this point, Sánchez provides thoughtful and generous readings of some of the field's major recent texts on identity, invention, and style, including Alex Reid's *The Two Virtuals: New Media and Composition*, Donna LeCourt's *Identity Matters: Schooling the Student Body in Academic Discourse*, Collin G. Brooke's *Lingua Fracta: Towards a Rhetoric of New Media*, Thomas Rickert's *Ambient Rhetoric: The Attunements of Rhetorical Being*, and John Muckelbauer's *The Future of Invention: Rhetoric, Postmodernism, and the Problem of Change*.

In all these works, despite their varied approaches and topics, despite their focus on writing as a fundamentally relational process, a space remains for the writing subject, an agent who is responsible for producing new text, or for making stylistic decisions. Rather than see this as a product of incomplete or faulty reasoning in the works analyzed, Sánchez suggests that this space, what he refers to as identity or interiority, is a fundamental if undertheorized property of writing. Perhaps writing, he argues, demands this space, this function that we call identity. Sánchez is not really interested in whether or not identity exists as identity (he acknowledges postmodern critiques that it doesn't). Rather, he is interested in what function identity continues to play in writing, especially at the moment of inscription. This shift in emphasis, according to Sánchez, moves theorizing about identity out of philosophy—where it has remained even in writing studies, and which focuses on what identity is—and into rhetoric, which focuses on what effects identity might have.

After reviewing the postmodern critique of identity and some responses to it, most notably from "post-positivists" Satya P. Mohanty and Linda Martín Alcoff, Sánchez provides his own theory of identity as event, a term he borrows nominally from Alain Badiou and substantively from Jacques Derrida. The event, Sánchez writes, "[describes] the encounter between the functions of exteriority and interiority," and identity "[describes] that encounter as it is said to take place at moments of inscription" (112). Drawing primarily on Derrida's lecture, "A Certain Impossible Possibility of Saying the Event," Sánchez argues that every act of writing is compelled by identity, that is, that writing necessarily carries identity with it. This is distinct from postmodern axioms about the nonexistence of a neutral language, in its suggesting that every act of writing also calls out, so to speak, to identity as a concept. As Sánchez argues, "We should think of identity as a feature, a function, a symptom of every act of inscription, at work in every scene of writing" (72-3). If, as Sánchez argues, identity is a Derridean event, then identity befalls the writer in the act of writing as a singular expression, and yet in its repeatability is not purely singular, but relatable, a symptom of language use. Neither an expression of who one (really) is, nor a violent, oppressive constraint, identity names the feature of writing that, qua writing, compels us toward a notion of agency.

Sánchez ends the book by writing, "I have not been trying to say something new about writing. I have, instead, been trying to say something new about what we say—and how we think—about writing" (113). This is why *Inside the Subject* draws so extensively on interpretations of many of the last decade's seminal works in writing studies, in order to recontextualize arguments as they relate to identity. Despite this, or perhaps because of it, this reviewer would have appreciated greater development of Sánchez's event-based theory of identity itself. Many of the book's central questions overlap significantly with those of philosophy, but Sánchez makes clear that he wants to leave philosophical grounds for rhetorical ones. This move is understandable, but the task of severing questions of identity, reality, exteriority and interiority, and the event (and, indeed, rhetoric) from philosophy is a staggering (if not impossible) one, hence done incompletely here. The result is an occasional ambiguity of terms. For instance, the interrogation of the interiority/exteriority binary is sometimes slippery, substituting for inside subject, identity, writer, and discourse, and for outside reality, empiricism, essentialism, and event. This very binary—specifically as it relates to identity—is the subject of Alcoff's *Visible Identities*, but regrettably—perhaps to veer away from philosophy—Sánchez draws only on her earlier essay, "Who's Afraid of Identity Politics?"

Ultimately, Sánchez's *Inside the Subject* is a compelling nudge for writing scholars to bring identity into the study of writing itself, to see identity not as a purely theoretical construct, a lens that ought to shape our studies of writing, but as an empirical feature of writing at the point of inscription. Identity, Sánchez argues, is observable. This claim is profoundly valuable for writing studies, not only for its methodological implications but also because it reveals how philosophy's longstanding animosity toward identity has influenced work in our field. Identity is not a false construct, not a narcissistic delusion, not a source of bias. Instead, Sánchez argues, identity is a real and productive effect observable in acts of writing.

Ithaca, New York

Facing the Sky: Composing through Trauma in Word and Image, by Roy F. Fox. Parlor Press, 2016. 298 pp.

Reviewed by Christy Goldsmith, University of Missouri

In his foreword to *Facing the Sky: Composing through Trauma in Word and Image*, Peter Elbow notes how his own 1973 book, *Writing Without Teachers*, spoke to the benefits of freewriting in much the same way that Roy F. Fox's 2016 text speaks to the benefits of trauma writing. Yet, he says (and Fox would clearly agree), the debate of "whether freewriting and personal writing can improve writing" (xi) still rages in composition and rhetoric scholarship. In this way, *Facing the Sky* begins with a clear thesis: While trauma writing is both useful and necessary, the method, characteristics, and rhetorical advantages of trauma composition remain largely unexplored.

Beginning with a short story recounting his grandfather's death, Fox realizes, for his then ten-year-old self, "word and image did not exist" (5) to help him deal with the trauma because it never occurred to him to write—or talk—about the loss. Several decades later, though, he witnesses the power of language to support the grieving process as he watches his daughter face the death of their family cat through the lens of *Charlotte's Web*. In these early anecdotes, Fox makes it clear that he practices what he preaches, and this authenticity only adds richness to the text's theoretical and practical outcomes.

We've long known that literacy activities help us cope with life's difficulties (see Allen; Anderson and MacCurdy; Borrowman; DeSalvo; Pennebaker), but through his diverse case studies, Fox explains how—and, more importantly, why—*composing through trauma* is especially powerful for the healing process. In his first pages, Fox details the most significant benefit of trauma writing, one which makes his text applicable to a wide readership. Trauma writing, he says, allows us to work through difficult circumstances, but it also allows us to "generate more and different thinking" (33). The act of writing about trauma not only works psychologically, creating a "less fragmented self" (24), but also allows educators to look beyond students as "learning machines" (43) in order to reinforce the value of expressive writing at all levels and in all disciplines.

Throughout the text, Fox focuses simultaneously on the humanity and the practicality of trauma writing. In chapter one, he provides a thorough and diverse review of the literature, citing studies from rhetoric, medicine, and history, which fully immerse the reader in the current conversation surrounding trauma writing. Exemplifying the theoretical lens he often employs for analysis, Fox then moves down Hayakawa's Ladder of Abstraction—a diagram adapted from Alfred Korzybski's work, which illustrates connections between language, perceptions, and meaning. Moving to the bottom of the

Ladder to provide concrete examples of trauma writing, Fox includes bits of letters from Presidents Jefferson, Lincoln, and Truman to anchor his literature review. These examples from our collective history combined with Fox's own stories of personal trauma showcase his readable prose and set the stage for the diverse set of participants and writing presented later.

In chapter two, the author outlines his methodology and describes his extensive background in teaching trauma writing to rural American high school students, developmental writing college students, and South African HIV-patient writers. This rundown of Fox's career as a writing teacher adds depth—and, again, Hayakawan concreteness—to his already extensive review of the literature. One of Fox's strengths is his ability to connect with people, and as such, the case study represented here spans five years and fourteen participants, all of whom were some level of literacy expert. Fox tells us that his friendships with his participants led to the raw, deep, and honest data his study produced, but it quite often left him feeling like "a phony priest . . . exploiting the tragedies of others" (76). Fox represents research as a highly personal endeavor much like the subject of his study itself. This honesty and reflexivity allow the author to enter his data through multiple points, apply different lenses, and produce a text as authentic as the words and images within it.

In chapter three, Fox showcases the trauma writing of Lucy, one of his former doctoral students, who was diagnosed with stage four metastatic breast cancer at age 42. More than a beautiful and heartbreaking story, this chapter demonstrates the forms trauma writing can take—emotional, rational, and professional—and the role of audience within these forms. Lucy's letters, emails, posts on a cancer website, and journals depict trauma writing as the most reliable external representation of the internal process of coping. Through her skillful and imagistic language, we can see Lucy rejecting society's typical depiction of a breast cancer patient: the bescarved smiling woman taking a selfie from a chemo chair. Fox describes the effect of Lucy's identification as a cancer patient and subsequent rejection of the typical cancer patient trope, giving us a peek into the verbal mind of his participant.

Again showcasing his reflexivity, Fox discusses his interview transcription process, noting how his choice to include Lucy's hesitations emphasizes the semantic process of verbalization. It is here that Fox makes his first suggestion of how trauma writing leads to improved writing across all genres: The power of this passage is in Lucy's "highly specific language," which allows the action to slow down and grants the author time to more completely process the situation (84). In this section, Fox also applies James Moffett's theory of simultaneous differentiation and integration to suggest that trauma writing is effective even beyond its ability to improve writing skills. He notes how Lucy often seeks to distance herself from typical cancer images, and in doing so, "the presence of some *other thing* . . . helps to *ground* and *anchor* those feelings being tapped from our internal reservoir" (146). The *other thing* is a theme which re-emerges throughout the text, manifesting in words and images from multiple writers.

Much of the strength of Fox's book is his refusal to adhere to overly prescriptive qualitative methods; his experimentation in chapter structure and content allows for his theoretical foundation to find a practical application. Chapter four is one such break from the traditional structure as he moves from focusing on a single case study participant to analyzing texts produced in his trauma writing graduate course. He provides brief explanations for fascinating assignments like The Monster and the Angel through which students like Minji were able to "crystallize" their traumatic incidents by refashioning their traumatic images (The Monster) into images of hope (The Angel) (126). Through his discussion of his students' work, Fox makes a clear point about the nature of trauma writing: Though the intensity of traumas varies, some seemingly less severe forms, like one graduate student who writes about his loan debt, might be more "subtle and insidious" than they seem on the surface (141).

Chapter five highlights another singular case study participant in Kate, a woman who lost her husband to a tragic motor scooter accident. While audience is featured prominently in Lucy's chapter through her differing forms of writing, Kate's chapter covers only one form of trauma writing—her personal journals. The intimate nature of this chapter forefronts the unique mutability of trauma writing. For example, in one entry, Kate lists and describes her husband in a format which turns him into characters of Hank the ___ (the blank filled with multiple labels like "gourmet" and "wordsmith"). Fox uses this opportunity to discuss naming, images, and metaphors as framing devices, which serves to unpack the implicit meanings communicated in text. Throughout this chapter, Fox peels back the layers of Kate's situation, drawing parallels to Lucy's situation and providing clear examples of key trauma writing themes such as "tapping into the inner stream," differentiating and integrating to discover selfhood, and, like in Lucy's case, using *the other thing* to process the traumatic event (202).

These varied and interesting case studies come together in the final chapter wherein Fox connects the themes across the various forms and authors. Some outcomes can be applied across many genres of writing. Elements leading to writers' perseverance and internalized principles of rhetoric, for example, speak to the ways trauma writing improves all writing. Other outcomes reveal the unique benefits of trauma writing—the writers' ability to gain control and pursue oppositions—and make a strong case for increased trauma writing in both educational and medical environments. Most importantly, though, Fox makes an effective case for integrating trauma composing into our academic courses. He lists a myriad of "characteristics heralded by academic thinking," which he also identifies in trauma writing (231).

As a writing program administrator, when I read this book, it struck me that so many of the texts we read in the classroom concern trauma, but so few we write do. Clearly, trauma writing is already venerated in our culture, and as such, Fox suggests we need also revere it in our writing classrooms. Trauma writing—unlike many other types of academic writing—allows us to start in the middle and work our way to a sound conclusion, prompting thinking all along the way. After all, as Fox says, "If we *begin* with a judgment or conclusion, why go further?" (170).

Columbia, Missouri

Works Cited

Allen, Guy. "Language, Power, and Consciousness: A Writing Experiment at the University of Toronto." *Writing and Healing: Towards an Informed* Practice, edited by Charles Anderson and Marian MacCurdy, NCTE, 2000, pp. 249-91.

Anderson, Charles, and Marian MacCurdy, editors. *Writing and Healing: Towards an Informed Practice*. NCTE, 2000, pp. 58-82.

Borrowman, Shane. *Trauma and the Teaching of Writing*. SUNY P, 2006.

DeSalvo, Louise. *Writing as a Way of Healing: How Telling Our Stories Transforms Our Lives*. Beacon P, 1999.

Hayakawa, S. I., and Alan R. Hayakawa. *Language in Thought and Action*, 5th edition, Harcourt, Inc., 1990.

Moffett, James. *Coming on Center: English Education in Evolution*. Boynton/Cook, 1992.

Pennebaker, James W. *Writing to Heal*. New Harbinger Publications, 2004.

Announcement

2019 Spilman Symposium on Issues in Teaching Writing

The Institute Writing Program at Virginia Military Institute in Lexington, Virginia invites faculty, instructors, and graduate students interested in the teaching of writing to join this one-day symposium on February 9, 2019. Presentations by Cheryl Glenn (Penn State), Robert Asen (U of Wisconsin-Madison), and Ann George (TCU) will initiate conversations among participants about this year's theme, Discourse for Democracy: Teaching Writing and Rhetoric for Civic Life. Participation is limited to the first 80 registrants. Registration is $40 and runs from November 15, 2018 to January 15, 2019. Register at www.vmi.edu/iwp

Contributors

Michelle Ballif, professor at University of Georgia, teaches courses in rhetoric, composition and contemporary literary and cultural theory. She is co-editor of *Women's Ways of Making It in Rhetoric and Composition* (Routledge, 2008), which details success strategies for women academics in the field. Ballif has edited several books on rhetorical histories and is currently President-elect of the Rhetoric Society of America.

Katie Bramlett is a doctoral candidate at the University of Maryland, College Park where she teaches writing courses and currently works as a Writing Center Administrative Fellow. Her scholarly interests include public memory studies, cultural rhetorics, and writing pedagogy.

Meaghan H. Brewer is assistant professor at Pace University (NYC), where she teaches courses in composition and literacy and directs the writing across the curriculum program. Her research includes training for graduate students, literacy, and women's science education. She recently published an article on the latter in *Peitho*.

Tessa Brown is a lecturer in Stanford's Program in Writing and Rhetoric, where she teaches and researches digital and hip hop literacies, critical whiteness studies, and histories of higher education. Her research has most recently appeared in *Peitho*. Find her on twitter @tessalaprofessa.

Carolyn Commer is assistant professor of English at Virginia Tech. Her research examines the rhetoric of U.S. higher education policy and local public leadership. She teaches courses in classical and modern rhetorical theory, critical theory, and professional writing.

Ana Cooke is assistant professor of professional writing at The Pennsylvania State University. Her research interests include professional writing, digital rhetoric, contemporary public discourse, and writing pedagogy. She teaches rhetoric, composition, and professional writing.

Jacob W. Craig is assistant professor at College of Charleston where he teaches courses in digital rhetoric and composition theory. Examining the relationship between writers and materiality, his work has appeared, among other places, in *Literacy in Composition Studies* and *Computers and Composition Online*.

Diane Davis is professor and chair of the Department of Rhetoric and Writing and affiliate faculty with English and communication studies at University of Texas at Austin. Her work is situated at the intersection of rhetorical theory and continental philosophy.

Kristen di Gennaro is assistant professor of English and Director of Composition at Pace University (NYC) where she teaches writing, composition theory, and language and linguistics. Her scholarly interests include second-language writing, sociolinguistic aspects of writing, and the interaction of language and gender.

Patricia Fancher is a lecturer at University of California, Santa Barbara, where she researches rhetoric and composition with a focus on feminist rhetoric, embodiment, and digital media. She teaches courses on multimedia composition, gender studies, and rhetorical theory. Dr. Fancher serves as the Director of Outreach and Digital Media for the Coalition of Feminist Scholars in the History of Rhetoric and Composition.

Thomas Girshin is assistant professor of writing at Ithaca College, and author of the forthcoming volume, *The Creative Argument* (Hackett).

Christy Goldsmith is assistant director of the Campus Writing Program at the University of Missouri. Her research is twofold as she investigates the teaching of disciplinary literacy at the secondary and post-secondary levels and explores narratives of secondary English teachers-as-writers.

Michelle Graber teaches writing and communication studies at Mitchell Technical Institute, specializing in composition and professional communications. Her pedagogical interests include teaching workplace-specific genres to students seeking technical or trade degrees and studying how fyw practice transfers into applied contexts.

Jacob Greene is assistant professor of English at Arizona State University. His research and teaching explores the effects of mobile writing technologies on how we perceive and interact with physical locations. His work has appeared in *Kairos* and *enculturation*, among other places.

Mike Haen is a doctoral candidate in the composition and rhetoric program at the University of Wisconsin-Madison. He currently works as the assistant director of the Writing Across the Curriculum program. His research interests include writing instructional talk and teacher training. His work has appeared in *WLN: A Journal of Writing Center Scholarship*.

Amy J. Lueck is assistant professor at Santa Clara University, where she teaches courses on writing, rhetoric, digital historiography, and public memory. Her historical research focuses on rhetorical education and practice in the U.S., particularly at the intersection of secondary and post-secondary institutions. She has published her work in *College English, Rhetoric Review,* and elsewhere.

Katelyn Lusher is a doctoral student and graduate instructor at the University of Cincinnati, where she teaches composition courses. Her research interests include community writing and publishing, activist rhetoric, and archival research methods.

Justin Mando is assistant professor of science and technical writing and chair of the writing studies committee at Millersville University of Pennsylvania. His research interests include environmental rhetoric, rhetoric of publics, placed-based pedagogies, and teaching-for-transfer models for themed composition courses.

Ryan McCarty is a PhD candidate at the University of Michigan, where he studies moments of translation that take place in new learning situations. He has taught in high schools, community colleges, jail, and universities.

Peter Wayne Moe is assistant professor of English and Director of Campus Writing at Seattle Pacific University. His work has appeared in *College Composition and Communication, Rhetoric Society Quarterly,* and *Leviathan: A Journal of Melville Studies,* among other places.

Roxanne Mountford is professor and director of rhetoric and writing studies, director of the First-Year Composition Program, and affiliate faculty in women and gender studies at the University of Oklahoma. She studies rhetorical education, rhetoric and religion, and women's rhetoric.

Ann Penrose is professor and Director of Graduate Programs in English at North Carolina State University. Research interests include writing pedagogy, program administration, cognitive processes in writing, and socialization in disciplinary communities. Her work has appeared in *College Composition and Communication, Written Communication, Writing Program Administration* and other venues.

Ethan Philbrick is a composer and writer based in Brooklyn, New York. His research interests include histories of the avantgarde; critical accounts of race, gender, and sexuality; and experimental critical writing. His book manuscript, *Group Works: Art and Politics in New York City 1960-1980,* explores the work of artists who turned to the small group as a medium for artistic and political experimentation in the 1960s and 1970s. He is currently a visiting assistant professor of theatre and performance studies at Muhlenberg College.

Gwendolynne Reid is assistant professor and director of the writing program at Oxford College of Emory University. Her research examines digital and multimodal composing in the disciplines. Her writing can be found in *Across the Disciplines*, *WPA-CompPile Research Bibliographies*, and a number of edited collections.

Laura Rosche is a doctoral student and associate instructor at Indiana University whose research explores the intersections of composition pedagogies, sexual violence rhetorics, and affect theory.

Anna Sicari is assistant professor of English and director of the writing center at Oklahoma State University. Her scholarship focuses on writing centers and feminist work. Anna is co-editor of a forthcoming collection, *Out in the Center: Public Controversies, Private Struggles* (Utah State UP, 2018).

Alexis Teagarden is assistant professor and director of the first-year English program at the University of Massachusetts Dartmouth. Along with intellectual risk, her research focuses on information literacy and research skills, discourse synthesis, and faculty development and evaluation.

Missy Watson is assistant professor at City College of New York, CUNY, where she teaches undergraduate composition and graduate courses in composition pedagogy, language, literacy, and linguistics. Her research lies at the intersection of composition and second-language writing and revolves around seeking social and racial justice.

Ellen O'Connell Whittet teaches in the writing program at the University of California, Santa Barbara. Her writing explores embodiment in performance and pedagogy, and she teaches classes in writing for visual arts and humanities, creative nonfiction, and magazine writing.

PARLOR PRESS
EQUIPMENT FOR LIVING

New, in Living Color!

Type Matters: The Rhetoricity of Letterforms ed. Christopher Scott Wyatt and Dànielle Nicole DeVoss (**BEST DESIGN AWARD-Ingram**)

Rhetoric and Experience Architecture ed. Liza Potts & Michael J. Salvo

Suasive Iterations: Rhetoric, Writing, and Physical Computing David M. Rieder

New Releases

Networked Humanities: Within and Without the University edited by Brian McNely and Jeff Rice

The Internet as a Game by Jill Anne Morris

Identity and Collaboration in World of Warcraft by Phillip Michael Alexander

Best of the Journals in Rhetoric and Composition 2017

Rhetorics Change / Rhetoric's Change edited by Jenny Rice, Chelsea Graham, & Eric Detweiler (Rhetoric Society of America

Congratulations, Award Winners!

Strategies for Writing Center Research by Jackie Grutsch McKinnie. **Best Book Award, International Writing Centers Association (2017)**

Antiracist Writing Assessment Ecologies: Teaching and Assessing Writing for a Socially Just Future by Asao Inoue, **Best Book Award, CCCC, Best Book, Council of Writing Program Administrators (2017)**

The WPA Outcomes Statement—A Decade Later edited by Nicholas N. Behm, Gregory R. Glau, Deborah H. Holdstein, Duane Roen, & Edward M. White, **Best Book Award, Council of Writing Program Adminstrators (2015)**

www.parlorpress.com

www.ingramcontent.com/pod-product-compliance
Lightning Source LLC
Chambersburg PA
CBHW031316160426
43196CB00007B/561